# 60 HIKES *within* 60 MILES
# PORTLAND

## SECOND EDITION

# 60 Hikes within 60 MILES

## PORTLAND

SECOND EDITION

## Paul Gerald

**MENASHA RIDGE PRESS**
Birmingham, Alabama

Copyright © 2001 Paul Gerald
All rights reserved.
Manufactured in the United States of America
Published by Menasha Ridge Press
Distributed by The Globe Pequot Press
Second edition, first printing, 2004


Library of Congress Cataloging-in-Publication Data

Gerald, Paul 1966-
  60 hikes within 60 miles, Portland/by Paul Gerald
  p. cm.
  Includes index
  ISBN 0-89732-571-0 (alk. paper)
  1. Hiking—Oregon—Portland Region—Guidebooks.  2. Portland Region (Or.)—
Guidebooks.  I. Title: Sixty hikes within sixty miles, Portland. II. Title
GV199.42.O72 P6738 2001
917.95'4904'44—dc21
00-068369
CIP

Cover design by Grant M. Tatum
Text design by Karen Ocker
Cover photo by Dennis Coello
Maps by Steve Jones and Scott McGrew
Author photo by Drea Brandom
All other photos by Paul Gerald

Menasha Ridge Press
P.O. Box 43673
Birmingham, AL 35243
www.menasharidge.com

**With immense gratitude and respect, this book is dedicated to the people who build and maintain trails.**

# TABLE OF CONTENTS

# TABLE OF CONTENTS

# ACKNOWLEDGMENTS

Books don't just come from authors. They come from a lot of work by a lot of people. This book wouldn't have happened without the work and assistance of a number of groups and individuals, whom I'd like to thank. I processed a lot of information for this book, much of which came from the United States Forest Service, Oregon State Parks, the Columbia Gorge Visitors Center, the Mount Hood Visitors Center, The Mazamas, The Crag Rats, and the amazing book *Oregon Geographical Names* from the Oregon Historical Society Press. I own the sixth edition, revised and updated by Lewis L. McArthur, and recommend it highly. Other helpful tidbits and charm came, along the way, from Laurie Mac-Arthur at Opal Creek, Walt Dunn and Carole Wendler at Mount Saint Helens National Volcanic Monument, the "flower ladies" I met on the trail to Paradise Park, and all the nice people at Nature of the Northwest.

The book includes words I wrote, maps I drew, and photographs I took, but many others have put it all together, including Russell Helms, Mopsy Gascon, Annie Long, Steve Jones, and Travis Bryant. Without these folks, the book is just a set of files on my Macintosh.

Of course, a hike is a lonely experience without good friends to share it with. Here—listed alphabetically to avoid controversy—is a list of the folks who made "researching" this book such an enjoyable experience: Keanu Allridge, Brenda Atkins, John Chandler (and Ruby), Dana Cuellar (and "Mister Stinky"), Kerri Dee (and Carlos), Christie Dewey, Majken Elek, Mike Fesenmeyer, Elisa Fink, Craig Frerichs, Diane Gage, Kathy Gural, Trevor Hollingsworth, Shelda Holmes (and Roxy), Beth Keegan, Seanna Kerrigan, Don Mcintosh, Eric Miller, Steve Moellering, Lida O'Donnell, Melissane Parm, Dustin Riggs, Diana Robinson, Eliza Rowley, Brandon Rydell, Jerome Schiller, Toni Schimming, Craig Schuhmann, The Shias (Beth, Mark, Megan and Colin), Chip Shields, Maria Shindler, Monica Siewert, Jeff Thomas, Betsy Tucker, Rick Vazquez, Tino and Collette Versoza, The Westovers (Mike, Michelle and Emily) and Chela Zini-Caban.

Special thanks, and a #42 at Pho Hung, to Drea Brandom for taking my author photo. Thanks and some ribs next time I'm in Memphis go to Terre Gorham for applying her legendary editing skills. Also big-time thanks must go to David Lyons and Ed Lawrence for putting me in touch with Menasha Ridge in the first place.

And finally, a lifetime of love and thanks to my family back East—Marjorie and Barry Gerald, Lee and Lela Gerald, Max Bellows, Lucy and Charlie Cook, and their great kids, Becky, David, and Jeffrey—and to my family here in Oregon, the Thursday Night Boys.

—*Paul Gerald*

# FOREWORD

Welcome to Menasha Ridge Press's *60 Hikes Within 60 Miles*, a series designed to provide hikers with information needed to find and hike the very best trails surrounding cities usually underserved by good guidebooks.

Our goal was simple: First, find a hiker who knows the area and loves to hike. Second, ask that person to spend a year researching the most popular and very best trails around. And third, have that person describe each trail in terms of difficulty, scenery, condition, elevation change, and all other categories of information that are important to hikers. "Pretend you've just completed a hike and met up with other hikers at the trailhead," we tell each author. "Imagine their questions; be clear in your answers."

An experienced hiker and writer, author Paul Gerald has selected 60 of his favorite hikes in and around his hometown of Portland. From the civilized hikes of downtown Portland to the rugged trails of volatile Mount St. Helens, Gerald provides hikers (and walkers) with a great variety of trails—and all within 60 miles of Portland.

You'll get more out of this book if you take a moment to read the Introduction explaining how to read the trail listings. And since this is a "where-to," not a "how-to" guide, even those of you who have hiked extensively will find the Introduction of particular value. The "Maps" section will help you understand how useful topos will be on a hike, and will also tell you where to get them.

As much for the opportunity to free the mind as well as to free the body, let Paul Gerald's hikes elevate you above the urban hurry.

*All the best,*
*The Editors at Menasha Ridge Press*

# ABOUT THE AUTHOR

Paul Gerald's writing career began in the sports department of the much-missed *Dallas Times Herald*. He later worked for the Memphis *Commercial Appeal* and the *Memphis Flyer* before setting out as a freelancer. Since then, he has written more than 200 travel articles for the *Flyer,* and along the way his work has also appeared in Northwest Airlines' *WorldTraveler, The Oregonian, Dish Magazine,* Nike. com, Weissmann Travel Reports, and numerous newspapers around the country.

He's also worked in and around landscaping, restaurants, public relations, social work, an amusement park, Alaskan fishing boats, the Portland Metro YMCA, and a host of temporary-agency gigs. All of that was back in his wayfaring days. Now, alas, he works in the marketing department at a Portland-based insurance company; his cubicle is the one with pictures of mountains all over it.

His hiking life started at age 12, when he went to a summer camp in the Absoraka Mountains of Wyoming. He became a trail and road hound at that point, and his hometown of Memphis never looked the same. He's hiked extensively in the Rocky Mountains from New Mexico to Montana, as well as Appalachia, Alaska, Nepal, and Argentina. In 1996 he moved to Portland to be close to the ocean, the mountains, and the big trees.

This is his first book, and he has greatly enjoyed meeting people using it out on the trails. He's also grateful that none of them appeared to be lost or angry. He does hope, however, that any feedback will be directed to him, care of the publisher. And he hopes people will continue to enjoy and benefit from the fruits of his labor.

# PREFACE

It's early March in Portland, and the rising sun glows directly behind Mount Hood. Aside from being an inspiring sight—the rays of sun spreading out from behind the mountain, the red glow on the underside of the clouds, the shadow stretching across the city—it's also an inspiring sign. It's confirmation that the sun is moving northward through the sky; warm and dry days are coming, and another hiking season is dawning.

I usually see this wonderful sight from a StairMaster at the YMCA on Barbur Boulevard, where I try to keep my legs and lungs strong over the winter so I can walk up and down hills for the next eight months or so. Sure, you can hike in the winter around here, but who needs it? Short days, muddy trails, rainy skies, few views—I get out there occasionally, because I'm addicted to trails. But the true hiking season starts when that March morning sun rises behind the mountain. That's when I know that very little snow will fall below 3,000 feet, the wildflower show will start in the eastern end of the Columbia River Gorge, the waterfalls will start to go nuclear, and somewhere, up on a hill or out on a trail, a trillium soon will bloom. And once the trillium blooms, I know it's time to get out and hike.

The book you're holding is intended to accompany you into the wonderful world that is dayhiking in and around the Portland area. Within these pages are 60 trails that you can hike between breakfast and dinner in the City of Roses. Sixty hikes: At one per week, you've got more than a year of hiking here.

Compared to the pantheon of trails in the area, 60 doesn't seem like much. This corner of America is a hiker's dream, with a wide variety of accessible, well-maintained trails and no shortage of places to find maps, gear, and walking companions. But here are 60 select trails which give you a little of everything there is to enjoy around Portland: mountain views, forest solitude, picturesque streams, strenuous workouts, casual strolls, fascinating history, fields of flowers, awesome waterfalls, and ocean beaches.

This book makes it a point to tell you much more than just which direction to go. Think of it as a pack-sized hiking partner, something you can learn from and enjoy as you go. It points out not just which turns to take, but also what to look for along the way. And it strives to educate: Why is Dog Mountain called Dog Mountain? Why are there cables attached to trees along the Clackamas River? Where do all these trails on Lookout Mountain go? What's with that trail above McNeil Point, the one that's not on the official map? Where is the tallest tree in Portland? How do I find the hidden waterfall near the "Throne of the Forest King?" And new in this second edition, I've included driving times to the trailhead and elevations for each trail.

Sunrise over Mount Hood and downtown Portland, from Washington Park Rose Garden

Even if you've hiked some of these trails, hiking them with this book will be a new experience for you. And if you've never laced on a pair of hiking boots, or you've just arrived in Portland, here are 60 great places to start. Whether you want a convenient city bus ride to the flat and fascinating Washington Park, a bumpy drive to Lookout Mountain, or the thigh-burning experience that are Kings and Elk Mountains,this book will tell you what to bring, how to get to the trailhead, where to go on the trail, and what to look for while you're hiking.

In fact, here's one of my favorite hints—just to get you going—that is not found elsewhere in this book (or any other): When driving to Mount Hood, don't follow the signs that say "Mount Hood." I know that sounds odd, but if you're traveling east on I-84, Exit 16/Mount Hood leads you right through the heart of Gresham, a tangle of strip malls, fast food joints, and traffic lights that only slow you down. Forget that. Take Exit 17/Troutdale, turn right at the second light onto 257th Avenue, and after four miles turn left onto SE Orient Road. It will drop you back onto US 26 just one mile before Sandy, after taking you through the kind of country that Gresham replaced: farms, nurseries, country stores, creeks, and a plain two-lane country road. Every time I take people this way, they usually say two things: First, "Where are we?" and, later, "Man, this is much nicer than the way I usually go."

I suppose that if I am to be your guide, you may want to know some things about me. While hiking has long been one of my favorite activities, I find that when inviting people to come along, I must often assure them that I am not embarking on a major expedition or a speed event. I am, to put it simply, not fast. The hiking times listed in this book are the times I would spend on a trail if I weren't stopping to make notes for a book. But even when I'm not "working," and that's a real stretch of the word, I also stop to eat, drink, look around, relax, take pictures, and eat some more. In other words, I hike to enjoy myself; I go elsewhere for my workouts. Out on the trail, I average about two miles an hour with stops included, but the times in the book take into account factors beyond my natural pace: hills, trail condition, altitude, and the number of times needed to stop and say, "Man, look at that (view, waterfall, creek, meadow, etc.)!"

Suspension bridge over Drift Creek Falls

I had hiked more than these 60 trails before I wrote this book, and the toughest decisions I had to make were which hikes to leave out. The range of the book—a rough circle of 60 miles as the crow flies from the edge of the Portland metro area—is bordered on the north by the south side of Mount St. Helens, on the south by Detroit Lake, on the east by OR 35, and on the west by the Pacific Ocean. Hiking these trails, you'll glimpse everything from desert to coastal rain forest, from volcanic aftermath to 1,000-year-old trees.

These things are on my mind when I'm indoors exercising; all the beauty is out there, just waiting. Maybe, during the winter, we hikers slip out a few times, like when we get a "sunbreak," a word surely made up by weather forecasters in the Pacific Northwest— the same people who distinguish between "rain" and "showers." These "sunbreaks" call us out to the city trails like Forest Park, Washington Park, or the Marquam Trail to Council Crest. Or, we just put on our raincoats to see wild birds in Oaks Bottom or if the steelhead run has made it to Tryon Creek. Sometimes we get tantalizingly clear days, when our eyes glaze over and we say foolish things like, "Is it spring?" Then, we insist on going out to the coast to look for whales from Cape Lookout, into the Gorge to see what Angels Rest is like without 57 other people up there, or down to Silver Falls State Park to see the waterfalls at full blast.

But for the most part, winter is a time to stay in shape at the gym or go play on the snow. March is when the snow starts to melt in lower elevations, especially on south-facing slopes like the Washington side of the Gorge. March is when you go to Beacon Rock State Park to warm up for Table or Dog Mountains. It's when you get the pay-off for your winter work-out. Or you wallow in the moisture and go see the great waterfalls of the Gorge or hike the Multnomah/Wahkeena loop, Triple Falls, or Eagle Creek before the summer crowds inundate them. Or you drive east of the Rain Shroud, out where it really is spring, to see the wildflowers at McCall Preserve or Catherine Creek, or stroll the pavement on the Historic Columbia River Highway.

As the snow line rises, so do the hikers. April means you can drive to the Lewis River Trail, or to Siouxon Creek, or to many of the great hikes in the Clackamas and Santiam watersheds—whether it's the old-growth majesty of Opal Creek or the rolling splendor of the Clackamas River itself. April also means there will be Spring Chinook spawning in the Salmon River, and you might even glimpse some in the underwater viewing structure at Wildwood. And when your legs get those early-season blues, there are always the hot springs at Breitenbush and Bagby.

May means the meadows on top of places like Saddle Mountain, Kings Mountain, and Dog Mountain are exploding with flowers—as well as weekend crowds, so steal away on a weekday. It also means those trails just a little farther up are about to be snow-free, and that the roads to places like Lava Canyon, Ape Cave, Ramona Falls, and Larch Mountain will be open.

By June the hiking panorama is practically wide open, and the problem becomes where to go. The coast is nice for the duration, so the views are clear from Tillamook Head and Mount Hebo. But back to the east the rhododendrons are blooming on the trails to Salmon Butte, Laurel Hill, and Mirror Lake. You can probably tackle south-facing Ape Canyon on the flanks of Mount St. Helens by now, too. And if you really want to see how well you're conditioned, go take a shot at some of the Mazama trails at Trapper Creek—and remember, when you're done, there are more hot springs just across the river in Carson.

On July 16, a red-letter date on the hiker's calendar, the road opens to the mind-boggling bluffs of Cascade Head out on the coast. And not long after that the rising temperatures make a splash in Trillium Lake or Serene Lake seem like a good idea.

And then there's August, which to me means one simple thing: wildflowers up high. Every time I arrive in Wy'east Basin, Paradise Park, Elk Meadows, or the ponds below McNeil Point on an August morning, I say to myself, "This is why I live here!" When people in other places say to me, "How can you handle all that rain?" I answer with one word: "August."

In August, it's sunny and around 85 degrees. You're in shape; the meadows on Hood are snow-free and flower-filled; the butterflies are flitting among the blooms; and all is right with the world. And as August yields to September, the sadness is more than made up for by the ripening huckleberries. Anybody who goes for a late-August walk around 5,000 feet elevation in the Pacific Northwest and doesn't want to move here is either stubborn or insane.

The nice thing about fall is that most people think hiking season is over, so the trails—compared to summer weekends, at least—are practically empty. And September is, in some ways, a sad month, because you know the clear skies are about to end. It feels that way, at least; the truth is that you've still got at least two months before the snows come again, and in the meantime there are the fall colors—the big-leaf maples on the Historic Columbia River Highway, the vine maples at Opal Creek, and the Mountain Ash on the ridge above the Toutle River. The blackberries on the way to Warrior Rock are so numerous you'll think it's an industrial crop, and it's always nice to go back to Silver Falls for a look at the trees and the falls without the throngs of people.

What starts with the sun glowing behind Mount Hood ends with me high up on it. I love the energy of a mountain under threat of winter, and my favorite way to say thanks to the trail gods at the end of the hiking season is to make the long drive to

# PREFACE

Cloud Cap Saddle, then the long hike to Cooper Spur. I like to sit there with most of the state below me, the October wind blowing a cloud off the summit above me, the Eliot Glacier calving next to me, and about ten of the hikes I've done in my field of vision. I sit there and remember the morning when I was on the StairMaster, looking up at this mountain and saying, "I can't wait to get up there."

Now, I'm there, and it's time to go back down. By early November, the little rock-walled sitting area at the top of Cooper Spur will be under a foot of snow, and I'll pant once more at the gym, or maybe I'll stroll along the Clackamas or in the Gorge, stealing a few more miles of hiking before the first "showers" turn to "rain." Then I'm living for "sunbreaks" once again, dreaming of flowers and butterflies and meadows and waterfalls, watching the rising sun retreat back to the south through the windows of the YMCA.

# HIKING RECOMMENDATIONS

## ▶ HIKES GOOD FOR CHILDREN

Ape Cave (lower cave)
Lost Lake
Oaks Bottom
Salmon River (lower portion)
Silver Falls State Park

Trillium Lake
Triple Falls (lower section)
Tryon Creek State Park
Washington Park/Hoyt Arboretum
Wildwood Recreation Area

## ▶ FLAT HIKES

Ape Cave (lower cave)
Lost Lake
Oaks Bottom
Salmon River (lower portion)
Sauvie Island

Trillium Lake
Tryon Creek State Park
Washington Park/Hoyt Arboretum
Wildwood Recreation Area

## ▶ STEEP HIKES

Cooper Spur
Dog Mountain
Kings Mountain/Elk Mountain
Larch Mountain
Mount Mitchell

Neahkahnie Mountain
Saddle Mountain
Table Mountain
Trapper Creek Wilderness
Wahkeena Falls to Multnomah Falls

## ▶ URBAN HIKES

Forest Park
Macleay Trail
Marquam Trail to Council Crest

Oaks Bottom
Tryon Creek State Park
Washington Park/Hoyt Arboretum

## ▶ RURAL HIKES

Breitenbush
Cape Falcon
Cascade Head
Cooper Spur
Mount Hebo

Opal Creek
Salmon Butte
Siouxon Creek
South Fork Toutle River
Trapper Creek Wilderness

## ▶ SECLUDED HIKES

Bull of the Woods
Cooper Spur
Mount Mitchell
Serene Lake

Siouxon Creek
Table Mountain
Vista Ridge

# HIKING RECOMMENDATIONS

## ▶ HIKES GOOD FOR WILDLIFE WATCHING

Cape Lookout State Park
Cascade Head
Elk Meadows
Macleay Trail
Mount Hebo

Oaks Bottom
Salmon River
Sauvie Island
Trapper Creek Wilderness
Wildwood Recreation Area

## ▶ SCENIC HIKES

Cape Falcon
Cape Lookout State Park
Cascade Head
Cooper Spur
Eagle Creek
Elk Meadows

Larch Mountain
Lookout Mountain
McNeil Point
South Fork Toutle River
Vista Ridge

## ▶ TRAILS GOOD FOR RUNNERS

Cape Lookout State Park
Clackamas River
Forest Park
Historic Columbia River Highway
Lost Lake

Macleay Trail
Marquam Trail to Council Crest
Salmon Butte
Serene Lake
Trillium Lake

## ▶ MULTI-USE TRAILS

Barlow Pass
Forest Park
Historic Columbia River Highway
Laurel Hill

Lookout Mountain
Opal Creek
Serene Lake

## ▶ HISTORIC TRAILS

Beacon Rock State Park
Cooper Spur
Historic Columbia River Highway
Larch Mountain
Laurel Hill
Lava Canyon

Macleay Trail
Opal Creek
South Fork Toutle River
Tillamook Head
Warrior Rock

# HIKING RECOMMENDATIONS

## ▶ TRAILS FEATURING WATERFALLS

Eagle Creek
Larch Mountain
Lava Canyon
Lewis River
Ramona Falls

Silver Falls State Park
Siouxon Creek
Tamanawas Falls
Triple Falls
Wahkeena Falls to Multnomah Falls

*In the following categories, parentheses indicate a shorter option within a longer hike.*

## ▶ LESS THAN 1 MILE

Ape Cave (lower cave)
Forest Park (several options)
Laurel Hill (to chute or Little Zigzag Falls)
Lava Canyon (upper loop)
Lewis River (to Lower Falls)
Oak Island
Silver Falls State Park (South Falls Loop)

Timberline Lodge (to White River Canyon overlook)
Triple Falls (to Ponytail Falls)
Tryon Creek State Park (several options)
Washington Park/Hoyt Arboretum (several options)
Wildwood Recreation Area

## ▶ 1 TO 3 MILES

Ape Cave
Bagby Hot Springs
Beacon Rock State Park (Beacon Rock or Rodney Falls)
Bull of the Woods (to Pansy Lake)
Cascade Head (to Nature Preserve)
Eagle Creek (to Punchbowl Falls)
Historic Columbia River Highway
Lewis River (to Middle Falls)
Lookout Mountain (from High Prairie)
Macleay Trail (to Audubon Society)

McCall Nature Preserve
Mirror Lake (to lake)
Neahkahnie Mountain (to summit from US 101)
Oak Island
Oaks Bottom
Silver Falls State Park (several options)
Tillamook Head (several options)
Timberline Lodge (to Silcox Hut)
Trillium Lake
Tryon Creek State Park

# HIKING RECOMMENDATIONS

## ▶ 3 TO 6 MILES

Angels Rest
Breitenbush
Cape Falcon
Cape Lookout State Park
Cascade Head
Elk Meadows (to meadows only)
Historic Columbia River Highway
Kings Mountain (without Elk Mountain)
Laurel Hill
Lava Canyon
Lewis River
Lost Lake
Macleay Trail

Marquam Trail to Council Crest
Mount Mitchell
Saddle Mountain
Salmon River (lower)
Silver Falls State Park
Tamanawas Falls
Timberline Lodge (to Zigzag Canyon)
Triple Falls
Vista Ridge (to Wy'East Basin)
Wahkeena Falls to Multnomah Falls
Washington Park/Hoyt Arboretum

## ▶ MORE THAN 6 MILES

Ape Canyon
Barlow Pass
Beacon Rock State Park
Bull of the Woods
Clackamas River
Dog Mountain
Eagle Creek
Elk Meadows
Forest Park
Kings Mountain/Elk Mountain
Larch Mountain
Lookout Mountain
McNeil Point
Mirror Lake

Neahkahnie Mountain
Opal Creek
Ramona Falls
Salmon Butte
Salmon River
Serene Lake
Silver Falls State Park
Siouxon Creek
South Fork Toutle River
Table Mountain
Tillamook Head
Timberline Lodge
Vista Ridge
Warrior Rock

# INTRODUCTION

Welcome to *60 Hikes within 60 Miles: Portland*. If you're new to hiking or even if you're a seasoned trail-smith, take a few minutes to read the following introduction. We explain how this book is organized and how to use it.

## ► HIKE DESCRIPTIONS

Each hike contains six key items: a locator map, an In Brief description of the trail, directions to the trail, a trail map, a hike narrative and a Key At-a-Glance Information box. Combined, the maps and information provide a clear method to assess each trail from the comfort of your favorite chair.

### LOCATOR MAP

After narrowing down the general area of the hike on the overview map (see inside back cover), the locator map, along with driving directions given in the narrative, enables you to find the trailhead. Once at the trailhead, park only in designated areas.

### IN BRIEF

This synopsis of the trail offers a snapshot of what to expect along the trail, including mention of any historical sights, beautiful vistas, or other interesting sights you may encounter.

### DIRECTIONS

Check here for directions to the trailhead. Used with the locator map, the directions will help you locate each trailhead. Driving times begin at the first landmark listed (I-205, for example), and are based on going the speed limit and not stopping on the way.

### DESCRIPTIONS

The trail description is the heart of each hike. Here, the author has provided a summary of the trail's essence as well as highlighted any special traits the hike offers. Ultimately the hike description will help you choose which hikes are best for you.

### NEARBY ACTIVITIES

Not every hike will have this listing. For those that do, look here for information on nearby dining opportunities or other activities to complete your day.

## ► KEY AT-A-GLANCE INFORMATION

The Key At-a-Glance Information boxes give you a quick overview of each hike.

LENGTH   The length of the trail from start to finish. There may be options to shorten or extend the hikes, but the mileage corresponds to the described hike. Consult the hike description to help decide how to customize the hike for your ability or time constraints.

# INTRODUCTION

**CONFIGURATION**  A description of what the trail might look like from overhead. Trails can be loops, out-and-backs (that is, along the same route), figure eights, or balloons. Sometimes the descriptions might surprise you.

**DIFFICULTY**  The degree of effort an "average" hiker should expect on a given hike. For simplicity, the level of difficulty is described as "easy," "moderate," or "hard."

**SCENERY**  Rates the overall environs of the hike and what to expect in terms of plant life, wildlife, streams, or historic buildings.

**EXPOSURE**  A quick check of how much sun you can expect on your shoulders during the hike. Descriptors used are self-explanatory and include terms such as shady, exposed, and sunny.

**TRAFFIC**  Indicates how busy the trail might be on an average day. Trail traffic, of course, will vary from day-to-day and season to season.

**TRAIL SURFACE**  Indicates whether the trail is paved, rocky, smooth dirt, or a mixture of elements.

**HIKING TIME**  How long it took the author to hike the trail. Paul says he makes about two miles an hour—a little quicker if it's flat, a little slower if it's steep. He can go faster, but he sees little reason to do so. Hiking, after all, is supposed to be fun.

**SEASON**  Times of year when this trail is accessible. In most cases, the limiting factor is snow on the trail or the road to the trailhead, but in some cases trails are closed for reasons relating to wildlife habitat. In any case, if it's a border time for the trail you want to hike, call the information number to be sure you can hike it.

**ACCESS**  Notes fees or permits needed to access the trail. Most Portland-vicinity trailheads on National Forest or National Monument lands require the Northwest Forest Pass, which can be obtained at many local outdoor shops and also at any Forest Service ranger station or information station. A day pass is $5, an annual pass is $30. For more information about the Pass, call (800) 270-7504.

**MAPS**  The best map for this hike in the author's opinion. See Appendix B (page 209) for places to buy maps.

**FACILITIES**  Notes any facilities such as rest rooms, phones, and water available at the trailhead or on the trail.

**SPECIAL COMMENTS**  Included in most hike information boxes, provides you with those little extra details that don't fit into any of the above categories. Here you'll find information on trail hiking options and facts such as whether or not to expect a lifeguard at a nearby swimming beach.

## ▶ WEATHER

For most folks, hiking season around Portland starts in March or April, when flowers and temperatures start to rise. Unfortunately, that's the least stable of seasons where

# INTRODUCTION

the weather is concerned. Weather forecasts are notoriously off the mark during spring, so if they aren't absolutely, positively sure it will be clear, plan for 50-something degrees and drizzling into June.

Snow is a different matter; the higher hikes in this book won't be completely clear most years until July. Also beware that in the Columbia River Gorge, wind is a constant reality, so even a sunny June day a hike like Dog Mountain can have you reaching for hat and gloves. By mid to late June, and all the way into October, you'll see mostly sunny skies, mild temperatures, and happy hikers. Then winter comes and, for all intents and purposes, it rains until spring. We try to think of it as waterfall-loading.

## AVERAGE DAILY (high) TEMPERATURES BY MONTH

| JAN | FEB | MAR | APR | MAY | JUN |
|-----|-----|-----|-----|-----|-----|
| 46  | 51  | 56  | 61  | 68  | 74  |

| JUL | AUG | SEP | OCT | NOV | DEC |
|-----|-----|-----|-----|-----|-----|
| 80  | 81  | 75  | 64  | 53  | 46  |

## ▶ MAPS

The maps in this book have been produced with great care and, used with the hiking directions, will help you stay on course. But as any experienced hiker knows, things can get tricky off the beaten path.

When used with the route directions in each chapter, the maps are sufficient to get you to the trail and keep you on it. However, you will find superior detail and valuable information in the United States Geological Survey's 7.5 minute series topographic maps (topos). Recognizing how indispensable these are to hikers and bikers alike, many outdoor shops and bike shops now carry topos of the local area.

If you're new to hiking, you might be wondering, "What's a topographic map?" In short, these differ from standard "flat" maps, indicating not only linear distance but elevation as well. One glance at a topo will show you the difference: Contour lines spread across the map like dozens of intricate spiderwebs. Each contour line represents a particular elevation, and at the base of each topo a particular contour interval designation is given. Yes, it sounds confusing if you're new to the lingo, but it truly is a simple and wonderfully helpful system.

Let's assume that the 7.5 minute series topo reads "Contour Interval 40 feet," that the short trail we'll be hiking is two inches in length on the map, and that it crosses five contour lines from beginning to end. What do we know? Well, because the linear scale of this series is 2,000 feet to the inch (roughly two and three-quarters inches representing one mile), we know our trail is approximately four-fifths of a mile long (2 inches are 2,000 feet). But we also know we'll be climbing or descending 200 vertical feet (5 contour lines are 40 feet each) over that distance. And the elevation designations written on occasional contour lines will tell us if we're heading up or down.

# INTRODUCTION

In addition to outdoor shops and bike shops, you'll find topos at major universities and some public libraries, where you might try photocopying the ones you need to avoid the cost of buying them. But if you want your own and can't find them locally, contact:

USGS Map Sales
Box 25286
Denver, CO 80225
(888) ASK-USGS (275-8747)
www.mapping.usgs.gov/esic

Visa and MasterCard are accepted. Ask for an index while you're at it, plus a price list and a copy of the booklet Topographic Maps. In minutes you'll be reading topos like a pro.

A second excellent series of maps available to hikers is distributed by the United States Forest Service. If your trail runs through an area designated as a national forest, look in the phone book under the United States Government listings, find the Department of Agriculture heading, and run your finger down that section until you find the Forest Service. Give them a call, and they'll provide the address of the regional Forest Service office, from which you can obtain the appropriate map.

## ▶ TRAIL ETIQUETTE

Whether you're on a city walk or on a long hike, always remember that great care and resources (from nature as well as from your tax dollars) have gone into creating these trails. Taking care of the trails begins with you, the hiker. Treat the trail, wildlife, and your fellow hikers with respect. Here are a few general ideas to keep in mind.

1. Hike on open trails only. Respect trail and road closures (ask if you're not sure), avoid trespassing on private land, and obtain permits and authorization as may be required.

2. Leave only footprints. Be sensitive to the dirt beneath you. This also means staying on the trail and not creating any new ones. Be sure to pack out what you pack in: No one likes to see trash on the trail.

3. Never spook animals. Give them extra room and time to adjust to you. Leave gates as you found them or as marked.

4. Plan ahead. Know your equipment, your ability, and the area in which you are hiking—and prepare accordingly. Be self-sufficient; carry necessary supplies for changes in weather or other conditions. A well-executed trip is a satisfaction to you and not a burden or offense to others.

5. Be courteous to hikers or bikers you meet on the trails.

# INTRODUCTION

## ▶ WATER

"How much is enough? One bottle? Two? Three?! But think of all that extra weight!" Well, one simple physiological fact should convince you to err on the side of excess when it comes to deciding how much water to pack: While working hard in 90-degree heat, we each need approximately 10 quarts of fluid every day. That's 2.5 gallons— 12 large water bottles or 16 small ones. And, with water weighing in at approximately 8 pounds per gallon, a one-day supply comes to a whopping 20 pounds. In other words, pack along one or two bottles even for short hikes. And make sure you can purify the water found along the trail on longer routes. If you drink it untreated, you run the risk of disease.

Many hikers pack along the inexpensive and only slightly distasteful tetraglycine hydroperiodide tablets (sold under the names Potable Aqua, Globaline, and Cough-lan's, among others). If you wait for these tablets to work their magic, usually about 30 minutes, and then add a few grains of vitamin C powder, your water will instantly clear up again. Some invest in portable, lightweight purifiers that filter out the crud. Unfortunately, even the best filters only remove up to 98–99% of all those nasty bacteria, viruses, and other organisms you can't see.

Iodine tablets or drops will knock off the well-known Giardia. If you are infected with Giardia, one to four weeks after ingestion you will be bloated, vomiting, shivering with chills, and living in the bathroom. But there are other parasites to worry about, including Cryptosporidium. "Crypto" brings on symptoms very similar to Giardia, but unlike that fellow protozoan it's equipped with a shell sufficiently strong enough to protect it against the chemical killers that stop Giardia cold. This means either boiling the water or using a water filter to screen out both Giardia and Crypto, plus the iodine to knock off viruses.

Some water filters come equipped with an iodine chamber to guarantee nearly full protection. Or you can simply add a pill or drops to the water you've just filtered (if you aren't allergic to iodine, of course). The pleasures of hiking—and the displeasure of getting sick—make this minor effort worth the few minutes involved.

## ▶ FIRST-AID KIT

A typical kit may contain more items than you might think necessary. But these are just the basics. Pack the items in a waterproof container such as a Ziploc bag.

Ace bandages or Spenco joint wraps

Antibiotic ointment (Neosporin or the generic equivalent)

Aspirin or acetaminophen

Band-Aids

Benadryl or the generic equivalent—diphen-hydramine (an antihistamine, in case of allergic reactions)

Butterfly-closure bandages

# INTRODUCTION

## ▶ FIRST-AID KIT (continued)

Epinephrine in a prefilled syringe of (for those known to have severe allergic reactions to such things as bee stings)
Gauze (one roll)
Gauze compress pads (a half-dozen 4 in. x 4 in.)
Hydrogen peroxide or iodine
Matches or pocket lighter

Moleskin/Spenco "Second Skin"
Snakebite kit
Sunscreen
Water purification tablets or water filter (on longer hikes)
Whistle (more effective in signaling rescuers than your voice)

## ▶ HIKING WITH CHILDREN

No one is too young for a nice hike in the woods or through a city park. Parents with infants can strap the little ones on with baby carriers. Be careful, though. Flat, short trails are probably best with an infant. Toddlers who have not quite mastered walking can still tag along, riding on an adult's back in a child carrier.

Children who are walking can, of course, follow along with an adult. Use common sense to judge a child's capacity to hike a particular trail. Always rely on the possibility that the child will tire quickly and have to be carried.

When packing for the hike, remember the child's needs as well as your own. Make sure children are adequately clothed for the weather, have proper shoes, and are properly protected from the sun with sunscreen and clothing. Kids dehydrate quickly, so make sure you have plenty of clean water and other drinks for everyone.

Depending on age, ability, and the hike length/difficulty, most children should enjoy the shorter hikes described in this book. To assist an adult with determining which trails are suitable for children, a list of hike recommendations for children is provided on page xv.

## ▶ THE BUSINESS HIKER

Whether you're visiting or a resident in the Portland area, these hikes are the perfect opportunity for a quick getaway from the your everyday demands. Many of the hikes are classified as urban and are easily accessible from downtown areas.

Instead of a burger down the street, pack a lunch and head out to one of the area's many urban trails for a relaxing break from the office or that tiresome convention. Or plan ahead and take a small group of your business comrades on a nearby hike in one of the area forests. A well-planned half-day getaway is the perfect complement to a business stay in Portland.

# ANGELS REST

## IN BRIEF

There's a reason they recently expanded the parking area for this one: it's one of the finer hikes around, with a gentle grade to a spectacular lookout point above the Columbia River. It also connects with the Wahkeena Trail, making longer loops or one-way hikes with shuttles possible.

## DESCRIPTION

As you drive out I-84, you can actually see Angels Rest, a flat-topped rock outcropping sticking out over the road at the end of a ridge. What looks like a building on top is actually a clump of trees. And if it looks like it's way up there, just remember that if you take your time on the way up you'll have plenty of breath left to be taken away by the view up top.

The trail starts with a moderate climb through the woods and has an early reward: a rare view down at a waterfall, in this case 100-foot Coopey Falls. Soon thereafter, the trail crosses on a wooden bridge over Coopey Creek and then starts climbing just a little more steeply.

After about a mile, you'll start switching back through an area that burned in 1991; note the blackened trunks of some of the bigger trees. It was mostly just the underbrush and smaller trees that burned, opening up the forest floor to the sun and letting wildflowers come in to take your mind off the climb. When the trail traverses a rock slide for 100 yards, you're almost done.

## KEY AT-A-GLANCE INFORMATION

**LENGTH:** 4.6 miles

**CONFIGURATION:** Out-and-back

**DIFFICULTY:** Moderate, due to altitude gain and a little rock scrambling at the top

**SCENERY:** Forest most of the way, waterfall, creek crossing, panorama at the top

**EXPOSURE:** Shady except for one section

**TRAFFIC:** Heavy; on a nice weekend day this trail will have more dogs on it than many trails have hikers.

**TRAIL SURFACE:** Packed dirt with some roots, rocks

**HIKING TIME:** 2.5 hours

**SEASON:** Year-round

**ACCESS:** No fees or permits needed.

**MAPS:** Trails of the Columbia Gorge; Green Trails #428 (Bridal Veil); USGS Bridal Veil

**FACILITIES:** Rest rooms and water one-half mile west at Bridal Veil State Park

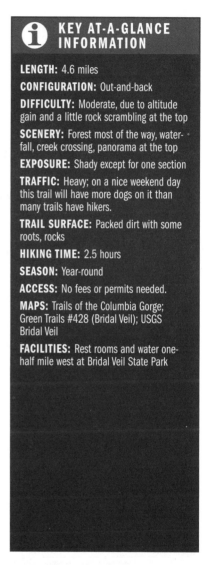

## DIRECTIONS

From Portland on I-84, drive 21 miles east of I-205 to Exit 28/Bridal Veil. After less than a mile, park in the sprawling parking area at the intersection with the Historic Columbia River Highway. The signed trailhead is just across the old highway. Driving time is 20 minutes.

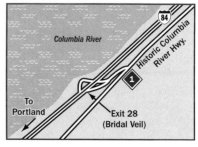

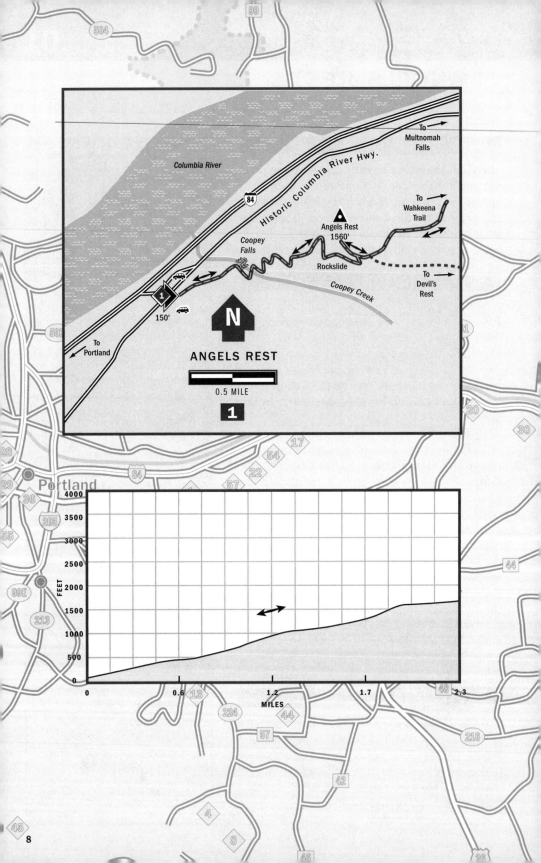

Columbia River

84

Historic Columbia River Hwy.

To
Multnomah
Falls

To
Wahkeena
Trail

Angels Rest
1560'

Coopey
Falls

Rockslide

Coopey Creek

To
Devil's
Rest

1

150'

To
Portland

**N**

**ANGELS REST**

0.5 MILE

**1**

FEET

4000
3500
3000
2500
2000
1500
1000
500
0

0    0.6    1.2    1.7    2.3
MILES

Just past the slide, the trail goes back into the woods briefly, and you turn left out onto the final ridge. This last stretch of the trail is why you might think twice about bringing small children: it gets a little narrow, with cliffs to the east falling away a few hundred feet, and in one spot you'll have to scramble up about ten feet of rocks. When a trail goes back and to the right on the ridge top, stay straight.

The reward for this small effort is a view to rival any other in the Gorge. To the east, you can see Beacon Rock and the high walls on either side of the river. To the west you can see the Vista House and the hills falling away toward Portland and the Willamette Valley. The Columbia River, right below you, seems so close that you could get a running start and jump into it. You might see some windsurfers out there; on one trip, I watched a float plane practicing touch-and-go landings on this stretch of the river. If it's really clear, you'll have a view of Silver Star Mountain right across the river. You can also see two hikes from this book: right next to Beacon Rock is the step-shaped Hamilton Mountain (See Beacon Rock State Park), and the big flat-topped mountain looming behind that is Table Mountain. There's even a nice new bench to sit on out there. All in all, it's hard to imagine a better place to have lunch.

If you're up for more hiking, you can turn this into a longer out-and-back or do a one-way hike with another car parked farther east. To do this, as you walk back down the ridge, veer left (east) instead of keeping straight, which is where you came from. After a few minutes you'll come to a junction; go left to head for the Wahkeena Trail or straight 1 mile up the Foxglove Trail to Devils Rest.

If you turn left in 2.6 miles you'll come to Wahkeena Spring, and 0.1 mile later you'll intersect the Wahkeena Trail (#420). Here, you can turn left (downhill) and follow Wahkeena Creek 1.6 miles down to the picnic area at Wahkeena Falls, or you can go straight and, in 1.2 miles, intersect the Larch Mountain Trail. Go down that one for 1.8 miles, and you'll be at Multnomah Falls. There's a more detailed description of this trail section in the hike Wahkeena Falls to Multnomah Falls (page 191).

## ▶ NEARBY ACTIVITIES

The Vista House, as well as the road that leads to it, is well worth a visit. To get there, simply drive back toward Portland on the Historic Highway, rather than on I-84. Follow the 85-year-old road and its moss-covered stone guardrails past a few other waterfalls and then up the hill to Crown Point, where you can step into the Vista House and get yourself an espresso while you take in a postcard view and historic displays about the building of the road. Keep going west on that road past the Vista House, and in a couple of miles you'll see a sign leading you down a steep hill back to I-84.

# APE CANYON

## KEY AT-A-GLANCE INFORMATION

**LENGTH:** 11.6 miles

**CONFIGURATION:** Out-and-back

**DIFFICULTY:** Moderate

**SCENERY:** Old-growth forest, a volcanic mudflow, a narrow canyon

**EXPOSURE:** Alternating shady and open on the way up, then wide open at the top

**TRAFFIC:** Moderate on summer weekends, light otherwise

**TRAIL SURFACE:** Packed dirt with roots and rocks, rock at the top

**HIKING TIME:** 5.5 hours

**SEASON:** June–October

**ACCESS:** Northwest Forest Pass required.

**MAPS:** USFS Mount St. Helens National Volcanic Monument

**FACILITIES:** None at trailhead; toilets at Lava Canyon trailhead. There's no water at the trailhead or on the trail.

## IN BRIEF

This trail visits two worlds not ordinarily seen: the upper reaches of a volcano and the edge of what they call the "blast zone." Without too much climbing, you can stand in a wonderful old-growth forest and be about 20 feet from an area that was completely obliterated barely 20 years ago. At the top, you'll have a sweeping view highlighted by an amazing geological oddity.

## DESCRIPTION

You'll get your first glimpse of the contrasts ahead when you have only walked 100 yards on this trail. You'll be at the top of a little bluff, looking out over a wide area of rocks. Those rocks used to be on the upper slopes of the volcano Mount St. Helens, but on May 18, 1980, they came down the hill at about 45 miles per hour, part of a landslide triggered when most of the Shoestring Glacier melted in a moment when the volcano erupted. But the mudslide stayed within the boundaries of the Muddy River, so the forest you're standing in—even though it was within feet of the slide—was spared. You'll spend the next 5 miles climbing this ridge, but don't worry: you'll only gain a little more than 1,300 feet along the way.

Before you leave this viewpoint, look down. You're standing on an example of stratigraphy; that's a fancy word for the fact that when the

## DIRECTIONS

From Portland on I-5, drive 21 miles north of the Columbia River and take Exit 21/Woodland. Turn right onto WA 503 (Lewis River Road), which after 31 miles (2 miles past the town of Cougar) turns into FS 90. Follow FS 90 for 3.3 miles and turn left onto FS 83. The trailhead is 11.2 miles ahead on the left, just before the Lava Canyon trailhead. Driving time is 1 hour and 20 minutes.

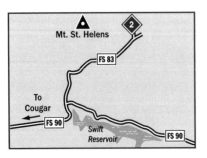

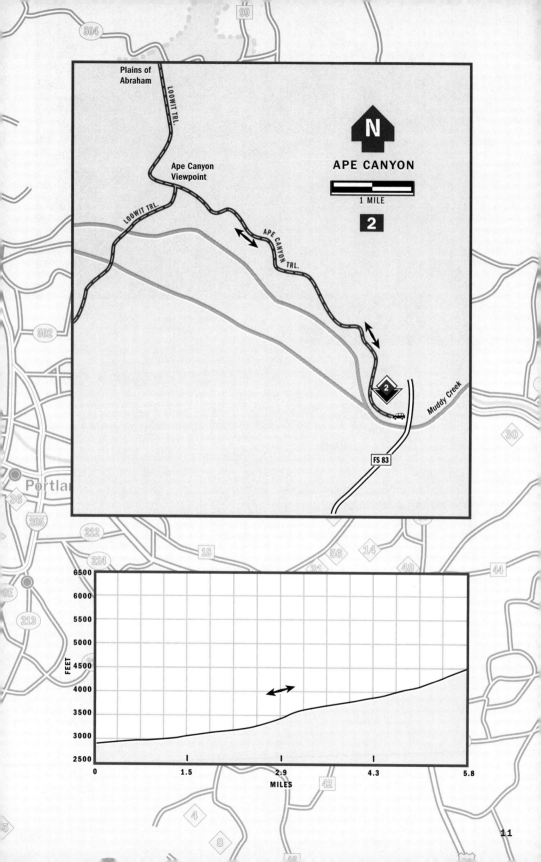

Plains of
Abraham

LOOWIT TRL.

Ape Canyon
Viewpoint

LOOWIT TRL.

APE CANYON TRL.

**N**

**APE CANYON**

1 MILE

**2**

**2**

Muddy Creek

FS 83

Portland

6500
6000
5500
5000
4500
4000
3500
3000
2500

FEET

0          1.5          2.9          4.3          5.8

MILES

South side of Mount Saint Helens, showing the lahar (mudflow) damage from 1980

1980 mudflow came through, it exposed several underlying layers of rock, which give scientists clues to the previous eruption history of the volcano.

If you're on this trail in September or October, you'll be in the world of the vine maple, and its red and orange explosion contrasts beautifully with the evergreen canopy. Keep an eye out for deer and elk, both of which are in the area. You won't see old-growth forest for about a mile and a half, but when you do you'll see some monster hemlocks. At this elevation they tend to get quite fat at the base but not as tall as usual, due to violent winter storms. I like to call them "Buddha Trees." Soon after you enter the old growth and climb some switchbacks, you'll get views out to the east of Mount Adams, the second highest peak in Washington at 12,276 feet. It's about 35 miles away. Mount Hood, 60 miles away to the south, is also visible, as is Mount Rainier to the north.

After five miles of gradual climbing, you'll come out into the open—and into the "blast zone" itself. You'll see trees that were killed by the super-heated gases produced when the mountain blew in 1980, and to the north (ahead of you) you will see the utter desolation the eruption created. (The explosion was actually "aimed" that way.)

When you come to a lookout point on the right, you can scramble down a bit (be very careful) and look into the 300-foot slot that lies at the head of Ape Canyon, which now stretches away to your right. If you work it right, it makes a heck of a foreground for a picture of Mount Adams. It's also visible from a little farther up the trail.

Just beyond this point, there's an intersection with the Loowit Trail, which goes all the way around Mount St. Helens. To your left, up a small rise, is an excellent viewpoint back down the mudflow toward your car. If you turn right and go 0.8 miles up the Loowit Trail, you'll come to the Plains of Abraham, which might as well have been lifted from the moon.

If you're wondering about the name of this hike, it comes from a 1920s incident in which an ape-like "Bigfoot" (decades later found to be a kid playing a prank) threw rocks at some miners in the area. The only connection between Ape Canyon and Ape Cave is in the name. Ape Cave was discovered by the Mount St. Helens Apes, who took their name from the Ape Canyon legend. For more information, contact the Mount St. Helens National Volcanic Monument office at (360) 247-3900.

Top of Ape Canyon with Mount Adams in the background

## ▶ NEARBY ACTIVITIES

If you'd like an even more dramatic view of the blast zone from the eruption of Mount St. Helens, drive around to the Windy Ridge Visitor Center, northeast of the mountain in the heart of the scene of destruction. In the summer, rangers give talks every hour on the half hour. To get there, when you get back to FS 90, turn left, and follow the signs; it's about 55 paved miles from there.

# APE CAVE

**LENGTH:** Lower cave is 1.6 miles round-trip; upper cave is 2.3 miles round-trip. Access trail adds 0.4 miles to both.

**CONFIGURATION:** Lower, out-and-back; upper, loop

**DIFFICULTY:** Lower cave, easy; upper, hard

**SCENERY:** Inside of a lava tube, with cave features and dripping water

**EXPOSURE:** None

**TRAFFIC:** Use is heavy all summer, especially in the lower cave.

**TRAIL SURFACE:** Pavement on the access trail; rock, packed dirt

**HIKING TIME:** 1 hour for lower cave; 3 hours for upper cave

**SEASON:** May–October

**ACCESS:** Northwest Forest Pass required.

**MAPS:** USFS Mount St. Helens National Volcanic Monument

**FACILITIES:** Rest rooms at the trailhead

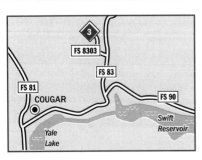

## ▶ IN BRIEF

If you've ever wanted to go caving, here's your chance. You have two options: one is an easy stroll with plenty of room; the other is more challenging and requires a little climbing here and there. Both are fun and fascinating for the whole family. Also, forest rangers lead hikes into the cave, so call ahead for the schedule.

## ▶ DESCRIPTION

This is no ordinary hike, to be sure, but it's something everyone should see. Even if you're claustrophobic and afraid of the dark, you should be able to handle the lower cave, which in the world of caving is a walk in the park.

Where did this cave come from? Technically it's a lava tube (the longest one in the continental United States), left behind after an eruption of Mount St. Helens 1,900 years ago. Lava on the surface cooled, but it kept running underneath, and when it was gone the tube was left behind. Since then, other eruptions have filled the bottom, making a nice floor to walk on, and earthquakes have shaken boulders loose from the ceiling of the upper cave. In places, you can make out ripple marks on the floor where lava cooled in waterlike patterns.

Now, as for the name. There are, of course, no apes here. A local band of Boy Scouts took

## ▶ DIRECTIONS

From Portland on I-5, drive 21 miles north of the Columbia River and take Exit 21/Woodland. Turn right onto WA 503 (Lewis River Road), which after 31 miles (2 miles past the town of Cougar) turns into FS 90. Follow FS 90 for 3.3 miles and turn left onto FS 83. Go 1.6 miles and turn left onto FS 8303, following a sign for Ape Cave. The well-marked trailhead is 0.9 miles ahead. Driving time is 1 hour and 10 minutes.

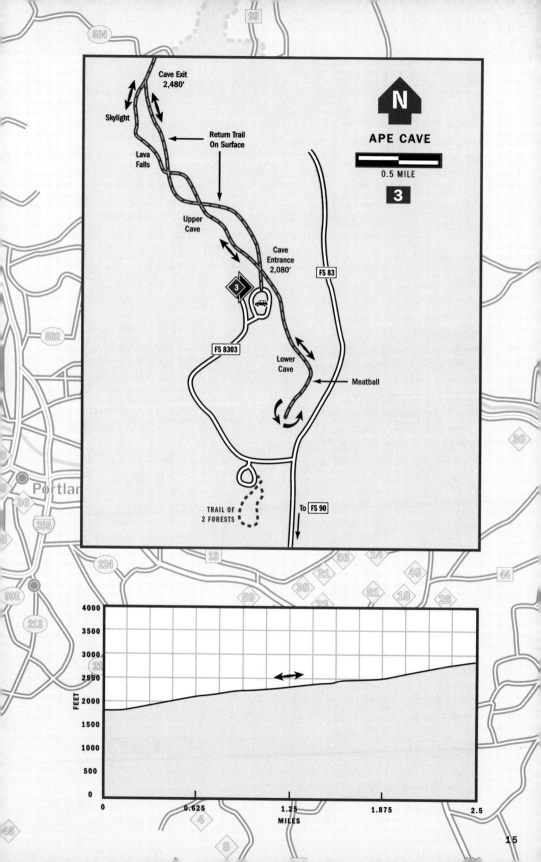

N

APE CAVE

0.5 MILE

3

Cave Exit
2,480'

Skylight

Return Trail
On Surface

Lava
Falls

Upper
Cave

Cave
Entrance
2,080'

3

FS 83

FS 8303

Lower
Cave

Meatball

TRAIL OF
2 FORESTS

To FS 90

FEET

4000
3500
3000
2500
2000
1500
1000
500
0

0        0.625        1.25        1.875        2.5

MILES

that name from a legendary (and staged) Bigfoot sighting in the 1920s. That "sighting" took place in what's now called Ape Canyon. The Scouts found the cave; hence, Ape Cave.

After walking a paved 0.2-mile trail from the parking lot, you'll arrive at the main entrance to the cave. Walk down the stone steps and pause to give your eyes some time to adjust. Even your flashlight beam will seem dim at first. Walk down a set of metal steps, and when you get to the bottom the lower cave will be in front of you. The upper cave starts behind the steps. Do the lower cave first.

As you walk along, look out for features such as "sand castles." Over the centuries before people came along, water washed away most of the sand on the floor but left some "castles" standing. Because there was no wind, they stood there for hundreds of years, until people came along and knocked most of them over. There are a few left, though, so watch your step. Also look along the ceiling for "lava-sicles," which look like tiny stalactites but were formed differently.

Stalactites are formed by dripping water, but these resulted when super-heated gases melted parts of the cave ceiling, which then dripped down to form lava-sicles.

Another thing that happened was that as the cave cooled, pieces of it broke off as large rocks and flowed with the lava. One of these pieces, known as "the meatball," was left wedged ten feet over your head toward the end of the cave.

Eventually, 0.8 miles from the start, the lower cave ends when the ceiling simply becomes too low to continue and pinches down to nothing. This happens because here the tube dips downhill, and the mudflow that made the floor so easy to walk on filled up the whole thing.

Now, for the upper cave. Less than 100 yards beyond the steps, you'll come to a big pile of rocks that you have to climb over; get used to it. In the next 1.4 miles, which will probably take you more than two hours, there are about a dozen of these rock piles. One thing should set you at ease, though: there is only one cave here, so even if you're up on a pile of boulders and briefly lose your sense of direction, you won't get lost.

Look for the same features here as described for the lower cave, with two additions. At just under a mile, you'll have to climb up two waterfalls of lava. The second one is a particular challenge. Somebody chipped a foothold into it a few feet off the floor, but after that you're on your own. The lava offers good traction, though, so trust that your shoes will hold. The best advice is to put your left foot in the hold, brace your right foot against the far wall, then put your hands on the rock and push up. Rock climbers might call this a chimney move followed by a mantle, but it's not as tough as it sounds.

A little bit past this point you'll come under a skylight, which is too high to climb out of, but when you get there you've only got 0.3 miles to go. At the end, a metal ladder on the left leads out into the world again, and the trail is an easy, downhill stroll of 1.2 miles back to the main entrance.

## ▶ NEARBY ACTIVITIES

For another look at the area's geological history, stop at the boardwalk Trail of Two Forests on the way back to FS 83.

# BAGBY HOT SPRINGS

## IN BRIEF

Unless you've got issues about being among naked people, this is one place you should positively visit. The hike isn't much of a challenge, but the destination is sublime: historic hot springs with cedar-log tubs, some of them private, surrounded by ancient-growth forest.

## DESCRIPTION

It seems everybody in the area knows about Bagby, even the folks who haven't actually been there. Just the word seems to stand for something about life in the Pacific Northwest: soothing, relaxing, a retreat from the hustle-and-bustle world, back into the days of the ancient forest and natural elements.

Well it's not just that. A nonprofit group called Friends of Bagby built two bathhouses on the property, and the chances you'll be the only people there are slim. On weekends you might have to wait to soak, unless you start early.

From the trailhead parking lot, start up the wide trail and cross a bridge over Nohorn Creek, named after the nickname of an early pioneer in the area. The hiking is pleasant, the pools in the river inviting, and the forest inspiring. If you happen to notice some old metal loops tacked high into the trees, those once held telephone wires that connected fire lookouts back in the 1930s. When you cross a bridge over Hot Springs Fork, you're almost to the springs.

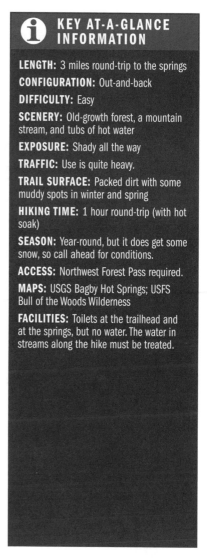

## KEY AT-A-GLANCE INFORMATION

**LENGTH:** 3 miles round-trip to the springs

**CONFIGURATION:** Out-and-back

**DIFFICULTY:** Easy

**SCENERY:** Old-growth forest, a mountain stream, and tubs of hot water

**EXPOSURE:** Shady all the way

**TRAFFIC:** Use is quite heavy.

**TRAIL SURFACE:** Packed dirt with some muddy spots in winter and spring

**HIKING TIME:** 1 hour round-trip (with hot soak)

**SEASON:** Year-round, but it does get some snow, so call ahead for conditions.

**ACCESS:** Northwest Forest Pass required.

**MAPS:** USGS Bagby Hot Springs; USFS Bull of the Woods Wilderness

**FACILITIES:** Toilets at the trailhead and at the springs, but no water. The water in streams along the hike must be treated.

## DIRECTIONS

From Portland on OR 224, travel 44 miles southeast of I-205, through the town of Estacada, to the ranger station at Ripplebrook. Turn right onto FS 46 and, 3.6 miles later, right again onto FS 63. Travel 3.5 miles and turn right onto FS 70. The trailhead is six miles ahead on the left. Driving time is 1 hour and 15 minutes.

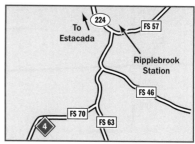

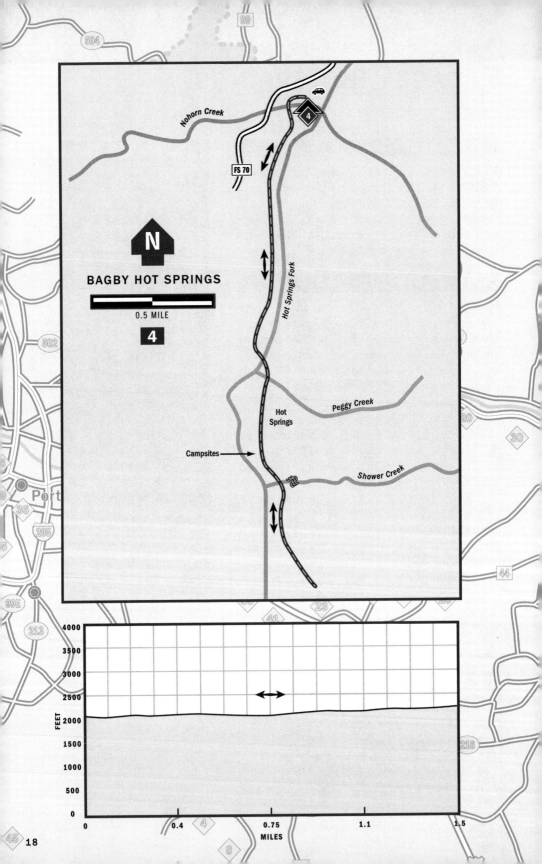

N

**BAGBY HOT SPRINGS**

0.5 MILE

4

Nohorn Creek

FS 70

Hot Springs Fork

Peggy Creek

Hot Springs

Campsites →

Shower Creek

FEET

4000
3500
3000
2500
2000
1500
1000
500
0

0    0.4    4    0.75    1.1    1.5
MILES

When you come to the springs area, the first thing you'll notice is the 1913 ranger cabin, which is listed on the National Register of Historic Places. It was a central communications station for those fire lookouts. I should mention that this cabin of 16-inch cedar logs was hand-built by one ranger, a certain Phil Putz, who first visited the area after walking 39 miles in one day. You think he was happy to find the springs? The path behind the cabin leads to a monumental downed tree; check out the inside, which was rotted away long before the giant was cut to keep it from squashing the bathhouses.

The bathhouse on the right has one big tub, with room for five or six adults. The one on the left has an open area with several tubs and five private rooms, each with a two-person log tub. The water comes out of the springs at 136 degrees and runs through a system of log flumes. To fill a tub, you just open up the valve and let the hot water in, then grab a bucket, fill it with cold water from a nearby tub, and get the temperature where you want it. Typically, a full tub needs four or five buckets of cold water to make it tolerable. As it cools off, just open up the valve and let some more hot stuff in. It's fantastic. About 50% of bathers don't wear swimsuits, but in areas other than the tubs you are requested to wear clothing. It's also requested that if people are waiting you limit your soaking to one hour.

Even if there's nobody around when you get to the springs, consider taking some time to explore farther up the trail before you soak. It's old growth all the way, up the Hot Springs Fork, past Shower Creek and Spray Creek, and eventually into the Bull of the Woods Wilderness. You should go at least as far as Shower Creek (0.3 miles past the springs and just 0.1 mile past a camping area on the right) to enjoy the 50-foot falls and a little wooden platform somebody built underneath it for folks to shower on.

As alcohol is allowed and the police are hours away, Bagby is best avoided on weekend nights, when partyers sometimes take over the place. So unless you too are a beer-swilling yahoo, go on a weekday or early on the weekends. For more information, call the Clackamas Ranger District office at (503) 630-4256.

# BARLOW PASS

## KEY AT-A-GLANCE INFORMATION

**LENGTH:** 8 miles

**CONFIGURATION:** Out-and-back

**DIFFICULTY:** Moderate

**SCENERY:** Forest, meadows, view of Mount Hood, and two river canyons

**EXPOSURE:** Forest on the way up, open on top

**TRAFFIC:** Use is light.

**TRAIL SURFACE:** Packed dirt with some roots

**HIKING TIME:** 3.5 hours

**SEASON:** June–October

**ACCESS:** Northwest Forest Pass required.

**MAPS:** USGS Mount Hood South; Mount Hood Wilderness; Green Trails #462 (Mount Hood)

**FACILITIES:** None; water on the hike must be treated

**SPECIAL COMMENTS:** Consider doing this hike as a one-way, 6-mile trek with a second car parked at Timberline Lodge.

## IN BRIEF

There's a great view of Mount Hood at the top, and a one-way car-shuttle option that ends at Timberline Lodge, but this convenient, not-too-tough hike is all about the forest. It goes through some of the finest high-elevation old-growth around.

## DESCRIPTION

There are more spectacular hikes in the Mount Hood area, but none has the combination of solitude and old-growth beauty that this one has. It's also perfect for a picnic, or just a dose of sunshine, in a high altitude meadow with Mount Hood looming over you. And if you do the one-way option with a shuttle, you can wind up at Timberline Lodge.

From the trailhead, walk across FS 3531 and into the woods on the Pacific Crest Trail (#2000). Stop to admire the relief map of the PCT in Oregon, and contemplate some of the distances on there. People who hike the whole PCT in a year average about 20 miles a day! You'll get in 4 miles on the PCT today; note that on the USGS Mount Hood South map, which was created in 1962, this trail is still labeled as the Skyline Trail, an old path that mostly got swallowed up when the PCT was created.

Take the left-most fork of the trails before you, walking north on the PCT towards Mount

## DIRECTIONS

From Portland on US 26, drive 51 miles east of I-205 and turn north on OR 35, following signs for Hood River. After 2.5 miles on OR 35, turn right onto FS 3531, following signs for Barlow Pass and the Pacific Crest Trail (PCT). The trailhead is 0.2 miles ahead on FS 3531. Driving time is 1 hour and 15 minutes.

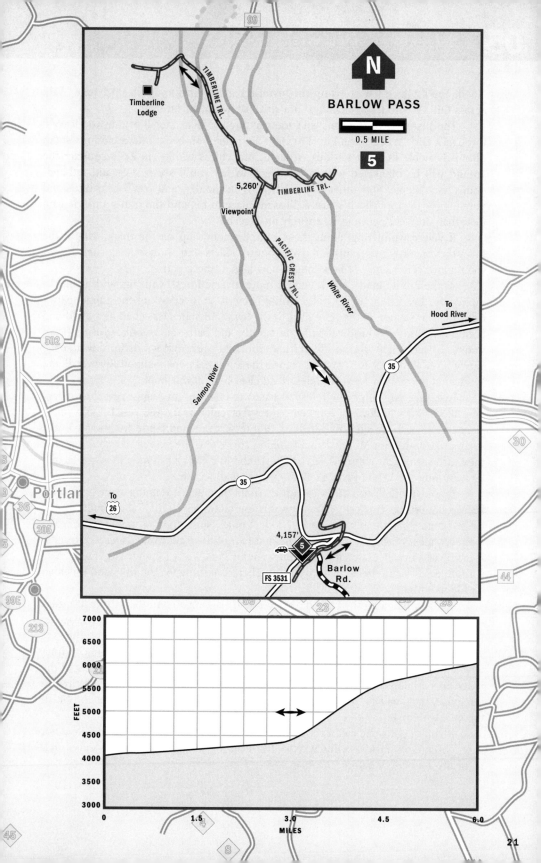

N

**BARLOW PASS**

0.5 MILE

5

Timberline Lodge

TIMBERLINE TRL.

TIMBERLINE TRL.

5,260'
Viewpoint

PACIFIC CREST TRL.

Salmon River

White River

To
Hood River

35

35

To
26

4,157'

5

FS 3531

Barlow
Rd.

Portlan

FEET

7000
6500
6000
5500
5000
4500
4000
3500
3000

0          1.5          3.0          4.5          6.0
MILES

Hood. You'll take a few steps on the historic Barlow Road and, after 0.1 mile, walk across OR 35. The trail continues in a small draw on the far side.

The first part of the trail isn't too exciting; in fact, after 0.5 mile you'll walk through a fairly recent clear-cut. But right after that you come into a glorious stand of mostly noble fir, with its long, straight, branchless trunks. In early summer the ground will be blanketed with wildflowers. In fall you'll see berries and red-and-orange vine maple. Stay quiet, especially early in the day, and you'll hear birds and possibly see deer or elk. It's just a pleasant place to be, and the trail's altitude gain (less than 300 feet per mile) is entirely manageable.

If you're wondering about those blue diamonds up on the trees early in the hike, they mark winter trails for cross-country skiers and showshoers. Their height should give you a sense of how much snow falls in these parts.

At the 2-mile mark, you'll enter a more diverse forest, with firs and hemlocks mixed together. Then, at 3.5 miles, you'll come to an overlook of the Salmon River Canyon. The Salmon is the only river in the lower 48 states classified as a Wild and Scenic River from its headwaters to its mouth, and here you're looking at its headwaters. It starts right up the hill at Timberline Ski Area, and winds up down at the Sandy River along US 26. Two hikes along the lower Salmon—Salmon River Trail and Wildwood Recreation Area—are described elsewhere in this book.

Just after this point, the forest will start to open up, in August revealing meadows filled with wildflowers, especially the spectacular beargrass, which looks like a giant cotton swab. In a few minutes, you'll intersect the Timberline Trail that's in just such a meadow, with Mount Hood looming above you. Relax here if you'd like and then turn around, or continue left on the Timberline Trail for .3 mile to a spectacular lookout onto the White River Canyon, hundreds of feet deep.

If you've opted to park a car up at Timberline and are doing a one-way hike, keep going up the Timberline Trail towards the mountain. It's 1.5 more miles to the lodge—miles that climb a little over 700 feet in all, so it's not too much more work. However, most of the climbing is in the first part of the trail, which is also, at points, as sandy as a beach. So it can get tedious. And if there's any rough weather anywhere around, it will be up here, so bring a coat. There's nothing to stop the wind this high on the mountain.

You go first along the edge of the White River Canyon and then through meadows and across the tiny Salmon River. This crossing has no bridge but is manageable. Look for views south to Mount Jefferson, some 45 miles away, and a sign on the PCT with mileages to Canada and Mexico. You'll also encounter the Mountaineer Trail, which loops up to the Silcox Hut, then back down to the Timberline Trail west of the lodge, in a section that's part of the Timberline Lodge chapter. When you get close to the lodge, trails will go every which way, so just aim for the hot chocolate and finish the hike with style.

If you've got some clearance on your vehicle, you can drive the Barlow Road for miles, eventually making your way to The Dalles—though the road improves dramatically a long way before The Dalles.

# BEACON ROCK STATE PARK

## ▶ IN BRIEF

One of the most recognized symbols of the Columbia River Gorge, Beacon Rock is also an amazing, if short, hiking experience—and it's not even all this state park has to offer.

## ▶ DESCRIPTION

Beacon Rock got its name—well, its white man's name—on Halloween 1805, when William Clark described it in his journal. For the Corps of Discovery as well as the people who then lived along the Columbia River, Beacon Rock meant two important things: the last of the rapids on the Columbia and the beginning of tidal influence on the river. Today, it means a unique hiking experience to its summit, and the state park around it means a chance for more nice views of the Columbia River.

To go up Beacon Rock, start walking at a sign on the south side of WA 14 and get ready to give thanks and admiration to a man named Henry J. Biddle. It was he who bought the rock (which is what's left of the inside of an ancient

## ▶ DIRECTIONS

From Portland on I-84, drive 37 miles east of I-205 and take Exit 44/Cascade Locks. As soon as you enter the town, take your first right to get on the Bridge of the Gods, following a sign for Stevenson, Washington. Pay a $1 toll on the bridge, and at the far end turn left (west) on WA 14. Proceed 6.6 miles to Beacon Rock State Park. To climb Beacon Rock, park on the left; to go toward Hamilton Mountain, turn right on the access road to the campground and drive 0.4 miles to the trailhead. The gate to the upper trailhead is closed in winter and spring, but the trail is open; you'll just have to park on WA 14 and walk 0.4 miles up the access road. Driving time is 55 minutes.

### ⓘ KEY AT-A-GLANCE INFORMATION

**LENGTH:** 1.6 miles to top of Beacon Rock; 7 miles to Hamilton Mountain

**CONFIGURATION:** Out-and-back

**DIFFICULTY:** Moderate (Hamilton Mountain is hard).

**SCENERY:** Overlooks of the Columbia River, close-up view of a waterfall

**EXPOSURE:** Fairly open

**TRAFFIC:** Heavy on weekends

**TRAIL SURFACE:** Packed dirt with rocks, pavement

**HIKING TIME:** 1 hour for Beacon Rock, 3.5 hours for Hamilton Mountain

**SEASON:** Year-round; call for trail conditions.

**ACCESS:** No fees or permits needed.

**MAPS:** Green Trails #428 (Bridal Veil)

**FACILITIES:** Water and rest rooms

**SPECIAL COMMENTS:** For more information, phone Columbia River Gorge National Scenic Area (541) 386-2333.

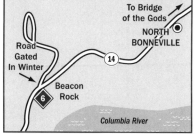

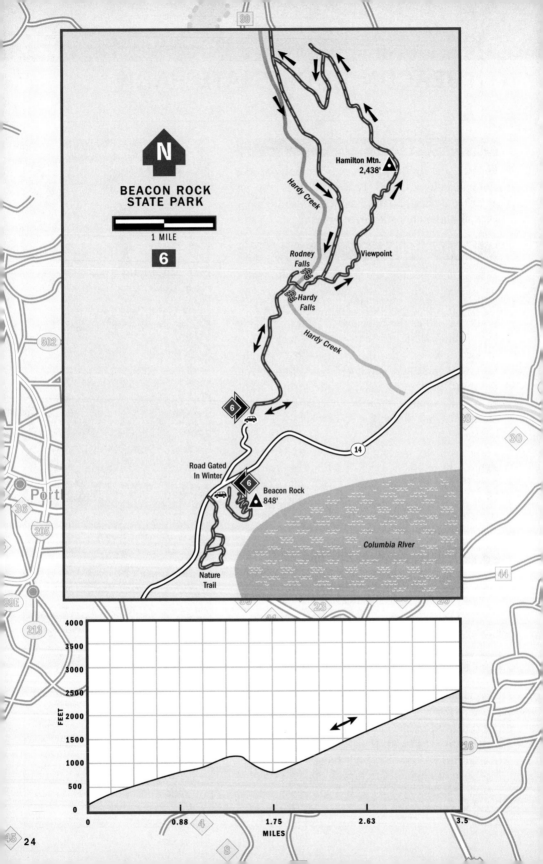

N

BEACON ROCK
STATE PARK

1 MILE

6

Hardy Creek

Hamilton Mtn.
2,438'

Viewpoint

Rodney
Falls

Hardy
Falls

Hardy Creek

6

14

Road Gated
In Winter

6

Beacon Rock
848'

Columbia River

Nature
Trail

FEET

4000
3500
3000
2500
2000
1500
1000
500
0

0        0.88        1.75        2.63        3.5

MILES

volcano) specifically to build the trail you're about to hike. That he did so is simply amazing; that he did it with the help of just one other person from October 1915 to April 1918 is almost beyond comprehension.

To get to the top, just keep it up and, if heights bother you, don't look down. It's virtually all rails and bridges and platforms until you're just below the summit, where you'll have a view east to Bonneville Dam, north to Hamilton Mountain, and straight down the other side to the boat docks of the state park. Keep an eye out for rock climbers, and don't throw anything from the top.

For a more challenging and more rewarding hike, drive (or walk, if the gate is closed) up the road across WA 14 to the campground and the Hamilton Mountain trailhead. You'll climb gently through forest until you reach a bench to take a break, although the power lines you're under aren't all that scenic. At half a mile, stay right at a trail junction, and 0.9 miles later you'll come to a sign saying Hamilton Mountain and pointing downhill.

For a sight to remember, and also if you'd like a soaking to cool you down, go left a couple hundred yards and check out Rodney Falls, which almost explodes out of a bowl in the rock face. You can get right in its spray, if you don't mind essentially wading throughout the last part of the trail.

If you don't feel like climbing anymore, turn back here, as it gets tougher quickly. For Hamilton Mountain, follow the signed trail as it crosses Hardy Creek and then heads up the hill. After 0.2 miles of climbing, you'll come to a trail junction; to the left is the return portion of a possible loop hike, but keep to the right, and after some sturdy climbing you'll reach a spectacular rock lookout. There's nothing wrong with turning around here, but be careful as you walk around on these rocks—in some spots it's more than 200 feet straight down.

But if you want the real view, keep going up—another 700 feet in just over a mile—until you reach a junction on top of the mountain. The view south is somewhat blocked by brush, but you can see up to Table Mountain (see page 162) to the northeast and Mount St. Helens to the northwest. The scenery is better on the route you just came up, but if you want to complete the loop, continue back along the ridge for 0.9 miles, turn left onto an old road, pick up another trail less than a mile later, and follow that trail through the woods for another mile. That puts you back at the junction mentioned above, just east of Rodney Falls. Turn right and you'll be back at the trailhead in 1.6 miles.

## ▶ NEARBY ACTIVITIES

The Columbia Gorge Interpretive Center, a few miles west on WA 14 in Stevenson, features historical displays ranging from the geological (formation of the gorge) to the steam engines used on railroads a bit more recently.

# BREITENBUSH

## ⓘ KEY AT-A-GLANCE INFORMATION

**LENGTH:** Recommended hike, 5.2 miles

**CONFIGURATION:** Out-and-back

**DIFFICULTY:** Moderate

**SCENERY:** Ancient forests and a raging river

**EXPOSURE:** Shady all the way

**TRAFFIC:** Moderate to light

**TRAIL SURFACE:** Packed dirt with a few roots

**HIKING TIME:** 2.5 hours

**SEASON:** Year-round

**ACCESS:** Northwest Forest Pass required. to park on FS 4685; day-use fee required to park at the hot springs.

**MAPS:** USGS Breitenbush Hot Springs; free maps available at resort office

**FACILITIES:** None at the trailhead; all are available at the hot springs.

**SPECIAL COMMENTS:** A one-way hike with a car shuttle will leave you at the hot springs.

## ▶ IN BRIEF

With its combination of old-growth majesty and New Age spirituality, the area around Breitenbush Hot Springs is one of the most peaceful and inspiring places in Oregon. The trails are easy, the surroundings are sublime, and the water is hot.

## ▶ DESCRIPTION

Like a bay of tranquility amid a sea of logging operations, the area along the South Fork of the Breitenbush River is often described with words like peaceful, magical, and special. The resort is a draw unto itself—with its pools, tubs, well-being programs, massage, and other healing arts—but the forest and the river beckon for easy, pleasant walks.

One option is to simply go to the hot springs resort, register as a day user, and start your hike on the Spotted Owl Trail, which starts across from the resort parking lot. After 1.1 mile on that trail, you'll come to a junction with the Cliff Trail. Turn right on the Cliff Trail for 0.7 fairly steep miles, including some exposed sections on a cliff, to an intersection with the Devils Ridge Trail, which climbs steeply to two lookouts. If you stay on the Spotted Owl Trail.] In a half mile, you'll come to the Emerald Forest Trail.

## ▶ DIRECTIONS

From Portland on I-5, drive 35 miles south of I-205 and take Exit 253/Stayton/Detroit Lake. Turn left (east) onto OR 22 and follow it 49 miles to Detroit. Turn left onto FS 46. For the roadside trailhead, travel 12.2 miles, turn right onto FS 4685, and go a half mile to the trailhead on the right. For the hot springs from Detroit, go 10 miles on FS 46 and turn right onto a one-lane bridge just past the Cleator Bend Campground. Over the next 1.5 miles, stay left at three junctions and you're there. Driving time is 1 hour and 45 minutes.

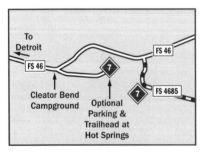

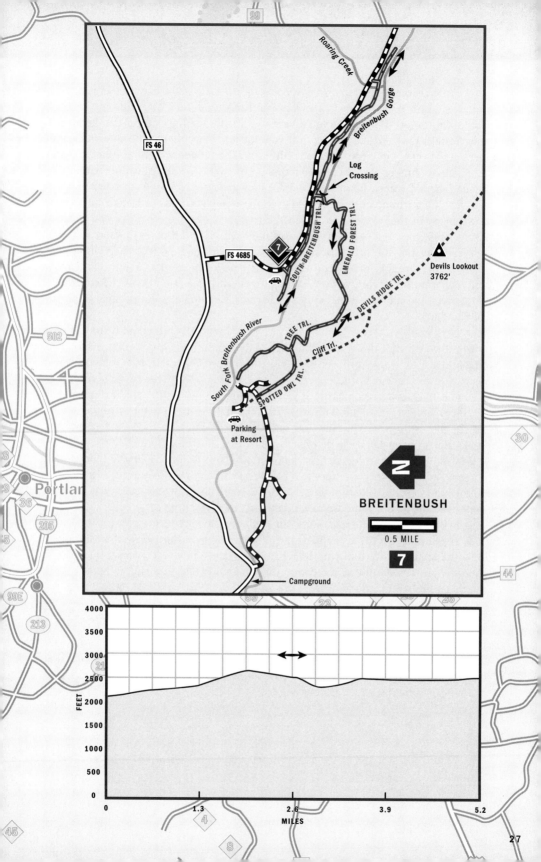

Roaring Creek

FS 46

Breitenbush Gorge

Log
Crossing

FS 4685

SOUTH BREITENBUSH TRL.

EMERALD FOREST TRL.

7

DEVILS RIDGE TRL.

Devils Lookout
3762'

South Fork Breitenbush River

TREE TRL.

Cliff Trl.

SPOTTED OWL TRL.

Parking
at Resort

BREITENBUSH

0.5 MILE

7

Campground

Portland

FEET

4000
3500
3000
2500
2000
1500
1000
500
0

0     1.3     2.6     3.9     5.2
MILES

From the parking area on FS 4685, walk 0.1 mile down the trail and turn left onto the South Breitenbush Gorge National Recreation Trail. You will only hear the river at this point, so for views you'll have to settle for the big Douglas firs, hemlocks, and Western red cedars towering over you and the clover-like oxalis and early-summer wildflowers below you. Rhododendrons will be blooming here in June.

After 0.7 miles, you'll come to a trail on the right, leading downhill, with a sign saying Emerald Forest. Ignore this one for now and keep going. In this area you will see what a big winter storm can do to even these mighty trees. In 1990 a storm blew down many of these trees and closed the trail for a year; another one, on Thanksgiving 1999, took out some bridges over the river. After 0.8 miles, a short side trail will lead down to the Breitenbush Gorge, a 100-yard-long, 40-foot-deep chasm that the river rips through. You can turn around here or go another half a mile on the main trail to a beautiful footbridge over Roaring Creek; this area also has much better views of the river. You might as well explore it, because the total elevation change is practically nothing.

Now make your way back to the first trail, the one you ignored before. Take it now, and go 0.1 mile down the hill to the South Breitenbush, which you used to cross on a bridge. The 1999 storm rolled this one-log bridge over on its side, officially closing it. But subsequent storms blew several trees down over the river. One of these logs is large enough to cross on easily. If you do so, on the other side, you'll climb briefly on the Emerald Forest Trail and then stroll through as pretty a forest as you'll ever see. By the end of the trail, one mile later when you intersect the Tree Trail and the Devils Ridge Trail, you'll be in what is known as a "climax forest." This, in other words, is what a forest looks like after thousands of years of being left alone—no humans, no major fires, no storms to blow everything down. If you put in about 0.1 mile on the Tree Trail, you'll walk between the rootballs of two trees that fell in opposite directions at the same time. You can also explore along the Devils Ridge Trail, which climbs some 900 feet in less than a mile to the lookouts.

If you parked a car at the hot springs, keep going on the Tree Trail until it intersects the Spotted Owl Trail, and in 1.1 mile on that one you'll be ready to soak. If, instead, you turn around at the end of the Emerald Forest Trail and go back to your car, that's the 5.2-mile loop.

▶ **NEARBY ACTIVITIES**

Breitenbush Hot Springs is open from 9 a.m. to 6 p.m. to day-use visitors, but advance reservations are required. You'll have access to the pools, steam room, and daily well-being programs. The cost is on a sliding scale (based on your ability to pay) and ranges from $8 to $15. Dinner is $8.

# BULL OF THE WOODS

This is like two great hikes in one: an easy stroll through old-growth forest and rhododendrons to two beautiful lakes, and a more challenging climb to a fire lookout tower with a panoramic view.

▶ DESCRIPTION

This trail has it all. Come in late June, as soon as the snow has cleared, and let your mind be boggled by the rhododendron show among the old-growth towers on the way to Pansy Lake.

Come in late summer and pick huckleberries up on the ridge. Or come in fall, when the ridge will be awash in color and the mountains might have their first coat of snow. Just make sure you get here.

The peak is the second-highest point in the 27,000-acre Bull of the Woods Wilderness, which boasts more than a dozen lakes bigger than an acre, 68 miles of hiking trails, and even the world-famous northern spotted owl, which you almost certainly won't see.

From the trailhead, you start right out through a beautiful forest, walking basically flat for 0.8 miles, across some nice little creeks and

▶ DIRECTIONS

From Portland on OR 224, travel 44 miles southeast of I-205, through the town of Estacada, to the ranger station at Ripplebrook. Bear right onto FS 46 and, 3.6 miles later, right again onto FS 63. After 5.7 miles, turn right onto FS 6340, following a sign for Bull of the Woods and Pansy Basin. At a junction 3.5 miles later, stay straight, still on FS 6340. Then, 4.4 miles past that junction (7.9 miles after FS 63), turn right on FS 6341, ignoring a sign to the left saying Bull of the Woods Trail. The parking area is 3.6 miles ahead on the right. Driving time is 1 hour and 45 minutes.

ℹ KEY AT-A-GLANCE INFORMATION

**LENGTH:** 2.2 miles round-trip to Pansy Lake; 7 miles round-trip to Bull of the Woods

**CONFIGURATION:** Loop

**DIFFICULTY:** Easy to Pansy Lake; hard to Bull of the Woods

**SCENERY:** Old-growth forest, a mountain lake, rhododendrons, huckleberries

**EXPOSURE:** In the shade to the top of the ridge

**TRAFFIC:** Moderate on summer weekends, light otherwise

**TRAIL SURFACE:** Packed dirt with some roots, then a few rocks up top

**HIKING TIME:** 1 hour to Pansy Lake, 4 hours for all

**SEASON:** June–October

**ACCESS:** Northwest Forest Pass required.

**MAPS:** USGS Bull of the Woods; USFS Bull of the Woods Wilderness

**FACILITIES:** None

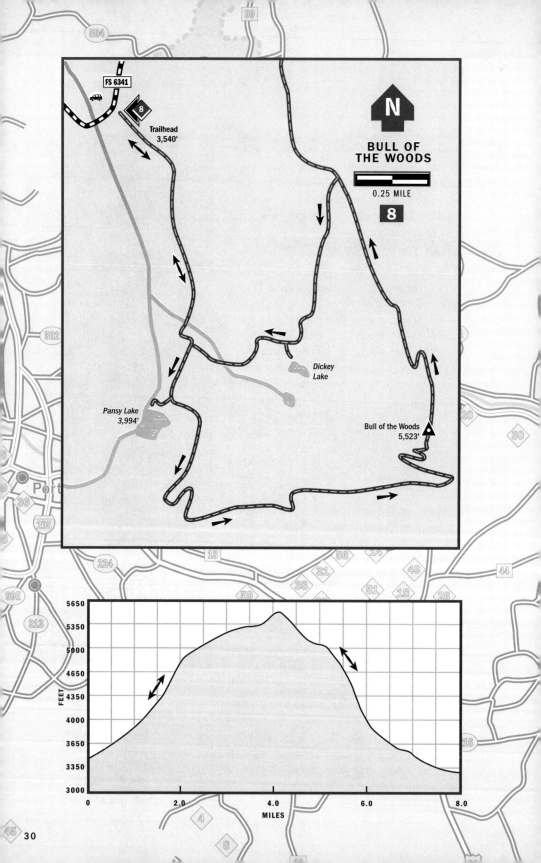

FS 6341

8

Trailhead
3,540'

N

BULL OF
THE WOODS

0.25 MILE

8

Dickey
Lake

Pansy Lake
3,994'

Bull of the Woods
5,523'

5650
5350
5000
4650
4350
4000
3650
3350
3000

FEET

0        2.0        4.0        6.0        8.0
MILES

through gauntlets of rhododendrons, until you reach a signed trail junction. Trail 549, coming down the hill from your left, is the return portion of our loop. We'll go right here, following a sign for Pansy Lake.

Just before the lake, you'll pass a sign that says TWIN LAKES, but ignore it and continue straight to visit Pansy Lake. There's a campsite on the right with excellent sitting rocks for a picnic or a quick rest and snack before you start up the hill.

Now, return to the trail and take what's now a right turn, following the Twin Lakes sign. You'll climb gradually for a while and then start into a series of switchbacks. In just less than a mile from the lake, you'll gain 800 feet before you intersect trail #558 in a saddle between Pansy Mountain and Bull of the Woods. Turn left onto 558.

While the switchbacks were obviously steep, this trail is what I call "sneaky steep," which means that it doesn't look like much, but you'll be able to feel the elevation gain. You're gaining about 700 feet in this mile of trail, and since you're now going over 5,000

Mount Jefferson from the lookout on Bull of the Woods

feet, you're probably starting to feel the relative lack of oxygen. The forest in here is beautiful, though, and should take your mind off the climb. And if you're wondering why the moss doesn't grow on the bottom 10 feet of the trunks, it's because that's where the average snow depth is.

When you gain the top of the ridge and intersect trail #554, turn left, and with one more push through some switchbacks you'll pop out at the top of Bull of the Woods, with its old forest service fire lookout tower. Walk up onto the deck and have a look around. You'll see Big Slide Lake below you, but Mount Jefferson, 20 miles away, is the dominant sight. On a clear day, you can see all the way from the Three Sisters on your right to Mount Rainier on your left. As the crow flies, it's about 175 miles from the Sisters to Rainier. Rest here and feel proud.

To continue the loop, find a trail junction in the trees on the opposite side of the watchtower from Mount Jefferson. This is the Bull of the Woods Trail (#550). Follow it to your right, along the ridge. You'll see occasional great views and many, many flowers for 1.1 mile, at which point you'll intersect Trail 549. Take 549 down and to the left, and your elevation loss will quickly get serious. Just past half a mile, keep an eye out through the trees on your left for Dickey Lake—a lake seen through trees is always a magical sight—and also for a trail that leads down to the lake itself. That trail is just past a meadow on Trail 549.

After another half mile, most of it through a sea of rhododendrons, you'll get back to the trail where this whole thing started, the Pansy Lake Trail (#551). Turn right there, and you'll be back to the car in no time.

# CAPE FALCON

## ⓘ KEY AT-A-GLANCE INFORMATION

**LENGTH:** 5 miles

**CONFIGURATION:** Out-and-back

**DIFFICULTY:** Easy

**SCENERY:** Old-growth forest, waterfalls, and several clifftop vistas of the sea

**EXPOSURE:** Shady until the last 200 yards

**TRAFFIC:** Use is heavy all summer, especially weekends; it's moderate otherwise.

**TRAIL SURFACE:** Packed dirt with some gravel; mud

**HIKING TIME:** 2.5 hours

**SEASON:** Year-round

**ACCESS:** No fees or permits needed.

**MAPS:** USGS Arch Cape

**FACILITIES:** There are toilets 0.1 mile down the road from the trailhead, but no water. The water on the trail must be treated.

## ▶ IN BRIEF

This is one of the best hikes on the Oregon coast. It's easy to get to, it's basically flat, and it offers great views and soothing forest. No wonder it's so popular!

## ▶ DESCRIPTION

Getting out of your car and onto the Cape Falcon Trail is what hiking on the Oregon coast is all about. You're barely an hour from the Portland metro area, and then after about five steps you're in a rare, coastal, old-growth forest, walking a wide, mostly flat path to a wonderful destination. You'll cruise along for 0.4 miles to a junction. Short Sand Beach with rest rooms in the campground will be to your left and down the hill about 0.3 miles; Cape Falcon will be to the right. Straight ahead will be a nice view of Smugglers Cove.

After turning right, you'll cross a small creek and start winding in and out with the contours of the land. One highlight along the way is a spectacular pair of downed trees sharing their root structures. The trail splits here for a few feet. The right fork is often muddy. The left fork is cooler: it includes climbing onto one of the downed trees and walking along its trunk for awhile.

Around 1.3 miles, where the trail makes a sharp left turn, there's a downed tree on the right

## ▶ DIRECTIONS

From Portland on US 26, travel 74 miles west of I-405 and turn south on US 101. The trailhead is 14 miles ahead on the right. There are actually three parking areas in succession here. The first (unmarked) one on the right is for Cape Falcon, distinguished by a small median strip along the highway. The second one, 0.1 mile farther on the left, is where the rest room is located. The third is one of the trailheads for Neahkahnie Mountain. Driving time is 1 hour and 35 minutes.

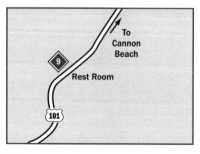

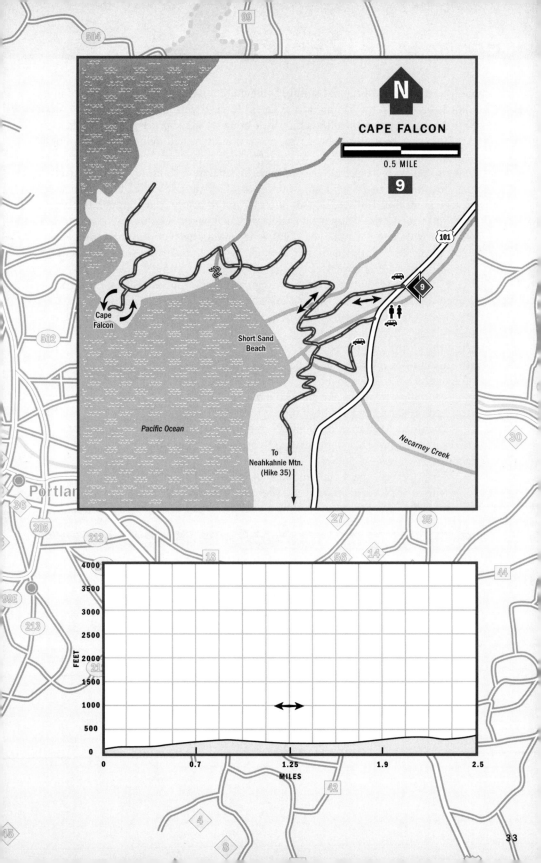

N

CAPE FALCON

0.5 MILE

9

101

9

Cape
Falcon

Short Sand
Beach

Pacific Ocean

Necarney Creek

To
Neahkahnie Mtn.
(Hike 35)

FEET

4000
3500
3000
2500
2000
1500
1000
500
0

0          0.7          1.25          1.9          2.5

MILES

that has left a large, disfigured stump. Some more imaginative hiking friends of mine dubbed this stump the Throne of the Forest King. If you assume the throne, you'll see that your kingdom includes a nice little grove of sitka spruce and hemlock.

With that goofiness behind you, proceed another half mile or so. You'll notice a series of trails plunging down to the left. These access the beach, but they're too steep to fool with—especially at the end. Just before a footbridge over a creek, a small, brushy trail to the left leads 100 feet to a hidden little waterfall in the creek. If you take it another 100 yards or so, often having to nearly crawl through the brush, you'll find yourself at the top of an even larger falls that goes right down to the ocean. Just be careful of your footing, or you'll wind up in a heap down on the rocks some 50 feet below. Back at the main trail, look for the big burls on the spruce in this area. You'll also get a different view of the first falls you visited on the side trail.

Just after this the trail starts out Cape Falcon itself for the last half mile. You'll get nice views back into Smugglers Cove and up to Neahkahnie Mountain (see page 118), then you'll dip through the trees once more to a junction at the edge of a brushy, largely treeless area. For the end of the cape, turn left, and walk about 0.2 miles through the gauntlet of brush. Out at the end, you'll be 200 feet above the sea, with Falcon Rock out in front of you. (At the end you'll be at the top of an unrailed 200-foot cliff.) There are some nice spots under the trees to spread out for a picnic. In late May and early June, the grassy bluffs here are awash in Indian Paintbrush and irises. Look for seals and sea lions on the rocks or in the water.

When you head back to the main trail, turn left for a bit and add some more scenery to your day. This is the Oregon Coast Trail, and in the next mile or so you'll get three more views of the sea.

When the trail starts climbing inland, you might as well turn back, unless the old-growth magic has you in its grips. There are no more ocean views for a while, but there are plenty of big trees and not many people.

## ▶ NEARBY ACTIVITIES

I feel quite strongly that the best clam chowder in the world is served at the Ecola Seafood Market in Cannon Beach, about 11 miles north of the trailhead on US 101. It's at the corner of Second and Spruce, right across from the visitor center.

Also, this hike is right next to the Neahkahnie Mountain Trail, so you could do both in the same day if you're feeling energetic. For more information, call the Oregon State Parks office at (800) 551-6949.

# CAPE LOOKOUT STATE PARK

## ▶ IN BRIEF

This park offers everything the Oregon Coast is all about: old-growth forest, secluded beaches, cliff-top views, and wildlife on land, wing, and water. You've got three options from the trailhead, and with a little energy you could do all three.

## ▶ DESCRIPTION

When you park at this trailhead, you will need to choose one of multiple options, and it's all down-hill from here. Of course, you'll have to come back uphill to get to the car, but even the 800-foot climb from the beach is so well graded you'll hardly be winded when it's done.

Start with the best of the trails, the one out the cape. Take the trail behind the sign at the far end of the lot, and when you get to a junction in 100 yards or so, stay straight. You'll be hiking through that rarest of treats, a coastal, old-growth forest. There are some nice sitka spruces and hemlocks in here, and the whole thing is as peaceful as can be. Just past half a mile out, you'll come to a plaque honoring the flight crew of a B-17

## ⓘ KEY AT-A-GLANCE INFORMATION

**LENGTH:** 5 miles round-trip to end of cape; 4 miles round-trip to South Beach; 4.6 miles round-trip to picnic area

**CONFIGURATION:** All three hikes are out-and-backs.

**DIFFICULTY:** All three hikes are moderate.

**SCENERY:** Old-growth forest, cliffs high above the sea, whales in winter and spring

**EXPOSURE:** Shady, then open at the end

**TRAFFIC:** Heavy on summer weekends

**TRAIL SURFACE:** Gravel, packed dirt, mud

**HIKING TIME:** 2 hours to the end of the cape; 1.5 hours to South Beach; 2 hours to the picnic area

**SEASON:** Year-round, with mud and possibly storms in winter and spring

**ACCESS:** No fees or permits needed.

**MAPS:** USGS Sand Lake

**FACILITIES:** None at the trailhead; rest rooms and water at the campground

## ▶ DIRECTIONS

From Portland on US 26, drive 20 miles west of I-405, then bear west on OR 6, following a sign for Tillamook. Drive 51 miles to Tillamook, and at the intersection with US 101 stay straight. At that intersection and from then on, you will be following signs for Cape Lookout State Park and the 3 Capes Scenic Route. After crossing US 101, go two blocks and turn left on Stillwell Street. Go two more blocks and turn right onto 3rd Street. Travel 4.9 miles and turn left. After 5.3 miles you'll pass the state park campground and day-use area; this is where you can stash a second car to do the shuttle. The trailhead is 2.7 miles past the campground on the right. Driving time is 1 hour and 35 minutes.

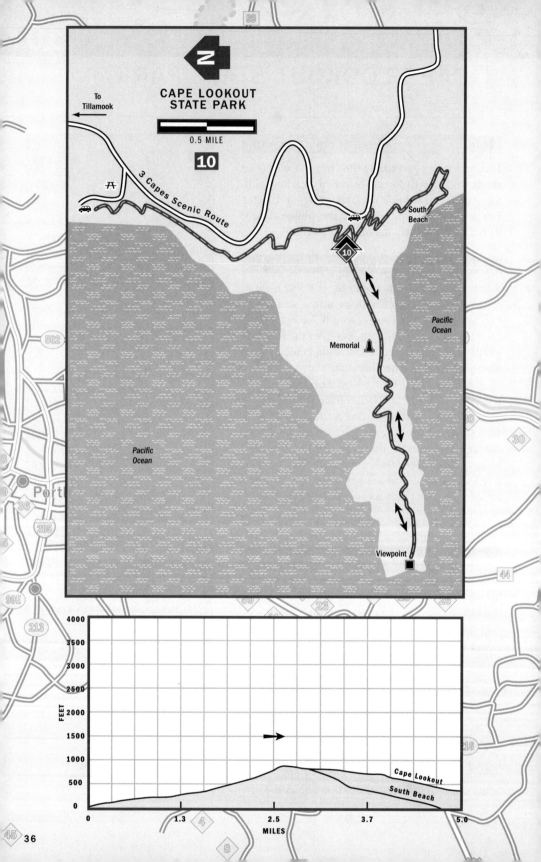

CAPE LOOKOUT
STATE PARK

0.5 MILE

**10**

To
Tillamook

3 Capes Scenic Route

South
Beach

**10**

Pacific
Ocean

Memorial

Pacific
Ocean

Viewpoint

4000
3500
3000
2500
2000
FEET 1500
1000
500
0

Cape Lookout

South Beach

0    1.3    2.5    3.7    5.0
MILES

South Beach and Cape Lookout

bomber that crashed into the cape just west of there in 1943. After another half a mile you'll get a view north; look for the three rocks just off Cape Meares and the town of Oceanside. You can make out an arch in the middle rock; in fact, all three have such arches, and they're called Three Arch Rocks. When you get to some moderately nerve-wracking drop-offs on the left, along with inspiring views south, you're almost done.

At the tip of the cape, you're looking 270 degrees around and 400 feet straight down at the crashing sea. On a calm day—which is rare in a place that gets 100 inches of rain per year—it's not uncommon to see seals or sea lions down there. But the main attraction is the gray whales. Thousands of them make the trip each year from the Bering Sea in Alaska to Baja California, a swim of some 6,000 miles. In late December and early January, when they go south, they tend to be farther out. But in March and April, they're on their way back north with newborn calves, so they go slower and stay closer to shore. At these times of year, bring binoculars (and a raincoat), and you might see dozens of whales in a day. For best viewing, go early in the day, when the sun will be behind you as you look out.

On your way back to the trailhead, when you reach the junction, turn right (downhill) and follow this trail down to South Beach. Avoid the temptation to take all the various cut-off trails, as they add to erosion. If the 2-mile, 800-foot-drop trail seems a little tedious (like when the beach looks like it's just right there below you but you're walking more sideways than down), just believe that you'll be thankful for this easier grade on your way back up.

There's often another kind of watchable wildlife on South Beach. My friend "Surfer John" informs us that the cape can really clean up a northwest swell, dude, and it's totally worth hauling the board down there when there are tubes coming in. You'll be stoked! You can also hike down the beach, which extends four miles south to Sand Lake, but eventually you'll get into an area where cars are allowed, which sort of takes away from the wilderness feeling.

The last option from the trailhead is located across the lot, going north on the Oregon Coast Trail. It's 2.3 miles, all downhill, to the picnic area and nature trail, down by the campground. You'll pass a couple of viewpoints on the way, including one of Sphinx Island.

If you left another car there, your whole day can be a total of 11.3 manageable miles. If you had only one car, you'll have to come back up to the car at the end of the day, stretching things out to almost 13 miles, so it might not be worth it.

*Note:* There is a protective cable at the end of the cape, but in other places you'll be right at the top of a 400-foot cliff. If you have two cars, put one down at the campground/picnic area. You'll have to pay a $3 day-use fee there, but at the end of the day you can walk downhill just 2.3 miles from the trailhead back to your second car. There's also a short nature trail there. For more information, call Cape Lookout State Park at (503) 842-4981.

## ▶ NEARBY ACTIVITIES

As long as you're in Tillamook, take advantage of its tourist stops, most notably the collection of World War II airplanes at the Air Museum south of town and the two cheese factories to the north. The Tillamook Cheese Factory is the best known, but there are slightly more exotic choices at the Blue Heron Cheese Factory.

# CASCADE HEAD

## ▶ IN BRIEF

Imagine standing high atop a windswept, flower-covered prairie, with the sea and the coast spread out below you and not a tree to block the view. Or imagine peeking into a hidden cove where sea lions bark, a waterfall plunges, and waves crash. Well, you don't have to imagine either scene: you can go to Cascade Head and make it happen.

## ▶ DESCRIPTION

First, the Harts Cove Trail. When it starts out, you might think you've got it made, because it's all downhill and steep—it loses about 500 feet in the first half a mile. Too bad you have to walk back up that at the end of the hike. The forest here is a young one of mostly sitka spruce; notice how only the tops of trees are green? That's because these lower portions don't get any sun, not because

## ▶ DIRECTIONS

From Downtown Portland on I-5, drive three miles south and take Exit 294/Tigard/Newberg. Bear right onto OR 99 West and follow it 22 miles. Just before the town of McMinnville, turn left onto OR 18 (following signs for the coast) and follow it for 51 miles to its intersection with US 101. Turn right (north) on US 101. Driving time is 1 hour and 35 minutes.

For the lower, year-round trailhead to the Nature Preserve, go one mile north and turn left onto Three Rocks Road. Follow this for two miles, turn left, and park at Knight Park. To reach the trailhead, follow a trail along the road.

For the two upper trailheads, go 3.8 miles north of OR 18 on US 101 and turn left onto unsigned FS 1861, just before the top of a hill on US 101. Stay left at 2.4 miles, still on FS 1861. The upper Nature Preserve trailhead is 0.8 miles after this turn, on the left. The Harts Cove trailhead is at the end of the road, one mile later.

## ▶ KEY AT-A-GLANCE INFORMATION

**LENGTH:** 5.4 miles round-trip to Harts Cove; 2 to 3.4 miles round-trip to the Nature Preserve

**CONFIGURATION:** Out-and-back

**DIFFICULTY:** Moderate, with an easy option

**SCENERY:** Old-growth forest, waterfalls, sea cliffs, wildflowers, and wildlife

**EXPOSURE:** In the forest at first, then open

**TRAFFIC:** Use is heavy on summer weekends but moderate otherwise.

**TRAIL SURFACE:** Packed dirt with some roots

**HIKING TIME:** 3 hours to Harts Cove; 1–1.5 hours for the Nature Preserve

**SEASON:** The upper trailheads are open July 16 through December 31. The lower trailhead is open year-round.

**ACCESS:** No fees or permits needed.

**MAPS:** USGS Neskowin

**FACILITIES:** No facilities; no water on the trail

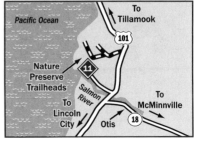

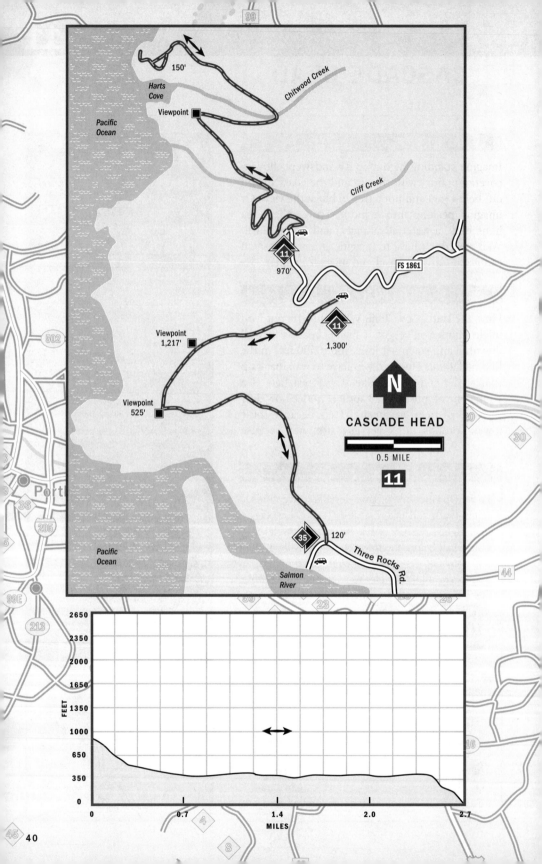

Harts Cove

Chitwood Creek

150'

Pacific Ocean

Viewpoint

Cliff Creek

11
970'

FS 1861

Viewpoint
1,217'

11
1,300'

Viewpoint
525'

N

CASCADE HEAD

0.5 MILE

11

35
120'

Three Rocks Rd.

Salmon River

Pacific Ocean

FEET

2650
2350
2000
1650
1350
1000
650
350
0

0       0.7       1.4       2.0       2.7

MILES

Looking south from the Nature Preserve at Cascade Head

they're unhealthy. Notice, also, the very large stumps around; there's one right on the side of the trail that you can get on top of and measure for yourself.

After 0.7 miles you'll cross Cliff Creek and walk into a different world. Here you can find out what a sitka spruce looks like after about 300 years. You'll also get to hear what hundreds of sea lions sound like—they're to the left, and you might get to see some of them later. Now the hiking gets flatter, as you go out to the end of the ridge to a bench with a view of Harts Cove ahead. Then you'll wrap back around to the right, through the drainage of Chitwood Creek. Half a mile after the bench, you'll walk under a massive blown-down spruce and then out into the meadows on top of the bluff—yet another world visited on this hike.

It's important to stay on the trails here; this area is fragile. If you come in August, you'll be wading through a view that looks like it was lifted from the upper reaches of Mount Hood: look for goldenrod, lupine, Indian paintbrush, and violets. Follow the trail that aims at some trees on the left; there's a wonderful spot to sit down there, and it has a front-row view into Harts Cove. The waterfall you see is that of Chitwood Creek, which you just crossed. As for the sea lions, louder than ever, they are mostly around the point to the south, but if you have binoculars you might be able to see some of them lounging on rocks or the far beach.

There's no real beach access here, but you can get close to the water. From the trees, walk west and stay to the left. There's a steep trail there, almost a slide in spots, that you can take down to the rocky shore. This rock, and all of Cascade Head in fact, is lava that flowed up through the water. If you make your way to the right 100 yards or so on the rock, you'll have a fabulous view of the headland and north to Cape Kiwanda and, farther off, Cape Lookout.

Now, for the Cascade Head Nature Preserve. If the upper road is open, start up there. The trail, actually an old roadbed, goes flat for one mile through a young and unexciting forest to the main-attraction meadow.

Over 30 years ago this meadow was slated to become a housing development, but conservation-minded folks banded together, bought it, and donated it to the Nature Conservancy. Now also designated as a United Nations Biosphere Reserve, it's protected as the home of the Oregon silverspot butterfly, whose caterpillar will eat only a rare violet that lives in these meadows. That's why FS 1861 and the upper part of the trail is closed from January 1 through July 15.

Once you're out in the meadow, you can go as far as you want. It's 1.7 miles down (and 1,200 feet of elevation loss) to the lower trailhead; just remember that you will have to walk back up. But you should go as far as a clifftop viewpoint that's just below the tree line in front of you. From there, you can see down to a secluded beach where the surf pounds and sea lions might be lounging.

If you started at the lower trailhead, you'll go through forest for just over a mile before coming out in the meadow. The top of the meadow (where the upper trail comes out of the woods) is 0.6 miles above you.

For more information, contact the Nature Conservancy at (503) 230-1221 or the Hebo Ranger District office at (503) 392-3161.

### ▶ NEARBY ACTIVITIES

Back on OR 18, a mile before you came to US 101, you went through the town of Otis. You might not have noticed it (it only has about a dozen buildings), but it's the home of an Oregon coast tradition, the Otis Café. It's got 28 seats, a line outside, and the biggest portions this side of a logging camp. They're famous for sourdough pancakes and whole-wheat molasses toast. If you're interested, the whole town of Otis is for sale—for $3 million.

# CATHERINE CREEK

## ▶ IN BRIEF

For ten months of the year, there's really no reason to go to Catherine Creek, but in April and May, there's no better place to be, for Catherine Creek at that time is wildflower heaven.

## ▶ DESCRIPTION

In a typical hiking year, there are usually some hikes that I do before Catherine Creek, but my personal hiking season really starts when the grass widows bloom at Catherine Creek in late March. It gets serious when the camas blooms. And my personal Easter Sunday tradition is to pack a lunch, hike up the hill to a certain spot, spread out my food, take in the view, and listen to the meadowlarks. Then I go back to rainy old Portland.

There's really not much to this hike, physically speaking. In fact, there's a paved and wheelchair-accessible section below the road that you could knock out in about 15 minutes. It's really all about the flowers. From the road, walk through a gate and choose a path that tends to the right toward a small canyon just up the hill. If you're like me, you'll stop within a few feet and start admiring flowers. One enthusiast has counted as many as 82 different species in bloom here on an April day, with such fantastic names as chocolate lily, common bastard toad flax, rough wallflower, Columbia gorge lupine, least hop clover, poet's

## ▶ KEY AT-A-GLANCE INFORMATION

**LENGTH:** Up to 3 miles

**CONFIGURATION:** Loop

**DIFFICULTY:** Easy to moderate

**SCENERY:** Wide-open vistas, a geological curiosity, and (at times) flowers, flowers everywhere!

**EXPOSURE:** Out in the open most of the way, optional trip to a clifftop

**TRAFFIC:** Heavy on weekends in late spring and early summer; light otherwise

**TRAIL SURFACE:** Dirt and some rock, also a small paved section

**HIKING TIME:** 30 minutes to 4 hours

**SEASON:** Year-round, but late March to early June is the time to go

**ACCESS:** No fees or permits required.

**FACILITIES:** Portable rest room at the trailhead, but no water around

## ▶ DIRECTIONS

From Portland on I-84, drive 57 miles east of I-205 and take Exit 64, the third exit for Hood River, Oregon. Turn left at the end of the ramp, following signs for White Salmon, Washington. Pay a $0.75 toll to cross the Columbia River, then turn right onto WA 14. Travel 5.7 miles and turn left onto Old Highway 8. The parking area is 1.4 miles ahead, on the left. Driving Time is 1 hour and 15 minutes.

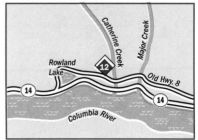

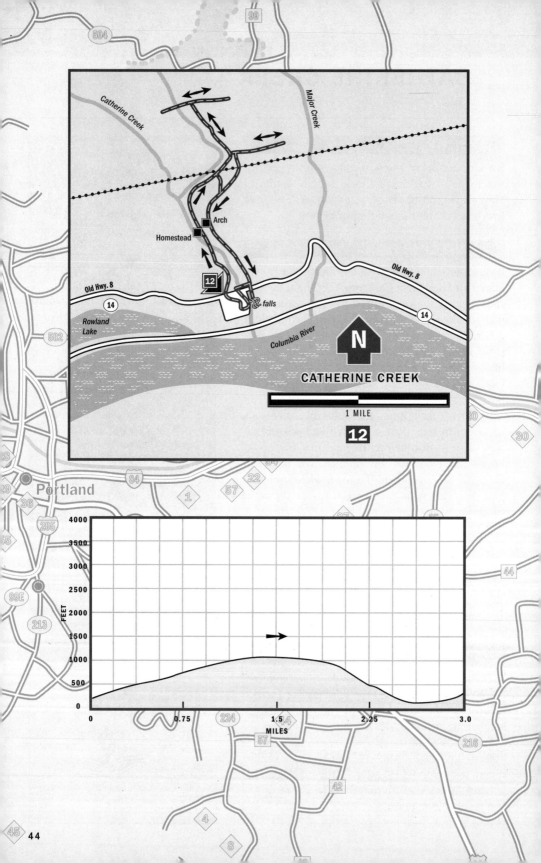

shooting star, rigid fiddleneck, great hound's tongue, slender popcorn flower, small-flowered blue-eyed Mary and chickweed monkey flower. I didn't make up any of those names! I can only identify about five kinds of flowers, but I love them all, and it seems like they're all at Catherine Creek.

Follow the path as it starts up the creek, and watch out for poison oak; it's everywhere, including a stand of it on the right just as you near the creek. After a quarter-mile, you'll cross the creek (either by fording it or on a cool, bouncy plank bridge) and 100 yards later arrive at an old homestead. The little white flowers that fill the corral here are called miner's lettuce, and you can eat them. Above you now is the geological curiosity, a natural arch that we'll visit later.

Past the homestead, you'll go up a slight rise and into a meadow. In May, under some of the bushes, you'll find dense thickets of irises. When you reach the power lines, you'll have your first decision to make. There are basically three options: a lower loop, an upper loop, and an exploration. For the lower loop, follow the road to the right here, and your hike will be less than a mile. I'll describe that section later, because you really should at least do the upper loop.

For this, follow a trail that continues up the ravine to your right (as you came up through the meadow). It will climb gradually for a half mile, through oak trees and past big, yellow balsamroot flowers (among many others), until it eventually pops out into the upper meadows. You might call this the "Catherine Creek High Country," but it's hardly 300 feet above the trailhead. Just go east into the meadows, and within 100 feet you'll encounter a trail heading up the hill. If you turn right and go downhill, this is the upper loop.

But now that you're up here, you really should do the exploration. You can strike out to the east and join the flower lovers, photographers, kids, dogs, and couples. I have fond memories of a guy I encountered out here who had a butterfly net and a big, boyish grin, practically skipping along. My favorite option here is to follow the trail up the hill (that's north) to the tree line, where another trail runs east and west. Turn left on that one, and it crosses another line of trees and enters yet another huge meadow. The trail sort of peters out in that meadow, but if you look up and to the right, you'll see a clump of trees that shelters a tiny spring. Just below that is a berm, created to capture the spring water. And on that berm a guy could have himself quite a fine Easter picnic, with the Columbia River laid out at his feet, flowers all around, and Mount Hood right across the way.

Now, for heading home. From the trail we first encountered in the upper meadow, just head downhill, and if all the trails confuse you (people tend to wander here) just aim between the island in the river and the orchards on the far side. You'll cross back under the power lines and come into a few more trees, then pick up a clearer trail that hugs the top of the ridge above Catherine Creek. Soon you'll get a view down into the canyon where the homestead is, and then you'll be at the top of the arch. You can get out on top of it (it's wider than it looks, but be careful), and you can also walk down through it to get back to the homestead. But why should you? There's more to see up here.

Keep going down the hill, and when in doubt stay close to the cliff edge. You'll enter a little draw filled with purple camas, with creek access on your right, and a few minutes later you'll be at the road—and probably as close to power lines as you'll ever be in your life. A little rock scramble will put you on the shoulder of the road, on which you'll cross the creek again and see the parking lot, just up the hill.

You could go up there and call it quits, but Catherine Creek has one more surprise for you. On the other side of the road, at the far end of the guardrail, take a little trail that goes back down towards the creek. You'll get to visit a lovely little waterfall down there, then you can climb a hill to a bench. That bench is on the paved section of the trail that's below the road where you parked, and if you keep turning right you'll be back at the car in no time. Be sure to stop and read some of the interpretive signs, especially the one that explains a little of the history of the area you've just wandered through.

# CLACKAMAS RIVER

▶ **IN BRIEF**

Convenient, not too tough, and not terribly long, the Clackamas River Trail is a perfect way to stretch out your legs and enjoy the scenery among old trees and along a beautiful river.

▶ **DESCRIPTION**

It's that rare nice day in winter or early spring—"nice" meaning it's not pouring—and you want to get out and do some hiking. Or it's blazing hot in summer and you want to visit a cool, shady place. Or it's autumn and you want to see the fall colors. Whatever the time, it's always a nice day to go out and hike the Clackamas River Trail. If you can work it out to bring a second car to be stashed at Indian Henry, it'll be that much better. Otherwise, you can do essentially the same distance and make a fine day of it.

From the trailhead, you'll start out in a flat section with the river a short distance to your left. After a half mile you'll come to a river access point with moss-covered rocks and a sandy beach—perfect for chilling out or, if you've brought small kids, perhaps for turning around. Soon after, you'll come into the first exceptional old-growth forest, with five-foot-thick Douglas firs and even

▶ **DIRECTIONS**

From Portland on OR 224, travel 33 miles southeast of I-205. Fifteen miles past the town of Estacada, just after crossing two bridges in quick succession, turn right onto Fish Creek Road. Go past the Fish Creek Campground, cross another bridge, and park in the parking lot on the right. The trail starts across the road on your left. To leave a car at the other end, stay on OR 224 for seven more miles and turn right into the Indian Henry Campground. The trailhead is a half a mile up on the right. Driving time to lower trailhead is 40 minutes.

### KEY AT-A-GLANCE INFORMATION

**LENGTH:** 7.8 miles one-way with a car shuttle or 7.2 miles round-trip to Pup Creek Falls

**CONFIGURATION:** Out-and-back

**DIFFICULTY:** Moderate

**SCENERY:** Old-growth forest, a white-water river, and a few waterfalls

**EXPOSURE:** Shady all the way

**TRAFFIC:** Use is heavy on summer weekends but light to moderate otherwise.

**TRAIL SURFACE:** Packed dirt with roots and rocks

**HIKING TIME:** 3 hours for either option

**SEASON:** Year-round; muddy in winter and spring

**ACCESS:** Northwest Forest Pass required.

**MAPS:** Green Trails #492 (Fish Creek Mountain)

**FACILITIES:** Toilets at the trailhead; the water along the way must be treated.

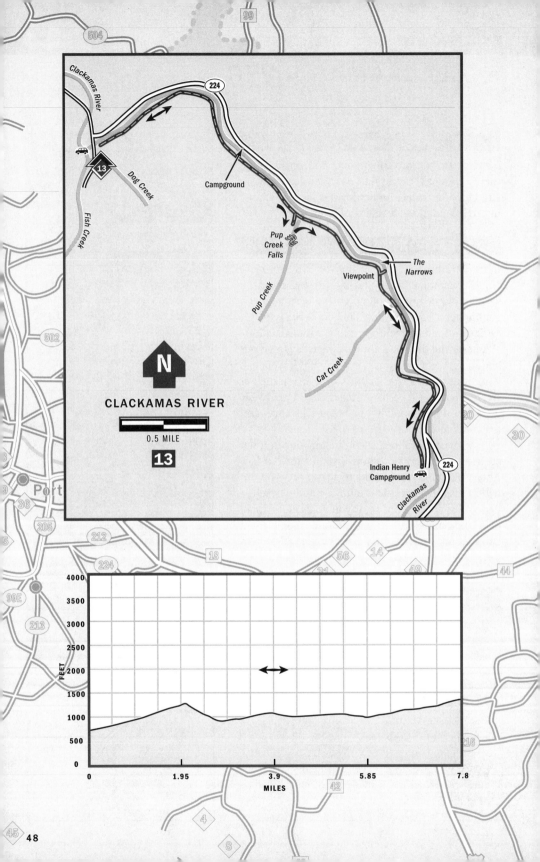

CLACKAMAS RIVER

0.5 MILE

**13**

224

Clackamas River

Dog Creek

Fish Creek

Campground

Pup Creek Falls

Pup Creek

*The Narrows*

Viewpoint

Cat Creek

Indian Henry Campground

224

Clackamas River

504

89

502

Port

36

9

205

212

224

18

56

14

49

44

99E

213

16

42

4

8

45

30

20

N

4000
3500
3000
2500
2000
1500
1000
500
0

FEET

0          1.95          3.9          5.85          7.8
MILES

bigger Western red cedars. In the next mile or so of trail, you'll do a little climbing and occasionally find yourself with some pretty serious drops to and views of the river to your left. Much of this early section burned in 2002, so you can check on how it's recovering.

If you're wondering about a good place to picnic, you'll find it 2.5 miles up in a campground. There's a stupendous western red cedar right by the water here and plenty of places to sit and contemplate the river. OR 224 is right across the river, by the way, but you'll rarely notice it. Again, if you've brought kids, think about turning around here, because during the next mile you'll go up, down, then up again (a couple hundred feet each time) and occasionally find the river some 200 feet far below you.

After a total of 3.5 miles, after you've dropped down the hill and found yourself under power lines, you'll come to Pup Creek, which the main trail crosses on a series of stepping stones. A side trail leads 0.1 mile up the creek to a view of beautiful Pup Creek Falls. If you didn't stash a car at Indian Henry, turn around here, and you'll have a 7.2-mile hike. If you did leave the second car there, keep on trucking.

In 0.9 miles a side trail will lead left to another beach—last chance to get to the river on this hike. Right after that you'll climb to a view up the Clackamas that includes The Narrows, a spectacular gouge in ancient lava. Down the other side of this hill, another side trail left will lead 0.1 mile to The Narrows themselves.

By the way, if you've seen some cables crossing the river in a few spots and wondered what that's about, they were put in by Portland General Electric for cable-car access across the river to maintain their power lines.

In the last three miles to Indian Henry Campground you'll cross several side creeks (the biggest one named Cat Creek, a nice complement to Pup Creek), see numerous big cedars, get sprayed by a waterfall, and go under a cliff. About half a mile before the end, keep an eye out for a large stump on the left with a cable wrapped around it leading to another large stump. The Forest Service does that to keep big stumps from rolling down into the river and squashing fishermen or boaters.

As of 1999, mountain bikes are no longer allowed on this trail. For more information, contact the Clackamas Ranger District office at (503) 630-4256.

## ▶ NEARBY ACTIVITIES

If it is one of those winter or spring days where the best you can say is "It ain't raining," or if the rain moves in and changes your mind about hiking, stop in Estacada at the Cada Corner coffee shop, where they have fresh cookies and a host of board games to play. It's in a little strip mall at the western end of town, right next to Hitching Post Pizza.

# COOPER SPUR

## ℹ KEY AT-A-GLANCE INFORMATION

**LENGTH:** 8.2 miles

**CONFIGURATION:** Balloon

**DIFFICULTY:** Hard

**SCENERY:** Old-growth forest, glaciers, the upper reaches of Mount Hood

**EXPOSURE:** Shady to sunny; plenty of wind

**TRAFFIC:** Use is moderate on summer weekends but light otherwise.

**TRAIL SURFACE:** Packed dirt, roots, sand, rocks

**HIKING TIME:** 4.5 hours

**SEASON:** July–mid-October

**ACCESS:** Northwest Forest Pass required.

**MAPS:** USGS Mount Hood North; USFS Mount Hood Wilderness; Green Trails #462 (Mount Hood)

**FACILITIES:** Outhouse and water at the trailhead

**SPECIAL COMMENTS:** Bring warm clothing. Weather at this altitude can change quickly.

## ▶ IN BRIEF

Though it's far from the toughest, this is the highest hiking trail in this book—right up into the realm of the mountain climber. You'll be in the world of rock and snow, and you won't even wear yourself out getting there—well, not completely. You'll also get to see the oldest buildings on Mount Hood and the results of a massive landslide.

## ▶ DESCRIPTION

If you want to get way, way up there, this is your hike. In the days before Timberline Lodge and the road to it were built, Cooper Spur was the standard climbing route to Mount Hood's 11,239-foot summit, and people still climb it that way today.

The whole area, in fact, is historically significant. Just up a hill from the trailhead, and at the end of the road, is the Cloud Cap Inn, built in 1889 by two prominent Portland families as a recreation destination. It's the oldest building on Mount Hood. The hotel venture never took off, and by World War II the property was given to the Forest Service. In 1956 the Crag Rats, a Hood River–based climbing and rescue organization, took it over, and they maintain it to this day. Although the public can't officially go in, if you're nice to some folks you see there, they might let you stick your head in for a bit.

## ▶ DIRECTIONS

From Portland on US 26, drive 51 miles east of I-205 and turn north on OR 35, following signs for Hood River. After 17 miles on OR 35, turn left at a sign for Cooper Spur Ski Area. After 2.4 miles, turn left, again following a sign for Cooper Spur Ski Area. In 1.4 miles, stay straight and leave the pavement. Go 8.3 winding miles to a T junction and turn right. The trailhead is half a mile ahead on the right, in the Cloud Cap Saddle campground. Driving time is 2 hours.

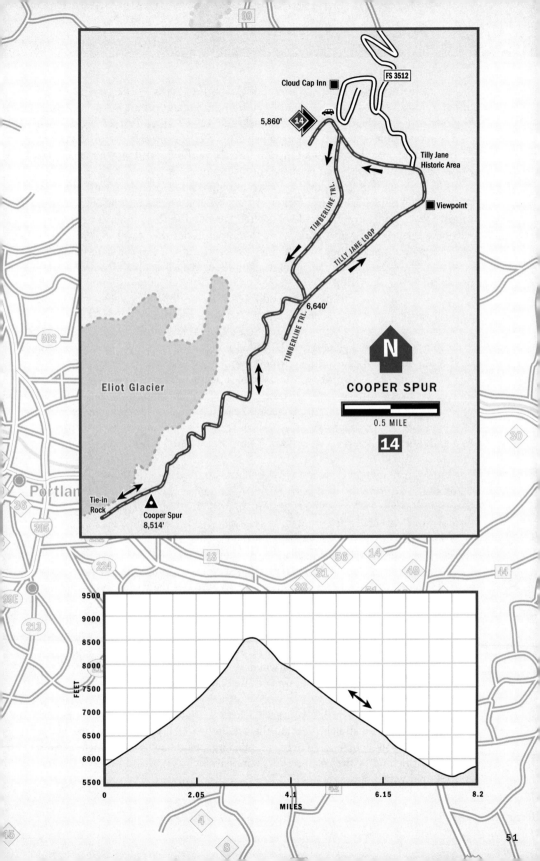

Cloud Cap Inn

FS 3512

5,860'

**14**

Tilly Jane
Historic Area

Viewpoint

TIMBERLINE TRL.

TILLY JANE LOOP

6,640'

TIMBERLINE TRL.

Eliot Glacier

**N**

**COOPER SPUR**

0.5 MILE

**14**

Tie-in
Rock

Cooper Spur
8,514'

FEET

9500
9000
8500
8000
7500
7000
6500
6000
5500

0          2.05          4.1          6.15          8.2
MILES

More history later; now, for the hiking. The trail starts at the far end of the campground. Take the Timberline Trail (#600) to the left and enter a rare, snow-zone, old-growth forest, where mountain hemlock and Pacific silver firs get bigger than you'd think possible in an area that usually has ten feet of snow by the end of November. In 1.2 miles you'll come to a junction just above the forest; following a sign for Cooper Spur, turn uphill—and get used to the climbing.

Just a couple hundred yards up, back among the twisted white bark pines on your right, sits the Cooper Spur shelter at the end of a small side trail. But for our purposes, keep going up. The trail will switch back and forth through the sand and rocks on a manageable grade, and slowly the Eliot Glacier will start to fill your view to the right. You'll hear it pop and rumble as it carves the side of the mountain, and if you're lucky, especially on late summer afternoons, you'll see big pieces of it calving and tumbling downhill.

After 2.3 miles of this climbing you'll come to the top of the ridge, where you should look for a rock with some impressive carvings and the date July 17, 1910. It commemorates a Japanese climbing party. Since you've climbed all the altitude at this point, you might as well go another 0.3 miles along the ridge top—just beware that this ridge is thin, rocky, and usually wind-swept.

Just before the snow line, you'll come to a plaque attached to the side of what they call Tie-In Rock; it's called that because it's here that climbers tie themselves to one another to venture out onto the glacier. Do not, under *any* circumstances (short of having ropes and crampons and relevant experience) go out onto the glacier. Be satisfied with being at the top of your local hiking world, and sit back among the sheltering rocks to take in the view.

From left to right, with Mount Hood behind you, we have the Eliot Glacier, and way off in the distance the bare face of Table Mountain in the Columbia River Gorge, Mount St. Helens, Mount Rainier, Mount Adams, Elk Meadows and Gnarl Ridge down at your feet. Lookout Mountain is on a ridge to the east, and then a building below you on a Mount Hood ridge, which is the top of a ski lift at Mount Hood Meadows Ski Area. Now do you feel like you're way up there?

Now look up at Mount Hood. The Cooper Spur climbing route begins on the snowfield right in front of you and proceeds up through the rocks above, tending slightly to your left. As climbers like to say, it's not as steep as it looks. Look for a prominent rock called The Chimney just below the summit and Pulpit Rock more to your right. The rocky area just below the right face of the summit is known as the Chisolm Trail because several members of a Chisolm family fell down it to their deaths. In fact, the Crag Rats say that whenever somebody falls on the Cooper Spur climbing route, they generally wind up within about 200 feet of the same spot at the top of the Eliot Glacier.

On your way down, when you get back to the junction where you originally turned right, now stay straight, leaving the Timberline Trail for the Tilly Jane Loop. After 0.6 miles, you'll come to an overlook of a large, bare bowl on your right. That's what was left behind by the Polallie Slide, a massive debris flow and flood in December 1980 that wiped out parts of OR 35.

A short while later you'll find yourself looking at some old buildings. This is part of the 1,400-acre Tilly Jane Historic Area. This area, by the way, is immensely popular with cross-country skiers and snowshoers, who come up a 2.7-mile trail from Cooper Spur Ski Area and spend the night in some of these buildings. And if you're wondering about that name, Tilly Jane was the matriarch's nickname of the Ladd family, one of the builders of Cloud Cap Inn.

Now, to get back to your car, just put Mount Hood on your left and follow the trail half a mile back to the trailhead.

▶ **NEARBY ACTIVITIES**

When you get back to OR 35, go north (left) and indulge yourself at some of the berry and fruit stands in the Hood River Valley. Some let you pick your own.

# DOG MOUNTAIN

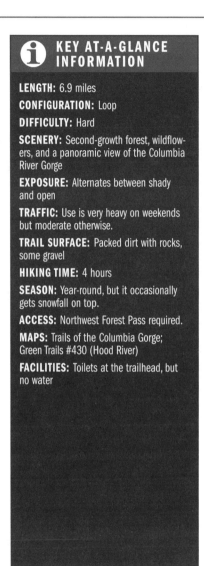

### ℹ️ KEY AT-A-GLANCE INFORMATION

**LENGTH:** 6.9 miles

**CONFIGURATION:** Loop

**DIFFICULTY:** Hard

**SCENERY:** Second-growth forest, wildflowers, and a panoramic view of the Columbia River Gorge

**EXPOSURE:** Alternates between shady and open

**TRAFFIC:** Use is very heavy on weekends but moderate otherwise.

**TRAIL SURFACE:** Packed dirt with rocks, some gravel

**HIKING TIME:** 4 hours

**SEASON:** Year-round, but it occasionally gets snowfall on top.

**ACCESS:** Northwest Forest Pass required.

**MAPS:** Trails of the Columbia Gorge; Green Trails #430 (Hood River)

**FACILITIES:** Toilets at the trailhead, but no water

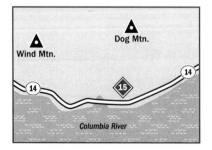

## ▶ IN BRIEF

This is probably the most popular of the real hiking trails in the Columbia River Gorge—"real" meaning it requires some real effort. But with an easy-access trailhead, great views of the river, and sunshine and wildflowers at a time when it's still raining in Portland. It's no wonder everybody on earth comes here.

## ▶ DESCRIPTION

It seems that everyone around Portland who hikes has been up Dog Mountain. Climbers use it as an early-season conditioner. Wildflower enthusiasts flock to it in early summer. In spring, when it's still raining in Portland, it tends to be sunny here. But most people take the main Dog Mountain Trail, which is therefore crowded, and which was also designed, it seems, to punish the legs and lungs of those who would hike it. This thing is steep! You can come down this way, if you want, but it's no bargain then, either.

Instead, from the parking lot, take the trail on the left, the Augsperger Mountain Trail. It's 0.6 miles longer, but whoever designed it had a much better grasp of the concept of "grade." That's not to say it's easy—it's 3.7 uphill miles, gaining 2,700 feet in elevation. But it's steady, whereas parts of the other trail are insane, and you'll

## ▶ DIRECTIONS

From Portland on I-84, drive 37 miles east of I-205 and take Exit 44/Cascade Locks. As soon as you enter the town, take your first right to get on the Bridge of the Gods, following a sign for Stevenson, Washington. Pay a $1 toll on the bridge, and at the far end turn right onto WA 14. Proceed 12 miles to the trailhead on the left. Start early in the day on this one, if only to make sure you get a parking place. Driving time is 1 hour and 15 minutes.

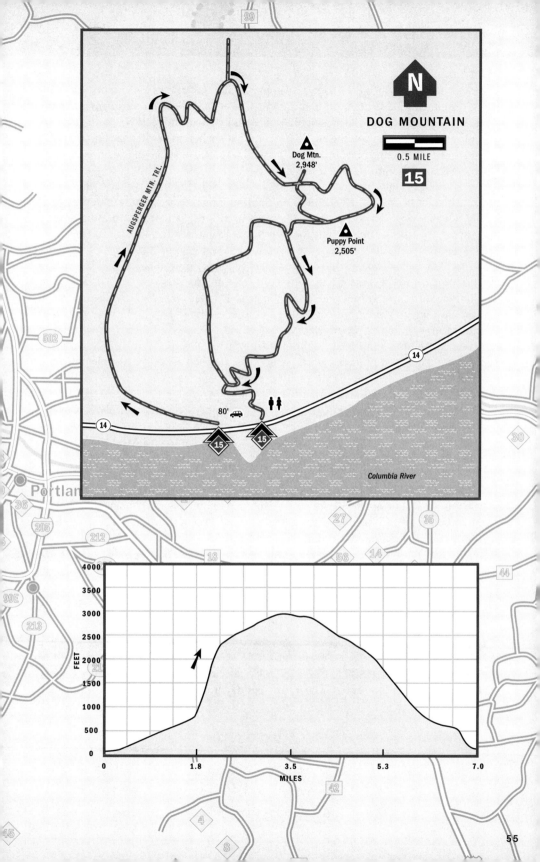

N

DOG MOUNTAIN

0.5 MILE

15

AUGSPERGER MTN. TRL.

Dog Mtn.
2,948'

Puppy Point
2,505'

14

15

14

15

80'

Columbia River

FEET
4000
3500
3000
2500
2000
1500
1000
500
0

0          1.8          3.5          5.3          7.0
MILES

55

spend more time in the Meadows up top. So take this one as it contours left, with ever-improving views of the river and Wind Mountain. When you turn right and away from the river, you will have gone 0.9 miles and gained 400 feet. Not so bad, right? In the next 1.3 miles you'll gain 1,200 feet. That's when the switchbacks start and it gets steep—just remember, this is the "easier" way. The next half mile gains some 700 feet. Then you'll turn right at a junction.

I'd like to take this moment to explain why Dog Mountain is called Dog Mountain. It's not because of all the dogs on the trail, nor is it because the climb is, well, like a female dog. It's because some pioneers in the area were forced to eat their dogs to avoid starvation. The town of Hood River, Oregon, was in fact first called Dog River, but the name was changed because nobody liked it. Imagine that.

With this knowledge in your head, enjoy a few minutes of flat trail before you climb again and pop out into the sun. Now it's time to claim your reward for all that climbing. In May and June, the open slopes of Dog Mountain are awash in flowers, especially big yellow balsamroot; but year-round, the views here of the river and other mountains—including Mount Hood, which peeks its head over the far side—are sublime. Stroll through this area and know that virtually all your climbing is done. You'll intersect the Dog Mountain Trail after 0.9 miles; turn left and, just 0.1 mile up, you'll be at the top of a sloped meadow with everybody and their dogs.

The view here stretches from the high desert of eastern Oregon to Beacon Rock in the west—look how small it is! Way to the right is Mount St. Helens. Directly across the way is 4,960-foot Mount Defiance, the one with radio towers on top—look how big it is! The highest point in the gorge, it seems to taunt, "Yeah right, you've climbed barely half of me."

To hike down Dog Mountain, take the scenic loop. From the summit, go left on a trail that soon ducks into the trees, some of which are surprisingly large. Keep an eye out for Mount Adams to the north. This trail rejoins the other branch of the Dog Mountain Trail at a lookout that's actually called Puppy Point (2,505 feet in elevation). Then the bottom drops out, and you lose 600 feet in the next half mile before a junction. You'll save 0.2 miles by going right, but it's worth it to go left for one last view of the river 0.6 miles down. Stay left at another junction 1 mile later, and after a final 0.5 miles you can finally rest your throbbing feet.

For more information, contact the Columbia River Gorge National Scenic Area office at (541) 386-2333.

## ▶ NEARBY ACTIVITIES

When you get back across to Cascade Locks, take a ride on the Sternwheeler Columbia Gorge, which has several scenic trips per day from mid-June through September.

# DRIFT CREEK FALLS

## ▶ IN BRIEF

This is a long drive, best done as part of a day at the coast, and there is just about nothing to this hike. If it weren't for the suspension bridge it crosses, nobody would ever hike it. But what a bridge! There are a couple of places to hang out by the stream, too . . . but what a bridge!

## ▶ DESCRIPTION

Like I said, there's nothing much to this trail. It's a long drive, so do it on a day when you're headed to the coast anyway—especially in spring or late fall, when there will be plenty of water in the creek. It's all about the bridge.

From the trailhead, you start down (what a novel concept!) and, in just over a mile, come to Drift Creek. There's a bridge here that was rebuilt in 2003, replacing one that was wiped out in the floods of February 1996. That was when, in a four-day period, 30 inches of warm rain fell on top of two feet of snow in the coastal mountains, and when it all came down, hell broke loose. Tillamook County alone suffered more than $50 million in damage. This little bridge was built to span the floodplain, so it should be around for a while.

## ▶ DIRECTIONS

From Downtown Portland on I-5, drive six miles south and take Exit 294/Tigard/Newberg. Bear right onto OR 99W and follow it 23 miles. Just before the town of McMinnville, turn left onto OR 18 (following a sign for Oregon Coast). Travel 49 miles down OR 18 and turn left onto Bear Creek County Road, following a sign for Drift Creek Falls Trail. In two miles you'll leave the pavement. At 3.3 miles, stay straight, again following a sign for the trail; you're now on FS 17. Follow FS 17 for 10 more miles; the trailhead is on the left. Driving time is 2 hours.

## ⓘ KEY AT-A-GLANCE INFORMATION

**LENGTH:** 3.5 miles

**CONFIGURATION:** Out-and-back

**DIFFICULTY:** Easy

**SCENERY:** Quiet forest, a meandering stream, and one seriously amazing bridge

**EXPOSURE:** In the woods, then on a narrow, high bridge—which you can get swinging, if you want

**TRAFFIC:** Moderate on summer weekends, light otherwise

**TRAIL SURFACE:** Packed dirt, muddy in winter and spring

**HIKING TIME:** 2 hours

**SEASON:** Year-round, but there could be snow in winter.

**ACCESS:** Northwest Forest Pass required.

**MAPS:** Siuslaw National Forest; USGS Devils Lake covers the area, but this trail isn't on it.

**FACILITIES:** Toilets at the trailhead

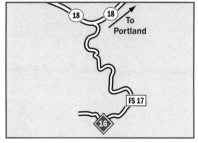

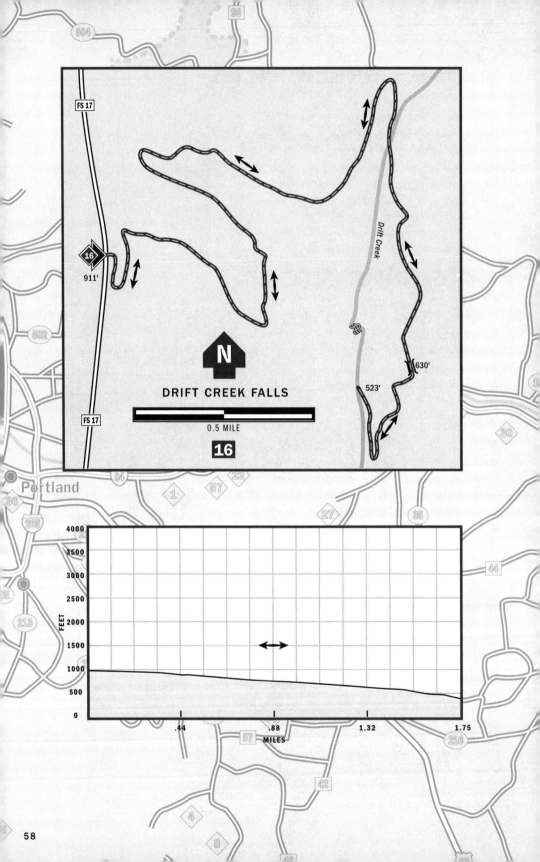

FS 17

FS 17

Drift Creek

16
911'

630'
523'

N

DRIFT CREEK FALLS

0.5 MILE

16

Portland

4000
3500
3000
2500
2000
1500
1000
500
0

FEET

.44        .88        1.32        1.75

MILES

A half-mile later you'll come to the real bridge. Built in 1997, the Drift Creek Falls Suspension Bridge is 240 feet long, 3 feet wide, and 100 feet above the canyon floor. The falls to your right are 80 feet high—and you're above them! A few more technical details: the towers are 29 feet tall and made of Douglas fir beams 12 by 18 inches thick. The anchors include 28 cubic yards of concrete and 10-foot rock bolts. The mainlines are 1-1/4 inch galvanized wire rope. Also of note is that the same company that built this bridge also built the one over Lava Canyon, another hike in this book.

And how do they build such a thing, you might wonder (I did). They flew in materials with a helicopter, and built the main span from a "skyline" more than 100 feet off the ground—not a business for anybody afraid of heights.

Enough with the technical talk. It's a wonderful bridge, spanning the canyon and at the same time visiting the tree canopy. And, if you're into such things, you can get

Sitting on the suspension bridge over Drift Creek Falls

it rocking back and forth. Just put a foot on each side and have at it. I couldn't get it to bounce, though—thanks to the stiffening truss underneath it. The bridge is dedicated to the late Scott Paul, a Forest Service trailbuilder who was foreman of this job and died in an accident during construction of the bridge.

If you keep going a quarter-mile past the bridge, you can get down to the creek and look up at both the falls and the bridge. There's a nice little pool where I saw some tiny trout kicking around, and a patch of grass across the creek that was pleasant for a picnic. I was there in October, though—probably the lowest water time of year. In the spring it would be a bit more of an adventure to cross.

## ▶ NEARBY ACTIVITIES

Perhaps you noticed another bridge on the way down Bear Creek Road. The Drift Creek Covered Bridge is one of only four in Lincoln County, and for a while it was thought to be the oldest in Oregon. There was a Drift Creek Covered Bridge (over Drift Creek) built in 1914 (hence the date on the sign), but it turns out the one still in existence in 1997 was built in 1933, after the original two got washed out. The County voted to tear it down, because it was beyond repair, but a couple named the Sweitzes offered to haul away the pieces and rebuild it here, over Bear Creek. The rest is a truly amazing story, related in a flier on the bridge, complete with miracles and a near-divorce and tears and more miracles. Seriously; you should read it. The bridge re-opened July 14, 2001 and is open to the public; the place across the way is the Sweitz home.

# EAGLE CREEK

**LENGTH:** 4.2 miles round-trip to Punchbowl Falls; 13 miles round-trip to Tunnel Falls

**CONFIGURATION:** Out-and-back

**DIFFICULTY:** Moderate

**SCENERY:** Waterfalls, old-growth forest, spawning salmon in the fall

**EXPOSURE:** Mostly shady

**TRAFFIC:** Use is heavy throughout the summer but moderate in the spring and fall.

**TRAIL SURFACE:** Packed dirt and rocks

**HIKING TIME:** 2 hours to Punchbowl Falls; 5.5 hours to Tunnel Falls

**SEASON:** Year-round, but it will be muddy in the winter and spring.

**ACCESS:** Northwest Forest Pass required.

**MAPS:** Trails of the Columbia Gorge

**FACILITIES:** Toilets at the trailhead, but no water

## ▶ IN BRIEF

One of the classic and most popular hikes in Oregon, seemingly everybody has done part of Eagle Creek. That's because this hike's easy to get to, easy to hike, and several kinds of beautiful. So start early, or go on a weekday, so you won't have to share it with everybody in the state.

## ▶ DESCRIPTION

The magic of this hike, at certain times of the year, begins before you even hit the trail itself. Eagle Creek has a small run of fall Chinook salmon—fish that spend their adult lives in the ocean, come more than 70 miles up the Columbia, swim through the fish ladder at Bonneville Dam, and then come here to spawn. A small dam blocks their further progress up Eagle Creek, but in October and November they spawn in little round pools cleared by volunteers to simulate conditions in a wild mountain stream.

The trail was built before 1920 to coincide with the opening of the Columbia River Highway. Although that historic roadway has mostly been gobbled up by I-84, the section from Bonneville Dam to Cascade Locks (which goes right by Eagle Creek) has been converted into a hiking and biking trail, as have a few other sections.

The work that went into the Eagle Creek Trail is a heroic feat; they chipped the trail into cliff faces, built High Bridge over the gorge, and put a tunnel behind a falls six miles up. It's work like this that inspired the dedication of this book.

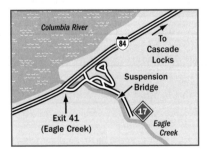

## ▶ DIRECTIONS

From Portland on I-84, drive 34 miles east of I-205 and take Exit 41/Eagle Creek. Go 0.2 miles and turn right, then 0.6 miles to the end of the road. If it's crowded, you might have to park closer to the highway and hike that much farther. Driving time is 35 minutes.

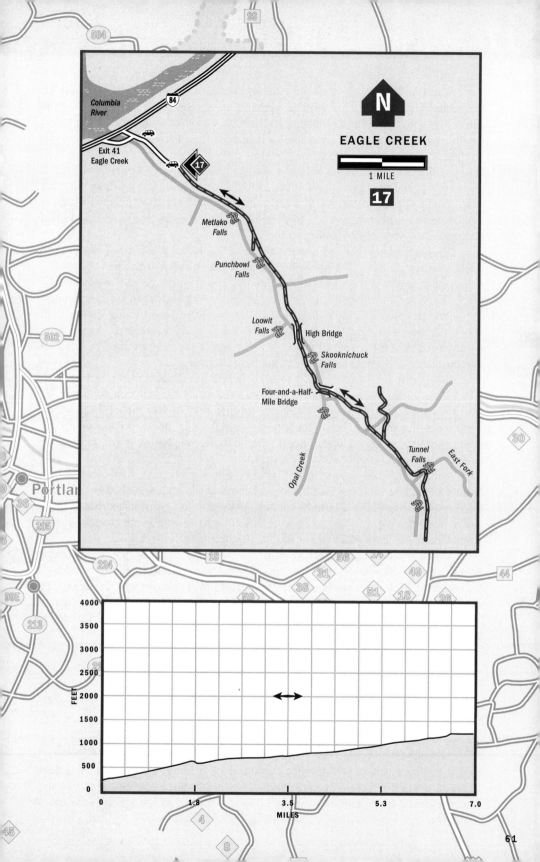

At just under a mile, you'll come to the first place where you walk a ledge with a cable to hang on to. If it's a summer weekend, things can get interesting here while you're trying to negotiate for cable space with dozens of other hikers. At 1.5 miles, you'll come to a viewpoint of Metlako Falls (named for a native goddess of salmon), the first of many such sights of your day. Just past the viewpoint is a bench for resting. At 1.8 miles and another bench, a side trail leads down to Punchbowl Falls, a must-see trip and the end of the line for a lot of people. Go 0.2 miles down this trail to an unnamed falls; just above that is a large clearing that's often filled with people swimming and sunbathing. At the upstream end of the clearing is a lovely (and often photographed) view of Punchbowl Falls.

If you turn back here, you will have done 4.2 miles, but it's not much more work to go at least as far as High Bridge, another 1.2 miles up. If you head up, in 0.3 miles you'll get a bird's-eye view of Punchbowl Falls; then the gorge narrows considerably. You'll see Loowit Falls on the right just before High Bridge; if you turn around at the bridge, you'll have a seven-mile day. But even if you are turning back, put in another 0.3 miles to a great picnic spot on the left and, 100 yards later, a rare chance for access to the creek itself, in this case at the top of Skooknichuck Falls. Just past that are some very impressive Douglas firs right on the trail.

Continuing up the trail, you'll soon cross what is officially known as Four-and-a-Half Mile Bridge. Now, even the map acknowledges that this is exactly four miles from the trailhead, so what gives? Well, the fish hatchery back at the trailhead wasn't there when the trail was built (there was no need for it, because Bonneville Dam didn't exist yet), so the trailhead used to extend half a mile farther north, to the edge of the Columbia River Highway.

Just past the bridge, look on the right for a double waterfall; that's Opal Creek, but it shouldn't be confused with the world-famous Opal Creek described elsewhere in this book (see page 125). About half a mile above that, a sign explains that the area you're now entering was burned in a 1902 fire; there are still some charred stumps around. So all the trees you'll see in this area are less than 100 years old.

After 1.5 more miles, bringing your total to 6, you'll come into a deep gorge where Tunnel Falls plunges 130 feet and the trail goes behind it through a 35-foot tunnel. Tunnel Falls is actually on East Fork Creek; to return to Eagle Creek and see one final, dramatic falls, go about 0.2 miles farther. This falls doesn't have a name, but it does have an interesting crisscross feature in its upper section. Perhaps it should be called Crisscross Falls.

You can keep going if you want, but if you head back at this point you'll wind up putting in 13 miles. That should be enough for a day, and besides, you get to see everything again on your way back.

For more information, contact the Columbia River Gorge National Scenic Area office at (541) 386-2333.

▶ **NEARBY ACTIVITIES**

Stop at the fish hatchery at Bonneville Dam on the way home. They have a fish ladder where at certain times of year you can see salmon and steelhead swimming up past the dam to spawn. It's one mile west on I-84, and there's no charge for admission.

# ELK MEADOWS

## ▶ IN BRIEF

One of the most spectacular sights in the Mount Hood area, sprawling and flower-filled Elk Meadows is relatively easy to reach. Beyond that, several side trips in the area invite you to soaring viewpoints.

## ▶ DESCRIPTION

If all you're doing is going to Elk Meadows, there's only one hill between you and your destination. But while you're at it, there are some other options worth checking out.

From the trailhead, you'll follow a flat trail through moss-draped forest, pocket meadows with wildflowers, and huckleberries that are ripe in late August. Ignore two trails on the left, the first #667 to Umbrella Falls and the second #646 up Newton Creek. After half a mile you'll cross Clark Creek on a bridge, and after another half a mile you'll cross Newton Creek on logs. This last one might be tricky for small children.

Now you are at the hill. In 0.6 miles you'll gain almost 700 feet in a series of long switchbacks—consider it your price of admission to Elk Meadows. Just over the top, you'll come to a four-way intersection. For Elk Meadows, go straight and you'll be there in about three minutes. For a side trip to Elk Mountain, turn right.

The trail to Elk Mountain is not spectacular in and of itself, but it's quiet and woodsy and leads to a nice view east across OR 35 to Mount

### ⓘ KEY AT-A-GLANCE INFORMATION

**LENGTH:** 4.5 miles round-trip to Elk Meadows; 11 miles to see it all

**CONFIGURATION:** Out-and-back with optional loops

**DIFFICULTY:** Moderate to Elk Meadows; hard to Gnarl Ridge

**SCENERY:** Meadows, mountain streams, close-up views of Mount Hood

**EXPOSURE:** Shady most of the way

**TRAFFIC:** Moderate use on weekends, light otherwise

**TRAIL SURFACE:** Packed dirt with some roots

**HIKING TIME:** 2.5 hours to Elk Meadows; 6 hours to see everything

**SEASON:** July–October

**ACCESS:** Northwest Forest Pass required.

**MAPS:** Mount Hood Wilderness; Green Trails #462 (Mount Hood)

**FACILITIES:** Outhouse at the trailhead; the water on the trail must be treated.

## ▶ DIRECTIONS

From Portland on US 26, drive 51 miles east of I-205 and turn north on OR 35, following signs for Hood River. After 7 miles on OR 35, turn left at the second entrance for the Mount Hood Meadows Ski Area (the one for the Nordic Center). The trailhead is half a mile ahead on the right. Driving time is 1 hour and 20 minutes.

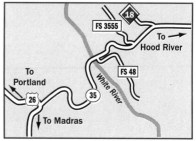

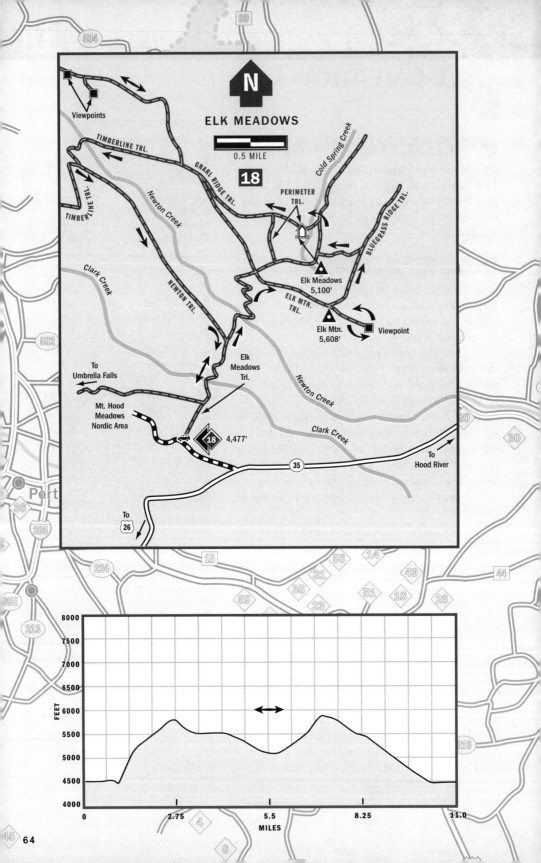

Jefferson to the south. Also, while staying quiet on an August morning hike, I briefly saw two elk up there, bounding through the forest away from me. To get to the lookout, go up 0.6 miles and stay straight at the junction with the Bluegrass Ridge Trail (#647). The lookout is 0.3 miles straight ahead. When you come back, take the Bluegrass Ridge Trail (it would now be a right turn) and follow it half a mile along the ridge top before turning left, at a large stone cairn, and plunging 0.4 miles down the Bluegrass Tie Trail (#647B) to Elk Meadows.

Elk Meadows is almost unbelievable. It's basically a circular area of meadows about half a mile in diameter, with islands of trees throughout and streams crisscrossing it. For the good of the flowers and grass, resist the temptation to go meadow-stomping, but by all means find a log or rock on the perimeter and have a sit-down. To complete a loop around the meadows or to explore the other loop available on this hike, turn right when you get to the meadows (regardless of whether you went to Elk Mountain or not).

When you come to a sign for Polallie Campground, stay left on the perimeter trail, and about 30 steps later you'll come to an unmarked trail leading left. That is the trail out into the middle of the meadows, where a stone shelter hosts backpackers most summer nights. It's worth a side trip, if only to be surrounded by the meadows.

Continuing on the perimeter trail, you'll cross Cold Spring Creek, and in about half a mile you'll come to a junction with the Gnarl Ridge Trail (#652). To go back to your car, turn left here, finish the loop around the meadows, and then turn right at the junction with the Elk Meadows Trail. But to go a little higher up toward Mount Hood, stay straight here on the Gnarl Ridge Trail.

After just less than a mile of gradual climbing, you'll come to a trail on the left; ignore it. Just past that you'll get to the Timberline Trail (#600). Here, you can turn right and climb 800 feet in 1.5 miles to a fantastic viewpoint atop Gnarl Ridge; or, you can turn left, stay at the same level, and make a loop back to the car. This way will take you along the west side of Gnarl Ridge (6,540 feet elevation) to a bridgeless crossing of Newton Creek. You can even explore up the creek by walking through the boulder field to your right; just be careful, as even the largest of the rocks can roll when you step on them.

To get back to the car, cross the creek, climb about a quarter of a mile, then turn left at the ridge top onto the Newton Trail (#646). Two miles down that heavily huckleberried trail, you'll intersect with the trail you started all this wandering on—the Elk Meadows Trail. Turn right and you'll be back at the trailhead in just over a mile.

For more information, contact the Mount Hood Visitor Information Center at (503) 622-7674.

## ▶ NEARBY ACTIVITIES

For a little piece of Oregon history, pay your respects at the Pioneer Woman's Grave, off of OR 35 just north of its intersection with US 26. Workers building the old Mount Hood Loop Highway found the woman buried beneath a crude marker; her remains have since been moved twice, and to this day people lay crosses or flowers on the pile of rocks marking her grave.

# FOREST PARK

## KEY AT-A-GLANCE INFORMATION

**LENGTH:** 28 miles one way—or loop hikes of any distance you wish

**CONFIGURATION:** Out-and-back or loop

**DIFFICULTY:** Easy

**SCENERY:** Mature forest, deep ravines, quiet creeks, views of far-away volcanoes

**EXPOSURE:** Shady

**TRAFFIC:** Heavy in the southern part of the park on weekends, otherwise light to moderate

**TRAIL SURFACE:** Packed dirt, rocks, roots

**HIKING TIME:** From 1 hour to 1 year

**SEASON:** Year-round

**ACCESS:** No fees or permits needed.

**MAPS:** A free Forest Park map can be obtained at Portland Parks and Recreation (1120 Southwest Fifth Avenue).

**FACILITIES:** Water and toilets available at points throughout the park

## IN BRIEF

Thanks to some very forward-thinking people of a century ago, assisted by the forces of nature and economics, Portland now has 4,900 acres of trees, creeks, and canyons within its city limits—something no other American city can claim. The heart of Forest Park is the Wildwood Trail, with access points and loops available along its length.

## DESCRIPTION

In 1903 a report to the city of Portland recommended setting aside the wooded hillside on the west side of Portland for a forest reserve. It was quite a vision for its time, especially considering the fact that to Oregonians then, deep forests were everywhere—and were a bother. Such things, they reasoned, needed to be destroyed for humans to prosper. But this report (and others in the decades that followed) realized that future generations wouldn't have so many of these big trees and uninhabited areas to contemplate, and they (we) would appreciate a chance to do so. They certainly were correct.

But what's now Forest Park almost got swallowed up by Portland's growth in the early twentieth century. Leif Ericson Drive was put in as part of a residential development plan in 1915, and a logging camp was set up to give work to the unemployed. But, thanks in part to the naturally occurring mudslides of the area, money became a

## DIRECTIONS

For the southern end of the Wildwood Trail, which is in Washington Park, the directions are the same as the Washington Park/Hoyt Arboretum hike. For the northern end of the trail, from Portland on US 30, drive six miles west of I-405 and turn left onto Germantown Road. Go 1.5 miles and park in the lot on the left. Driving time is 5 to 15 minutes, depending on the trailhead.

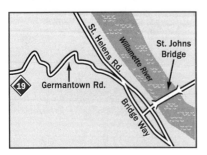

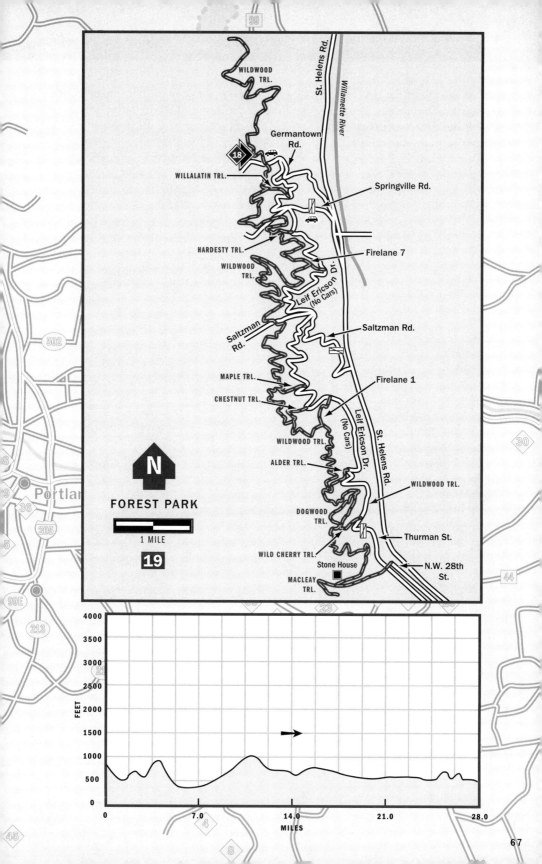

WILDWOOD TRL.

St. Helens Rd.

Willamette River

Germantown Rd.

18

WILLALATIN TRL.

Springville Rd.

HARDESTY TRL.

Firelane 7

WILDWOOD TRL.

Leif Ericson Dr. (No Cars)

Saltzman Rd.

Saltzman Rd.

MAPLE TRL.

Firelane 1

CHESTNUT TRL.

WILDWOOD TRL.

Leif Ericson Dr. (No Cars)

St. Helens Rd.

ALDER TRL.

WILDWOOD TRL.

N

FOREST PARK

1 MILE

19

DOGWOOD TRL.

Thurman St.

WILD CHERRY TRL.

Stone House

N.W. 28th St.

MACLEAY TRL.

Portland

problem. When the city started taxing the vacant lots to pay the bills, many of them went into foreclosure. Then came the Great Depression and World War II; it was only after these interruptions that the original idea of a forest park was resurrected. The city dedicated Forest Park in 1948, and then more or less left it alone, installing few (if any) plans or buildings or designs. Today it is an ever-expanding wild area of almost 5,000 acres, home to more than 100 species of birds and 60 species of mammals, including elk and black bear, who roam in on occasion through a wilderness corridor that connects the area to the Coast Range.

There are 60 miles of hiking trails in Forest Park, virtually all of them connected by the 28-mile-long Wildwood Trail and/or Leif Ericson Drive, a wide, multi-use path that runs for 11 miles parallel to the Wildwood Trail.

What follows is a brief description of the Wildwood Trail, but as you can see on the map, loop options abound. Several things are helpful about the Wildwood Trail: it's very well marked, it's accessible by car at several points, and throughout its length it is marked by mileposts every quarter mile.

The first few miles of the Wildwood Trail are covered as part of the Washington Park/Hoyt Arboretum hike. Just north of that, Wildwood connects to the Pittock Mansion, at the top of our Macleay Trail hike. After that, around Milepost 5, it drops down to the Audubon Society (also on the Macleay Trail), which can be reached by car as well. North of that, Wildwood crosses Balch Creek Canyon into an area thick with alder and maple.

Just past Milepost 9, Wildwood crosses Northwest 53rd Street, where car access is available. At Milepost 11 there's a large meadow. North of there, the forest turns to older cedars and firs, where woodpeckers roam and sign of deer and coyote may be found. At Milepost 16, the trail crosses Northwest Saltzman Road—again, car access is available here, though the trail is one mile up the road from a locked gate.

Now you're in a seldom-visited section of the park—an area where native trees and plants dominate. In many other areas of the park, introduced species—especially English ivy, which creates "ivy deserts," where nothing else grows—have taken over. At Milepost 18, you'll get a view of Mount Hood. At Milepost 19 you'll get views of Swan Island and the University of Portland across the Willamette River. Starting around Milepost 22, you'll start a long descent—through fantastic old-growth fir, hemlock, and cedar—until you reach Northwest Germantown Road, just past Milepost 24. That's where the northern trailhead parking, described above, is located.

There's still more to the Wildwood Trail, however, and in some ways what lies north of Northwest Germantown Road is the most spectacular part of Forest Park. This is the least-visited part of the park, and therefore it is the most inhabited by wildlife. From the parking area on Germantown Road, you can go south and explore some of the loops available, or go north for a 7.4-mile out-and-back to Northwest Skyline Boulevard at the northern terminus of the Wildwood Trail.

# HISTORIC COLUMBIA RIVER HIGHWAY

## ▶ IN BRIEF

When it was completed in 1922, the Columbia River Highway was an engineering marvel, known as the "King of Roads." Now it's a historic relic. Some of it can still be driven, but more than ten miles of it have been restored for hiking and biking only. It's an interesting way to see the Columbia River Gorge, and the Mosier Twin Tunnels (less than a mile from a trailhead in Mosier) are well worth a visit on their own.

## ▶ DESCRIPTION

The Columbia River Gorge is one of the most distinct climate border regions in the world. The

## ▶ DIRECTIONS

All the trailheads lie east of Portland on I-84. For the eastern section: Park at either Hood River or Mosier. For Hood River, take Exit 64, make two quick rights (the first right is unnamed; the second right is OR 35), and proceed 0.1 mile to the four-way stop. Turn left onto US 30 and travel 1.4 miles to the parking area. For Mosier, take Exit 69, turn right at the stop sign, then left in 0.1 mile. The trailhead is 0.8 miles ahead on the right, but parking is 0.1 mile beyond it on the left. For the middle section: park at either Starvation Creek State Park (Exit 55) or Viento State Park (Exit 56, then turn right). For the western section: park at either Bonneville Dam or Cascade Locks. To park near Bonneville Dam, take Exit 40 and turn right. If you're headed west to Moffett Creek, the parking lot is just ahead on the right; if you're headed east to Eagle Creek and Cascade Locks, the lot is 0.4 miles up a gravel road to the left. To park in Cascade Locks, take Exit 44 (37 miles east of I-205); and park under the Bridge of the Gods. Driving time is 1 hour to eastern section, and 30 minutes to western section.

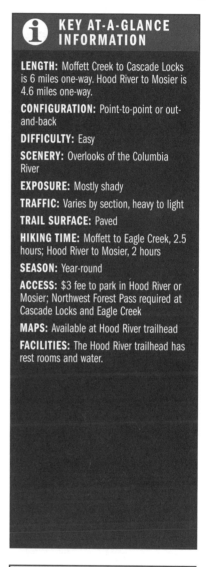

## ⓘ KEY AT-A-GLANCE INFORMATION

**LENGTH:** Moffett Creek to Cascade Locks is 6 miles one-way. Hood River to Mosier is 4.6 miles one-way.

**CONFIGURATION:** Point-to-point or out-and-back

**DIFFICULTY:** Easy

**SCENERY:** Overlooks of the Columbia River

**EXPOSURE:** Mostly shady

**TRAFFIC:** Varies by section, heavy to light

**TRAIL SURFACE:** Paved

**HIKING TIME:** Moffett to Eagle Creek, 2.5 hours; Hood River to Mosier, 2 hours

**SEASON:** Year-round

**ACCESS:** $3 fee to park in Hood River or Mosier; Northwest Forest Pass required at Cascade Locks and Eagle Creek

**MAPS:** Available at Hood River trailhead

**FACILITIES:** The Hood River trailhead has rest rooms and water.

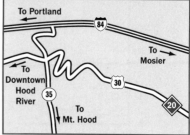

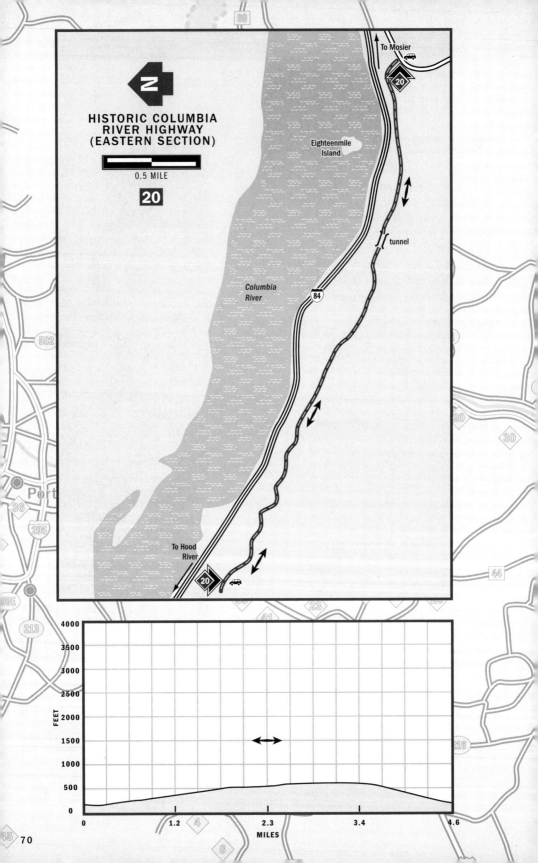

HISTORIC COLUMBIA
RIVER HIGHWAY
(EASTERN SECTION)

0.5 MILE

**20**

To Mosier

Eighteenmile
Island

Columbia
River

tunnel

To Hood
River

Columbia River just east of Mosier Tunnel from Historic Columbia River Highway

eastern end is a dry area of grasslands; the western end is a temperate rain forest. These trails explore the gorge in a unique way, and the section from Hood River to Mosier displays the climate transition in dramatic fashion.

The most interesting section is this easternmost one. If you just want to see the Mosier Twin Tunnels, park at Mosier; from there, it's 0.7 miles to the tunnels, a viewpoint looking east on the Columbia, and a grassy picnic area beside the road. (The latter two features were added for the 2000 opening of the trail.) Here you're well into the eastern gorge climate, where dry brush and lodgepole pine dominate rather than cedars and firs. But this scenery is even more dramatic if you start at Hood River and make the 3.9-mile trek to the tunnels.

From the Hood River trailhead, first take a quick stroll out to the lookout over the river, then duck into the new Information Center to get maps and brochures. Then start up the trail, renovated in 2000 and opened in grand style with a parade of antique cars. You'll walk through a section of firs and big leaf maples (spectacular in fall); around two miles out, a side trail on the left leads to a lookout over the river.

Just before the tunnel, you'll pass through a brand-new rock catchment structure, put in to keep rocks from the cliffs above from squashing hikers and bikers on the road below; this was also a problem when cars were on the road, especially when they got too wide and the tunnel had to be turned into a one-lane road, causing cars to have to wait their turn to enter. This fact should make you feel better: soon after it opened, the structure stopped a 5,000-pound rock that had fallen 200 feet.

The tunnels themselves took two years to complete and had to be put in because the builders of the road got into a dispute over right-of-way with owners of the railroad below. They're a combined 493 feet in length, and they feature several adits, or windows out onto the gorge. A walkway outside the adits, part of the original road, is now off limits.

One thing to look for in the tunnel is graffiti left by a 1921 traveling party when they were trapped in the tunnel for eight days by a November snowstorm. It's almost at the eastern end of the tunnel, on the northern side. (They were packed for a long camping trip, by the way, and had plenty of food.)

71

The western section of the Highway Trail connects Moffett Creek and Cascade Locks. This is in the heart of the western-gorge (rainforest) climate, with numerous creeks, countless moss-covered trees, and several fine views of the river.

The eastern (right-hand) parking lot at Exit 40 is also a trailhead for a lovely 1-mile hike to Wahclella Falls, a two-tiered 350-footer in a narrow canyon. The Highway Trail starts out on a bridge that crosses Tanner Creek, the home to fish released from the hatchery at Bonneville Dam. A lot of this 1.4-mile section is a little too close to I-84, but the bridge over Moffett Creek is worth a visit. It was built in 1915 and was, at the time, the longest flat-arch bridge in the world. It's now one of four bridges right next to each other, including the still-used 1906 railroad bridge. From our bridge, you can see, across the river, three of our hikes: Beacon Rock and Mount Hamilton in Beacon Rock State Park and, to the right, Table Mountain with its sheer face. As of this printing, by the way, the state's top funding priority for the HCRH trail is to extend it west from this bridge to Warrendale, a distance of some three miles.

The section from Tanner Creek to Eagle Creek, also 1.4 miles, starts out along I-84 but quickly gets into the woods. It climbs slightly and comes to a viewpoint of Bonneville Dam—and also the only stop sign on a trail in this book. It's there because a lot of people bike this trail, and just beyond the stop sign is a set of 62 steps leading down to Eagle Creek.

To continue west, walk between the fish hatchery and I-84, and after another small section along the highway, you'll climb in the woods to a crossing of lovely Ruckel Creek. The rest of the 2.4 miles to Cascade Locks is away from the highway and is quite serene. There's even a nice place to sit down next to a tunnel, and when it's all over, you're in the parking lot of the Charburger, where they do some pretty fine chow.

The middle section, from Starvation Creek to Viento State Park, is the least interesting, but it's also the least crowded. Starvation Creek Falls, right behind the rest rooms at Starvation Creek State Park, is worth stopping to see. The two names are somewhat interesting, too. Starvation Creek got its name when a train got stuck there by a snowstorm in 1884. Nobody starved, but after the local papers reported otherwise, the name stuck. Viento comes not from the Spanish word for wind (which would be appropriate for the area) but from a combination of the names of three men who ran a railroad there in Oregon Trail days. They were Villard, Endicott, and Tolman; hence, Viento.

▶ **NEARBY ACTIVITIES**

The town of Hood River is worth a visit while you're in the area. The downtown area is compact and interesting, and in keeping with modern Oregon tradition, you should swing by the Full Sail Brewery, where they have tours, a pub, and a tasting room.

# KINGS MOUNTAIN/ ELK MOUNTAIN

## ▶ IN BRIEF

There are two options here: the trip up Kings Mountain is simple but steep, but the loop that includes Elk Mountain borders on an adventure, with exposed scrambles and insanely steep hiking over a 13-mile good time.

## ▶ DESCRIPTION

This entire hike is in the Tillamook State Forest, which might not sound that impressive compared to a national park or wilderness area, but there is a fascinating story behind this forest.

On a hot August day in 1933, a fire started at a logging operation in Gales Creek Canyon. The temperatures had been in the 90s for weeks, and humidity was at an all-time low. The forest, therefore, was a bomb waiting to go off. The Gales Creek fire started as a fairly standard fire, but then a hot, dry wind came from the east, and the 40,000-acre fire turned, in less than 24 hours, into a 240,000-acre fire. This "explosion" threw up a mushroom cloud 40 miles wide that rained debris two feet thick on a 30-mile stretch of the Oregon Coast. Three more major fires would strike every six years until 1951 by which time 355,000 acres and 13 billion board feet of timber (enough for more than one million five-room homes) had been completely destroyed. Logging came to a halt, wildlife was decimated, rivers were choked with sediment and debris, and most importantly for the forest, seedcones were annihilated, meaning that the forest wouldn't even grow back on its own.

## ▶ DIRECTIONS

From Portland on US 26, drive 20 miles west of I-405, then bear west on OR 6, following a sign for Tillamook. Continue 26 more miles and, just before milepost 25, park at the trailhead on the right. Driving time is 50 minutes.

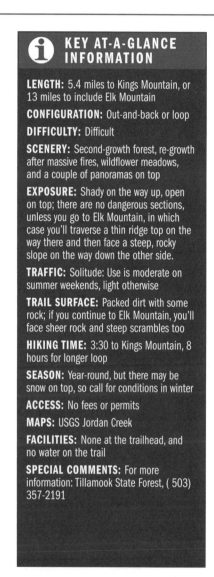

## ⓘ KEY AT-A-GLANCE INFORMATION

**LENGTH:** 5.4 miles to Kings Mountain, or 13 miles to include Elk Mountain

**CONFIGURATION:** Out-and-back or loop

**DIFFICULTY:** Difficult

**SCENERY:** Second-growth forest, re-growth after massive fires, wildflower meadows, and a couple of panoramas on top

**EXPOSURE:** Shady on the way up, open on top; there are no dangerous sections, unless you go to Elk Mountain, in which case you'll traverse a thin ridge top on the way there and then face a steep, rocky slope on the way down the other side.

**TRAFFIC:** Solitude: Use is moderate on summer weekends, light otherwise

**TRAIL SURFACE:** Packed dirt with some rock; if you continue to Elk Mountain, you'll face sheer rock and steep scrambles too

**HIKING TIME:** 3:30 to Kings Mountain, 8 hours for longer loop

**SEASON:** Year-round, but there may be snow on top, so call for conditions in winter

**ACCESS:** No fees or permits

**MAPS:** USGS Jordan Creek

**FACILITIES:** None at the trailhead, and no water on the trail

**SPECIAL COMMENTS:** For more information: Tillamook State Forest, ( 503) 357-2191

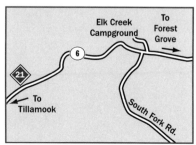

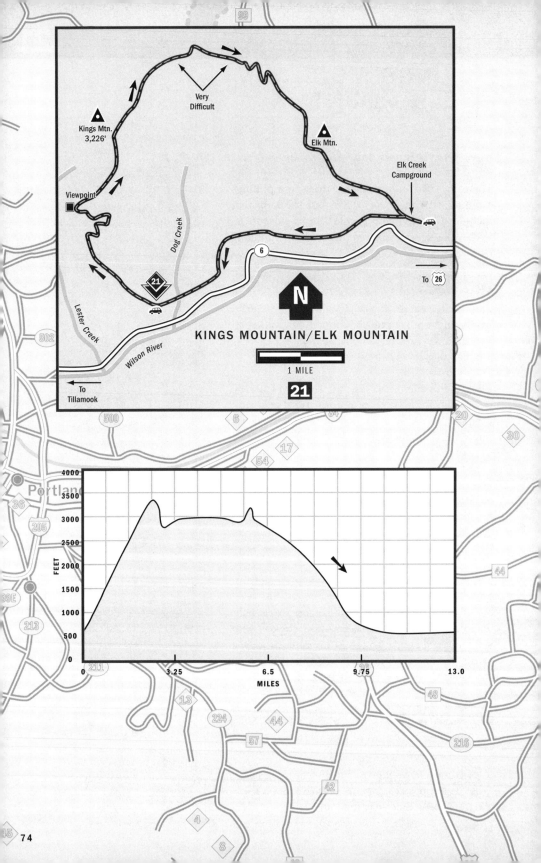

KINGS MOUNTAIN/ELK MOUNTAIN

1 MILE

21

But starting with a bond measure in 1949, a recovery effort was launched. Eventually, more than 72 million seedlings were planted by hand, and in 1973 what had been known as the Tillamook Burn was renamed Tillamook State Forest. Now the question facing the state is whether or not to start logging it again. You won't have to worry about that; your job is to explore one of the highest points in the forest and have a look at how the place has recovered. Keep an eye out for charred logs, for example, and remember that 50 years ago most of this area was bare of vegetation.

With an elevation of 670 feet at the trailhead and a climb to 3,226 feet at the top of Kings Mountain, get ready for a workout. This trail starts steep and gets steeper. But first you have to admire the signs at the trailhead. What do you suppose are the odds that it's exactly 2.46 miles to the summit of Kings Mountain? And I don't know who considers this a "one-quart trip," but I'd start out with more than that, especially if you're also going to Elk Mountain.

You begin in a forest of alder and fern with Dog Creek off to your right. At 0.1 mile, you'll see (but not take) the Wilson River Trail on your right; if you're going to Elk Mountain, you'll be coming back this way. Around 1 mile, things get nasty steep; the next mile gains about 1,300 feet, as opposed to the 800 feet you've gained in the first mile. When the trail makes a sharp turn to the right and a small trail goes left, go out there for your first real view to the north. Lester Creek, below you, flows into the Wilson River to your left; Kings Mountain is directly behind you, higher than the rocky peak you see to the north. There are also some large, charred stumps on this ridge. The live trees were all planted after the big fires.

The last 0.6 miles of this hike gain about 900 feet, so just take your time and believe it's worth the effort. If you're here in May or June, you'll have no doubt about that when you walk past a picnic table (many thanks to Troop 299 from Tigard!) and out into the meadows, which in early summer are filled with beargrass, lupine, Indian Paintbrush, and seemingly a billion other tiny flowers. The summit is now just 0.3 miles straight ahead, marked by a wonderful sign. The view stretches from the ocean to the Cascades; be sure and sign the register, one of the few in Oregon.

Now, if you've had enough, go back while you can. If you want to add 9 miles and tons of fun to your day, head on to Elk Mountain by continuing over the summit of Kings Mountain, traveling east. The downhill slope will get steep quickly, which might make you miss the trip up Kings Mountain. There are even some rock scrambles and ledges to keep things interesting. After 0.8 miles of this loveliness, you'll cross the ridge through a rock slot and join an old roadbed that traverses the ridge for 0.5 miles to a junction. Stay right for the last two miles to Elk Mountain, a tiny summit with a big view.

From here, you might wish you had a parachute. The Elk Mountain Trail is the steepest thing in this book. At times, you'll have to practically slide down rocky slopes, and in some places it will look like you're about to hike off the end of the world. Just take it easy, and you'll get down in one piece. When you reach the Wilson River Trail, turn right onto it, and you're 3.7 miles from the trailhead. There's a nice meadow on the way (this trail has it all!), and the only direction you need is that just after you cross a bridge, you'll encounter a road that you ignore; stay on the trail until you hit the Kings Mountain Trail, then turn left for 0.1 mile to the car. Whew.

# LARCH MOUNTAIN

## KEY AT·A·GLANCE INFORMATION

**LENGTH:** 8.6-mile one-way with a car shuttle; otherwise, 17.2 miles out-and-back. The upper loop is 6 miles.

**CONFIGURATION:** Out-and-back or one-way

**DIFFICULTY:** Hard to moderate

**SCENERY:** Waterfalls, creeks in wooded canyons, colossal trees

**EXPOSURE:** Mostly shady

**TRAFFIC:** Always heavy on lower stretches

**TRAIL SURFACE:** Pavement, packed dirt, some gravel

**HIKING TIME:** 4 hours one-way; 7 for the round-trip; 3 for the upper loop

**SEASON:** June–October

**ACCESS:** No fees or permits needed.

**MAPS:** Trails of the Columbia Gorge; USGS Multnomah Falls

**FACILITIES:** Full services at Multnomah Falls trailhead; rest rooms only at top of Larch Mountain

## IN BRIEF

Sure, you can drive to the top of Larch Mountain, but the trail between there and Multnomah Falls is one of the classic walks in Oregon—from the shores of the Columbia River to a high lookout in the Cascades, with old-growth forest on the way up and a view from Portland to several volcanoes on top. There's even a shorter loop hike that takes in the upper parts of the mountain only.

## DESCRIPTION

Pick a clear day to take in the view; or think about timing your arrival on top just as the sun is setting—you'll get to see Mount Hood bathed in pink light, and the lights of Portland are spectacular from there.

You can actually see Larch Mountain as you drive out I-84: it's just to the left of Mount Hood and has a notch in the top. The top of that notch is where you're headed.

## DIRECTIONS

To start at Multnomah Falls, take I-84 24 miles east of I-205 to Exit 31/Multnomah Falls, which leads to a parking lot. Park and walk under the expressway to the historic lodge. For the upper trailheads, take I-84 15 miles east of I-205 and take Exit 22/Corbett. At the intersection with the Historic Columbia River Highway, turn left. After two miles, veer right onto Larch Mountain Road. The uppermost trailhead is in the parking lot at the end of the road, 14 miles up. The middle trailhead is 11.5 miles on the left, where Larch Mountain Road makes a big turn to the right and a gravel road takes off to the left. If your vehicle has good clearance, you can drive 0.3 miles up this road. Driving time to lower trailhead is 25 minutes and to upper trailhead is 50 minutes.

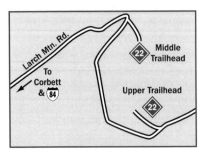

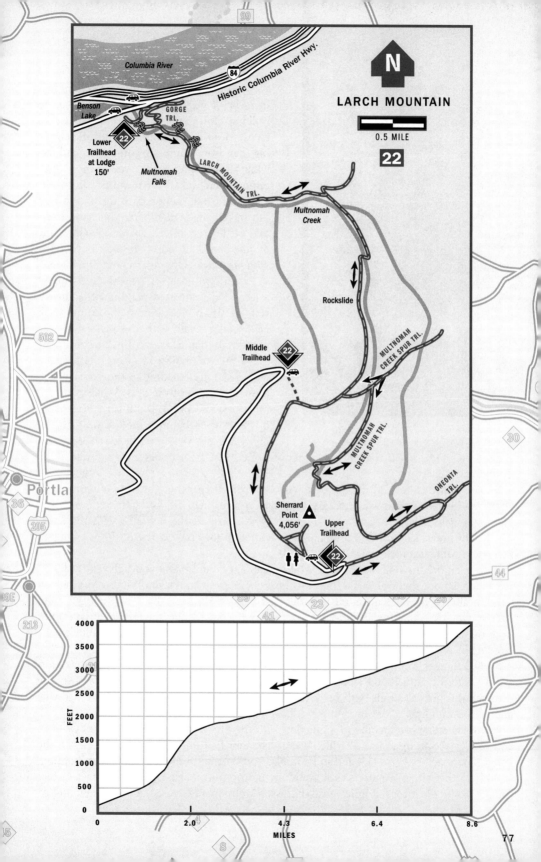

Columbia River

Historic Columbia River Hwy.

84

N

LARCH MOUNTAIN

0.5 MILE

22

Benson
Lake

GORGE
TRL.

22

Lower
Trailhead
at Lodge
150'

*Multnomah
Falls*

LARCH MOUNTAIN TRL.

Multnomah
Creek

Rockslide

MULTNOMAH CREEK SPUR TRL.

Middle
Trailhead

22

MULTNOMAH
CREEK SPUR TRL.

ONEONTA TRL.

Sherrard
Point
4,056'

Upper
Trailhead

22

30

502

Portla

36

205

99E

213

44

59

23

41

8

FEET

4000

3500

3000

2500

2000

1500

1000

500

0

0        2.0        4.3        6.4        8.6

MILES

Upper Multnomah Falls

As for the hike, I confess a certain bias in favor of walking up hills as opposed to walking down them. It seems easier to recover from losing your breath while climbing than from pounding your knees and feet while descending. Still, you've got three options here, all of them quite worthwhile. You can start at the top or at the bottom and put in 6.8 miles (assuming you have a second car for a shuttle), or you can start in the middle and do a loop that takes in the view with less work. Or you can combine these.

For our purposes, let's assume you put a second car at the top parking lot, and we'll start at the bottom. From the Multnomah Falls Lodge, walk with the masses up the paved trail that leads over the Benson Bridge and 1 mile (climbing 600 feet) to a junction with a side trail leading to the viewing platform at the top of the falls. When you continue past this point, you'll leave 90 percent of the masses behind; for the next several miles you may well have the Larch Mountain Trail (#441) to yourself. You will also enter one of the few areas of old-growth forest in the Columbia River Gorge.

The trail was built in the 1910s to coincide with the opening of the Columbia River Highway—and one thing we should get straight is that there are no larch trees on Larch Mountain. The name stuck when old-time loggers confused the noble fir with the larch, which only grows east of the Cascade Range (although they have a few in the Washington Park/Hoyt Arboretum; see page 195).

Staying on this trail, you'll cross Multnomah Creek and pass two lovely waterfalls. At 1.8 miles, ignore the Wahkeena Trail on the right. At two miles you'll cross Multnomah Creek again, then at 3.1 miles traverse the East Fork of Multnomah Creek. Just 0.6 miles later you'll cross a one-log footbridge, which, by pure coincidence, my friend Christie and I were the first people to cross. (The workers had just set the log in place and allowed the crossing before they started on the handrails.)

At 3.9 miles you'll cross a rockslide and then start climbing through an old-growth forest of western hemlock and Douglas fir trees that get as thick as five and six feet. In late summer, this area abounds with huckleberries, and in autumn the red/yellow/orange vine maple is astounding.

At 4.8 miles you'll come to a junction with the Multnomah Creek Way Trail (#444), and you'll have an option as to which way to go. Your first option is to simply stay on the Larch Mountain Trail (#441), and in two miles you'll come to the top. The second option, (#444) to the left, is a more scenic route to the top but is also 0.7 miles longer. If that sounds okay, take it for 0.2 miles until it crosses Multnomah Creek, then turn right and go

2.5 miles through a marsh and up the ridge of Larch Mountain. When you come to the Oneonta Trail (#424) at the top of the ridge, turn right and follow it 0.9 miles to the parking area atop Larch Mountain. You'll have to follow the road for the last little bit. Then follow a signed, paved trail to Sherrard Point for the big view.

Now, as for your other hiking options on Larch Mountain, you can either start at the top and go down to Multnomah Falls (following either the Larch Mountain Trail all the way down or the loop described above via the Multnomah Creek Way Trail) or you can park at the middle trailhead described above. This accesses the upper part of Larch Mountain without 3,000 feet of climbing from the Columbia. From that trailhead, either walk up the Larch Mountain Trail 1.5 miles to the top, or go down it half a mile, take the Multnomah Creek Way Trail (#444), and take the loop described above.

Any way you go, make sure when on top that you go out the paved trail to Sherrard Point and have a look around. You'll see (if it's clear) Portland, Mount Hood, Mount Jefferson, Mount Adams, Mount St. Helens, and Mount Rainier. You'll also notice that you're at the top of a cliff on a semicircular ridge. That's because Larch Mountain is what remains of an ancient volcano, and what you're looking down into is its former crater.

Millions of years ago lava flows from volcanoes like this used to occasionally dam the Columbia River, forming lakes that stretched back into Montana and occasionally broke through in catastrophic floods. At times like this there would have been some 400 feet of water where Portland is now—just a little something to think about as you walk back to your car. For more information, call the Columbia River Gorge National Scenic Area office at (541) 386-2333.

## ▶ NEARBY ACTIVITIES

If you did the one-way car shuttle, stop on the way to or from Multnomah Falls at the Portland Women's Forum Viewpoint on the Historic Columbia River Highway. It's a little farther west than the more famous Vista House, and it is therefore a less seen view up the Columbia River Gorge.

# LAUREL HILL

## KEY AT-A-GLANCE INFORMATION

**LENGTH:** 0.8 miles to 8 miles

**CONFIGURATION:** Out-and-back

**DIFFICULTY:** Easy to moderate

**SCENERY:** Forest, two abandoned historic roadways, a nice little waterfall

**EXPOSURE:** Shady all the way

**TRAFFIC:** Light use, but beware of mountain bikers on the Pioneer Bridle Trail.

**TRAIL SURFACE:** Packed dirt and one stretch of pavement that has cars and trucks on it

**HIKING TIME:** 30 minutes to see the chute, 4 hours to see it all

**SEASON:** April–November

**ACCESS:** Northwest Forest Pass required only on Road 2639.

**MAPS:** Green Trails #461 (Government Camp); USGS Government Camp

**FACILITIES:** None at the trailhead; the water in Little Zigzag River must be treated.

### ▶ IN BRIEF

Step back into Oregon's history on a section of the old Barlow Road, an Oregon Trail alternative to the then-dangerous Columbia River. Within just a few minutes you can see a fascinating piece of history; if you have a few hours, you can see that and more, including lovely Little Zigzag Falls.

### ▶ DESCRIPTION

It's tough to tell which is more amazing: the June rhododendron show in this area or the fact that the pioneers got through here in the 1840s and 1850s in cattle-pulled wagons. To decide, you'll want to have a look for yourself.

From the lower trailhead, you'll start up the Pioneer Bridle Trail, named because this section of the Barlow Road was so steep that travelers (going in the opposite direction) had to lower their wagons with ropes or brake them by dragging whole trees behind—and this is what they went through by taking the Barlow Road so they didn't have to go down the Columbia River by boat.

Take a few steps into the woods and then right at a junction. Soon you'll climb the hill the pioneers came down. If you do so in June, you'll be in a world of pink rhododendrons, which the pioneers thought were laurel (they came through in the fall, when the plants weren't blooming and, judging from their journals, it rained every

### ▶ DIRECTIONS

From Portland on US 26, drive 42 miles east of I-205. At FS 2639, which is 1 mile past the town of Rhododendron and marked by a sign: KIWANIS CAMP ROAD, the lower trailhead is on the left side of US 26. For the upper trailhead (to start near the Laurel Hill Chute), stay on US 26 for 2.1 more miles and pull over at the historic marker on the right side. There's parking for just a few cars. Driving time is 50 minutes.

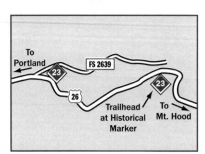

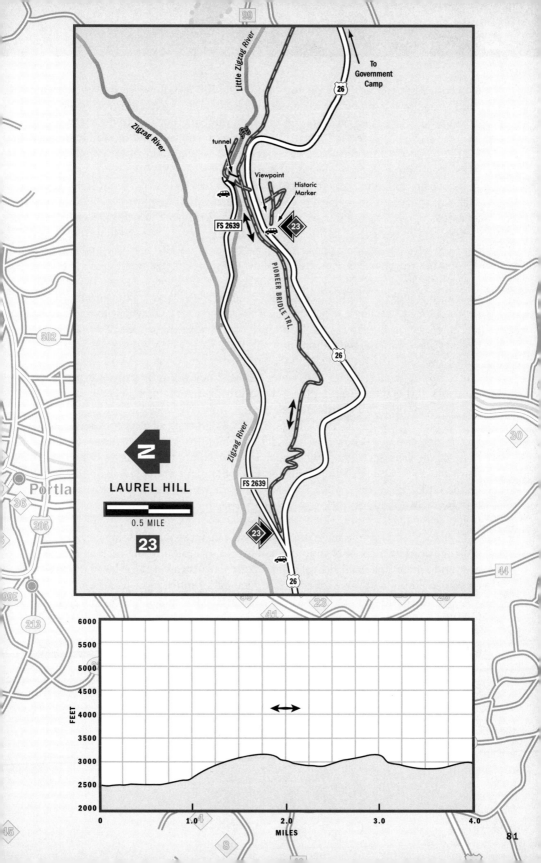

Little Zigzag River

Zigzag River

tunnel

Viewpoint

Historic
Marker

FS 2639

PIONEER BRIDLE TRL.

Zigzag River

FS 2639

To
Government
Camp

**N**

LAUREL HILL

0.5 MILE

**23**

FEET

6000
5500
5000
4500
4000
3500
3000
2500
2000

0        1.0        2.0        3.0        4.0

MILES

moment). After crossing over the top of the hill, 700 feet above where you started, you'll drop down to a point where a side trail leads to the right, out to US 26. To just head up to Little Zigzag Falls, stay on the main trail, and don't go to the highway.

If you want to see the Laurel Hill Chute, another steep (and incredibly rocky!) hill the pioneers came down, and also stay on the original route of the Barlow Road, cross US 26 and walk to the historical marker on the far side. From there, walk up a series of steps and turn right on an old road; this is the 1920s-era Mount Hood Loop Highway, which was abandoned decades ago when US 26 went in.

Just up the road, you'll see on the left the chute itself, which pioneers called "the longest and steepest hill from the States to Oregon." If you want to go to the top of it, you have two options: one is to take a steep shortcut that starts behind the sign just right of the chute; the other is to follow the more gradual trail that departs the road a little farther up. They wind up at the same four-way intersection. On the main trail, keep straight at that intersection (it would be a left if you took the shortcut) for the top of the chute and a nice view down the Camp Creek Valley. The fourth trail at that intersection, by the way, is the original Barlow Road route, but other than that fact and a lot more rhododendrons, it's not particularly worth visiting.

Now, for Little Zigzag Falls, walk back across US 26 and down to where you started on the Pioneer Bridle Trail, which as you'll now see is by a highway sign saying SLIDES NEXT 2 MILES. Re-enter the woods, turn right at the trail junction, and keep going straight until you get to a tunnel.

A tunnel? Yep. In the 1930s parts of the old Barlow Road were converted into a hiking trail, and this is how it went under the Mount Hood Loop Highway. To get to Little Zigzag Falls, go through the tunnel, loop back onto the old highway, and walk down the road 0.2 miles to a parking lot. From there, it's a simple walk of 0.3 miles up the Little Zigzag River, which in my mind is the perfect little mountain stream. If it's late August, you can pick some huckleberries on the way and eat them on the bench by the falls.

If your car is at the lower trailhead, you can save yourself some elevation by walking back down FS 2639 from the parking lot, instead of going back on the Pioneer Bridle Trail. You could also, of course, park here instead of at the lower trailhead. Or you could put a car here (or on US 26) and do a shuttle. Options abound.

For more information, contact the Mount Hood Visitor Information Center at (503) 622-7674.

## ▶ NEARBY ACTIVITIES

Below Laurel Hill, Barlow Road more or less followed the present-day route of US 26. Four miles below FS 2639, and 0.2 miles east of the Tollgate Campground, there's a replica of a Barlow Road tollgate. Brush, trees, and a padlock blocked the road, and for 25 cents the gate would be opened.

# LAVA CANYON

## IN BRIEF

An unparalleled look at geological forces at work, Lava Canyon is also a beautiful place to be, with several waterfalls, a dramatic bridge, some challenging hiking, and a short, barrier-free hiking loop.

## DESCRIPTION

First, a little history, so you'll know what you're looking at here. In ancient times, a forest covered a deep valley. Then, 3,500 years ago, Mount St. Helens erupted, sending a massive mudflow down through the canyon, filling it with volcanic rock. Over the years, the river cut its way through the rock, forming a canyon with waterfalls and deep cuts and towers of harder rock—Lava Canyon. Then other mudflows covered all of that, and eventually forest grew back over the whole thing.

Then on May 18, 1980, Mount St. Helens erupted again, melting 70% of its glaciers in an instant and sending millions of cubic feet of mud and rock blasting down the side of the mountain at about 45 miles an hour. That eruption scoured out the forest and rock, exposing Lava Canyon for the first time in thousands of years. As you drove in, you got a glimpse of this 1980 mudflow (also known as a lahar); now go see what it gave us.

From the trailhead, you start on a paved path that, although officially barrier-free, would

## DIRECTIONS

From Portland on I-5, drive 21 miles north of the Columbia River, and take Exit 21/Woodland. Turn right onto WA 503 (Lewis River Road), which after 31 miles (2 miles past the town of Cougar) turns into FS 90. Follow FS 90 for 3.3 miles and turn left onto FS 83. The Lava Canyon trailhead is at the end of FS 83, 11.3 miles ahead. Driving time is 1 hour and 20 minutes.

### KEY AT-A-GLANCE INFORMATION

**LENGTH:** 1 to 6 miles

**CONFIGURATION:** Out-and-back or loop

**DIFFICULTY:** Easy for the upper section, hard to do the whole thing

**SCENERY:** Waterfalls, canyon, lava, suspension bridge

**EXPOSURE:** Most of this hike is out in the open.

**TRAFFIC:** Use is very heavy on summer weekends, heavy during the week, and moderate the rest of the season.

**TRAIL SURFACE:** Paved, boardwalk, gravel, then packed dirt with rocks

**HIKING TIME:** 30 minutes to do the upper loop, 3 hours to do the whole thing

**SEASON:** May–October

**ACCESS:** Northwest Forest Pass required.

**MAPS:** USFS Mount St. Helens National Monument

**FACILITIES:** Toilets at the trailhead, but no water

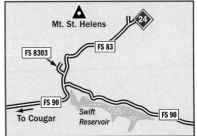

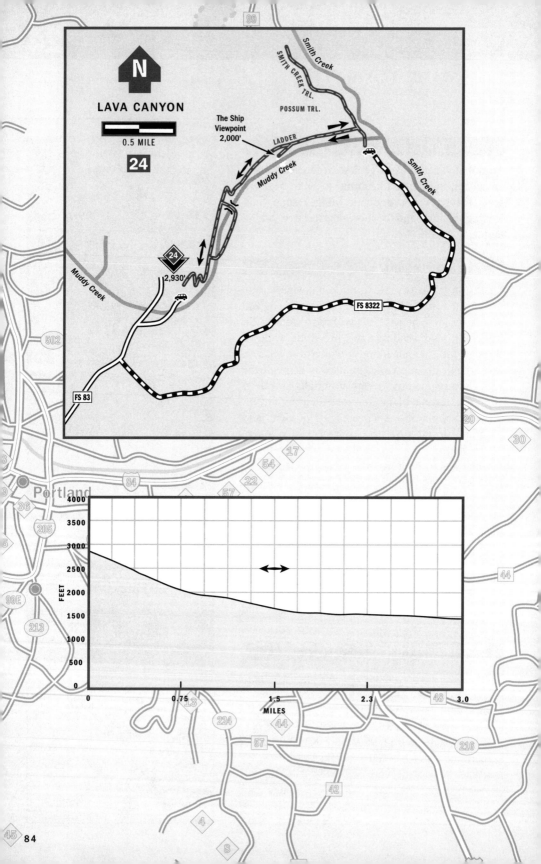

LAVA CANYON

N

0.5 MILE

**24**

The Ship
Viewpoint
2,000'

LADDER

Muddy Creek

SMITH CREEK TRL.

Smith Creek

POSSUM TRL.

Smith Creek

24
2,930'

Muddy Creek

FS 8322

FS 83

FEET

4000
3500
3000
2500
2000
1500
1000
500
0

0      0.75      1.5      2.3      3.0
MILES

require some work to push a wheelchair through. You can see here that the trees around you survived the 1980 eruption, but everything below was wiped out. Also, look around for trees that have rocks embedded in them—that's how strong the eruption was, and this point is some five miles from the crater. The pavement will soon give way to boardwalk, and two viewing platforms give both information and dramatic views of the upper canyon.

After 0.4 miles you'll come to a junction; stay straight for now, and in 0.2 miles you'll come to the suspension bridge. It's only 3 feet wide and 100 feet long, and it was also built by the same company that built the suspension bridge at Drift Creek Falls (page 57). Small kids probably shouldn't go below the suspension bridge, and everybody should be careful if it has rained recently. If you'd like to do only a 1.3-mile loop, cross the bridge and follow the trail back up; you'll wind up at the first intersection after crossing another small bridge.

Looking up Lava Canyon from "The Ship"

Follow the trail downhill (and I do mean down) from the suspension bridge.In the next section of trail, you'll go down steep slopes, along unguarded ledges, across a couple of bridgeless creeks, and down a 40-foot ladder. After that, you have to climb back up 900 feet in about a mile. So if it has been raining, or you're tired or nervous about heights, think twice before you go past the bridge.

After a steep half a mile down, passing several beautiful waterfalls and an area where the river flows through a chute just a few feet wide, the trail mellows somewhat. At 0.8 miles, you'll climb down a ladder (be careful if your shoes are wet!) and then cross a mossy stream. The rock formation on your right here is known as The Ship; it was one of the formations left standing thousands of years ago when the river cut a new course through the ancient canyon. The top of The Ship was the floor of the valley before 1980. There's a little perspective, eh?

It's worth the effort to get to the top of The Ship. A trail on the right leads 0.2 miles up it; it's pretty steep and includes rock steps and yet another (smaller) ladder, but there are late-summer huckleberries up there, and it's a heck of a place for a picnic.

At this point, you've seen the best of the hike, so it's a good spot to turn around. But if you'd like to keep going, the Lava Canyon Trail continues another 1.3 miles to the Smith Creek trailhead, losing 350 feet in elevation on the way. There's a bridge just before the end, another good chance to see the remains of the 1980 mudflow.

Whenever you head back, cross the suspension bridge, and take the loop hike back. You'll wind up out on a pre-1980 lava flow, with good roaming available off the trail. When you cross a small metal bridge, turn left, and you're 0.4 miles from the car. For more information, call the Mount St. Helens National Volcanic Monument office at (360) 247-3900.

# LEWIS RIVER

**KEY AT-A-GLANCE INFORMATION**

**LENGTH:** 5.6 miles

**CONFIGURATION:** Out-and-back

**DIFFICULTY:** Easy

**SCENERY:** Several waterfalls, stream flowing through a wooded canyon, old-growth forest

**EXPOSURE:** Shady all the way

**TRAFFIC:** Use is heavy all summer long, especially on weekends.

**TRAIL SURFACE:** Gravel at first, then packed dirt with some roots

**HIKING TIME:** 3 hours

**SEASON:** Year-round, although it might get snow in the winter

**ACCESS:** Northwest Forest Pass required.

**MAPS:** Green Trails #365 (Lone Butte)

**FACILITIES:** Toilets at the trailhead; from spring to fall there's drinking water in the campground.

## ▶ IN BRIEF

Here's a pleasant, mostly flat stroll along a beautiful river with three dramatic waterfalls. Chances are, they're unlike most falls you've seen, too. The long drive to the trailhead is worth it.

## ▶ DESCRIPTION

From the trailhead in the picnic area, follow a trail that starts just left of the rest rooms. In 100 yards turn right to reach several viewpoints above Lower Falls, one of the most dramatic falls around. The water looks like it's spilling off a shelf, and in fact it is—this is the edge of an ancient lava flow. Over the next stretch of trail, you're walking around the campground, so there are a lot of trails. Turning left will throw you off track and into the campground, but turning right will offer several opportunities to get right down to the river. Once you're above the falls there are some nice opportunities to swim.

About half a mile after you leave the campground area, look for a bridge (or, rather, half a

## ▶ DIRECTIONS

From Portland on I-5, drive 21 miles north of the Columbia River and take Exit 21/Woodland. Turn right onto WA 503 (Lewis River Road), which after 31 miles (2 miles past the town of Cougar) turns into FS 90. Follow FS 90 for 30 more miles (note that you'll have to turn right just past the Pine Creek Information Center to stay on FS 90) to the Lower Lewis River Falls Recreation Area. Take the first right off the entrance road for the trailhead. You may notice that a mile before the campground on FS 90 there's a Lewis River trailhead, just past a bridge. You can start there if you'd like, but it adds 3 miles to the round-trip hike, and doesn't add any waterfalls to the view. Driving time is 1 hour and 45 minutes.

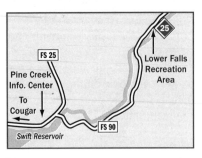

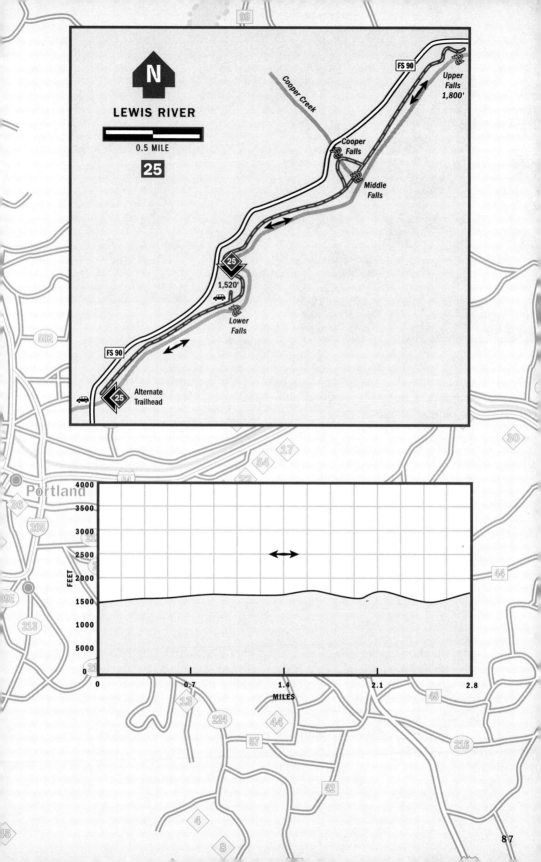

**N**

**LEWIS RIVER**

0.5 MILE

**25**

Cooper Creek

FS 90

Upper
Falls
1,800'

Cooper
Falls

Middle
Falls

25

1,520'

Lower
Falls

FS 90

25

Alternate
Trailhead

| FEET | | | | | |
|---|---|---|---|---|---|
| 4000 | | | | | |
| 3500 | | | | | |
| 3000 | | | | | |
| 2500 | | | | | |
| 2000 | | | | | |
| 1500 | | | | | |
| 1000 | | | | | |
| 5000 | | | | | |
| 0 | | | | | |

0        0.7        1.4        2.1        2.8

MILES

Lower Lewis River Falls

bridge) across the river. According to the 1965 USGS map of the area, the Lewis River Campground used to be on the far side of the river, so that bridge offered access from that campground to this trail.

Around 0.8 miles from the campground, you'll pass the top of a small waterfall, and then 1.2 miles out you'll cross Copper Creek Falls, which looks like a waterslide into the Lewis River (don't try it). You may notice, on the left, two trails leading up the hill, one just before Copper Creek and one just after. This is a half-mile scenic loop you can do on the way back, if you'd like. Just past the second of these trails, the main trail arrives at Middle Falls, another shelflike falls worth exploring. Just be careful, because the rock here is almost always wet and slippery.

Back on the main trail, you'll soon pass under some enormous cliffs, then drop down into an area with some seriously large trees. There are some Western red cedars here in the neighborhood of six feet thick, and one Douglas fir on the left that must be ten feet thick. Just past this area you'll come to a campsite on the right, then the amphitheater of Upper Falls, an 80-foot plunge. There are good logs and rocks in the sun here for picnicking or just general lounging. A trail to the left leads 0.2 miles up the hill to a platform at the top of Upper Falls, a very worthy side trip. Just a few moments above it, there's a view of yet another falls above Upper Falls.

On the way back, just past Middle Falls, go ahead and take the Copper Creek scenic byway. Just take the first right past Middle Falls, climb briefly to another water-fall up Copper Creek, then take a left at the fork (the road is to the right) and you'll be back on the main trail, 1.5 miles from the car.

For more information, call the Mount St. Helens National Volcanic Monument office at (360) 247-3900.

# LOOKOUT MOUNTAIN

> **IN BRIEF**

One of the easternmost points in this book, Lookout Mountain is also the widest and most wonderful viewpoint, stretching from south of the Three Sisters all the way to Mount Rainier, and including desert, lake, and river.

> **DESCRIPTION**

First, for the "studly" route, which is a whole lot more work but comes with a lot of benefits. From the Gumjuwac Trailhead on OR 35, the first couple of miles are relentlessly uphill. You'll gain 1,600 feet in less than two miles, then catch a little break over the last half-mile to Gumjuwac Saddle. There's also, at the top of the real climbing around two miles up, a wonderful rocky viewpoint back towards Mount Hood.

At Gumjuwac Saddle, you'll encounter several trails. The Gumjuwac Trail crosses FS 3550 and drops down the other side of the ridge into Badger Creek Wilderness. Coming in from the

> **DIRECTIONS**

From Portland on US 26, drive 51 miles east of I-205 and turn north on OR 35, following signs for Hood River. For the longer hike on the Gumjuwac Trail, go 10.5 miles on OR 35 and park on the right just after the road crosses the East Fork of Hood River. To drive to High Prairie for the shorter loop, go 2.5 more miles on OR 35 and turn right onto FS 44. After 3.7 miles, turn right (following a sign for High Prairie) onto gravel FS 4410. Over the next 4.6 miles, during which the road occasionally rides like a washboard, take the larger, more uphill road at all the junctions. At a sign for Badger Lake on the right, follow FS 4410 around to the left; the parking area is 100 yards ahead. Driving times are: High Prairie, 1 hour and 40 minutes; and Gumjuwac Trail, 1 hour and 20 minutes.

**KEY AT-A-GLANCE INFORMATION**

**LENGTH:** 2.2 or 9.2 miles

**CONFIGURATION:** Out-and-back or loop

**DIFFICULTY:** Easy or hard

**SCENERY:** One of the great vista points in Oregon

**EXPOSURE:** Shady, exposed rock at the top

**TRAFFIC:** Heavy use on weekends, moderate otherwise

**TRAIL SURFACE:** Packed dirt and rock; High Prairie is wheelchair-traversable.

**HIKING TIME:** 1 hour or 5 hours

**SEASON:** July–October

**ACCESS:** Northwest Forest Pass required at both trailheads

**MAPS:** Green Trails #462 (Mount Hood); USGS Badger Lake

**FACILITIES:** Outhouse at High Prairie; there are two springs on the way up from Gumjuwac and one more near the summit.

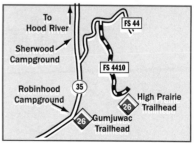

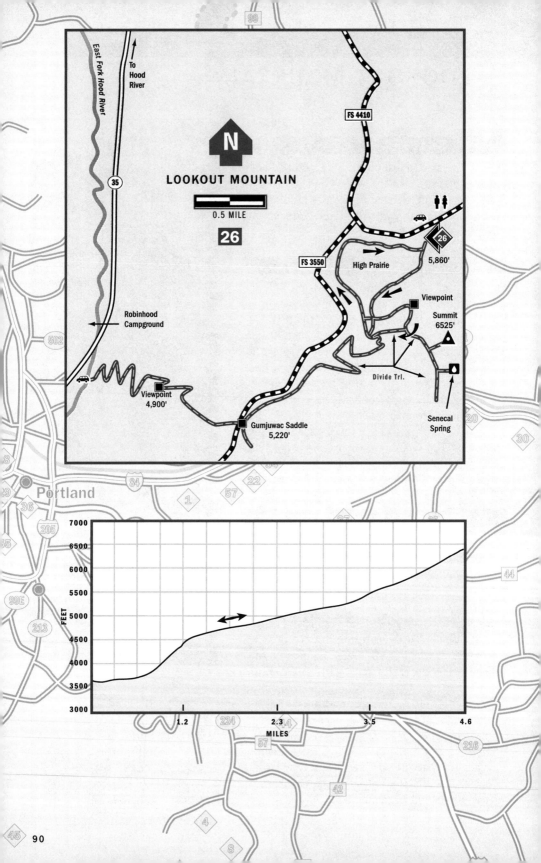

East Fork Hood River

To
Hood
River

35

N

LOOKOUT MOUNTAIN

0.5 MILE

26

FS 4410

FS 3550

High Prairie

26
5,860'

Viewpoint

Summit
6525'

Divide Trl.

Robinhood
Campground

Viewpoint
4,900'

Gumjuwac Saddle
5,220'

Senecal
Spring

FEET

7000
6500
6000
5500
5000
4500
4000
3500
3000

1.2    2.3    3.5    4.6

MILES

Mount Hood from the
Gumjuwac Trail

right is the Gunsight Trail, popular with mountain bikers because it's 4.5 miles along the ridge with very little elevation change. In case you're thinking of driving FS 3550 to this point, you'd better have some clearance. But if you insist, turn right at the Badger Lake sign mentioned in the directions to High Prairie and bounce about three miles to the saddle.

And if you're wondering about the name Gumjuwac, it comes from a sheepherder, Jack. Apparently Jack liked gum shoes, hence Gum Shoe Jack. Somehow that became Gumjuwac over the years. This is explained in what's left of the sign at the Saddle; that sign also refers to the Mount Hood Loop Highway, which hasn't existed for decades.

To keep going to Lookout Mountain, simply walk across FS 3550 and start to your left on the Divide Trail (#458), following a sign for Lookout Mountain. You'll encounter a lovely spring half a mile up, and during this time you'll also have a view straight ahead of Lookout Mountain. You'll also see why this trail is called the Divide Trail. Technically, it splits two watersheds—Hood River from The Dalles—but it's also an amazing sample of east versus west. Coming up the Gumjuwac Trail, it was all shady, with a view of snow-covered Mount Hood; but on this side you'll encounter meadows and flowers and views of the desert. As you climb with Hood on your left, look for views over your right shoulder to Badger Lake. Watch out for wildlife, too; I once saw two falcons chasing each other around here, and I scared up an owl in the woods.

Keep climbing, and just below the summit, stay straight when the High Prairie Loop (#493) cuts off to the left. This will put you on a rocky outcrop with an amazing view; this is where most people stop, but it's not the top of Lookout Mountain. To get there, put Mount Hood behind you and keep going, still on the Divide Trail. You'll walk along a rocky ridge looking down into the Badger Creek drainage, then climb briefly to a trail leading left to the wide-open summit. You'll know you're there when you see the foundation of an old fire lookout. For a description of the view, see below.

There's one more spring up here that's worth visiting. To reach Senecal Spring (named for a forest service ranger from the turn of the twentieth century) take the Divide

Trail 0.2 miles past the summit and turn left on a trail that's barely visible and whose sign is often lying on the ground. The (very cold) spring is a quarter-mile below the Divide Trail.

Now, if you're more into driving up long hills than walking up them, here's the High Prairie Loop. There are a lot of trails on Lookout Mountain, some of which are not on trail maps. So take our map with you and remember that just about all these trails go to the same two places: Lookout Mountain and the trailhead.

From the parking area, walk straight across FS 4410 and up the wide path, so well worn it's practically paved, into the meadows. The fields of daisies and lupine might make you want to stop there, but it's worth it to keep going. The trail you see immediately on your right, labeled for horses to follow, is the Loop Trail (#493) coming back to the trailhead. Ignore it for now.

Follow the wide trail ahead for one mile until, in an area of reddish rock, it splits into three trails. The faint one through the trees on the right is a cutoff to the return portion of the Loop Trail; ignore it. The one straight ahead (and up the hill) is a cut-off to the Divide Trail. If you stay on the wide trail, you'll loop around to the left to a point with a fine view east of the Cascades, out into the Oregon High Desert. The road then loops back around to the right and intersects the Divide Trail (#458). Turn left on the Divide Trail, climb briefly, and follow a small trail to the left to reach the summit.

The view from up here is one that you just can't get from the western side of the Cascades, or for that matter from most points in the Cascades. From left to right, on a clear day, you can see Diamond Peak, the Three Sisters, Jefferson, Hood (absolutely huge just seven miles across the way), St. Helens, Rainier, and Adams. From Diamond Peak to Rainier, as the crow flies, it is about 225 miles. You can also see, if you look closely, a stretch of the Columbia River to the northeast.

If only to see some new country, return to the trailhead by completing the High Prairie Loop. To do this, when you're on Lookout Mountain walk toward Mount Hood on the Divide Trail. At 0.3 miles down, take the signed Loop Trail to your right and follow it as it crosses the face of Lookout Mountain and dives into the woods. After 0.7 miles, turn right at a sign and walk back through the meadows to rejoin the wide, packed trail you started on just above FS 4410.

For more information, call the Barlow Ranger District office at (541) 467-2291.

# LOST LAKE

This is like a resort area, with boats for rent, picnic tables with grills, a campground, and a beautiful lake stocked with trout. It's also a lovely walk around the natural, 240-acre lake, including an interpretive, barrier-free Old Growth Trail and one of the most photographed views of Mount Hood.

## DESCRIPTION

Lost Lake has what you need—that's why there are often so many people there. But, as is always the case, their number decreases in direct proportion to how far you walk.

For the 3.3-mile trail around the lake, start right in front of the newly renovated General Store. Walk down to the boat dock and turn right. The first quarter mile of this trail, which parallels the road, is dotted with picnic tables tucked down by the lakeshore. Soon you'll come to a platform with the killer view of Mount Hood. It dominates the view from Lost Lake.

Beyond the platform, the trail leaves the road, and you start to feel like you're actually out in the woods. In late summer, your progress will be reduced by plump, ripe huckleberries; you can pick a handful or two to go along with your lunch,

## DIRECTIONS

From Portland on I-84, drive 55 miles east of I-205 and take Exit 62/W. Hood River. Turn right at the end of the off-ramp, then take an immediate right onto Country Club Road. At the end of Country Club Road, three miles later, turn left at a stop sign onto Barrett Drive. After 1.3 miles, turn right onto Tucker Road (the second stop sign you'll come to on Country Club Road), which turns into Dee Highway. Go 8.5 miles and turn right onto Lost Lake Road (FS 13). The resort is 14 miles ahead at the end of the road. Just keep following the LOST LAKE signs. Driving time is 1 hour and 30 minutes.

## ⓘ KEY AT-A-GLANCE INFORMATION

**LENGTH:** 3.3 miles around the lake; an additional 4 miles to Lost Lake Butte

**CONFIGURATION:** Loop with an out-and-back option

**DIFFICULTY:** Easy to moderate

**SCENERY:** Lake beaches, a great view of Mount Hood, huge trees

**EXPOSURE:** Shady, unless you get on the lake or climb to the top of the butte

**TRAFFIC:** Heavy on summer days, very heavy on weekends

**TRAIL SURFACE:** Packed dirt and boardwalk; Lakeshore Trail is wheelchair-traversable.

**HIKING TIME:** 1.5 hours around the lake; another 2 hours to Lost Lake Butte

**SEASON:** May–October

**ACCESS:** $6 day-use fee per vehicle

**MAPS:** USGS Bull Run Lake; free maps at Lost Lake General Store

**FACILITIES:** Full-service camping resort

**SPECIAL COMMENTS:** If you want to fish, a license costs $8.25.

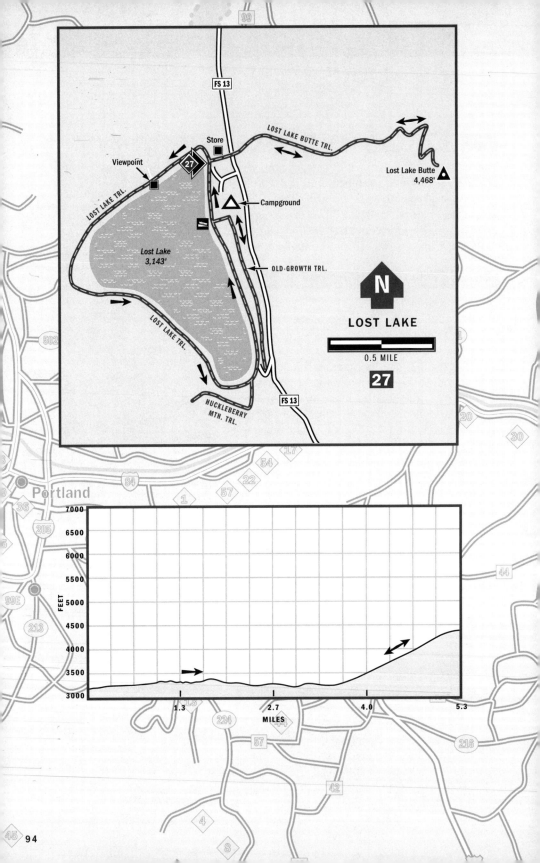

Viewpoint

Store

**FS 13**

LOST LAKE BUTTE TRL.

Lost Lake Butte
4,468'

**27**

LOST LAKE TRL.

Campground

Lost Lake
3,143'

OLD-GROWTH TRL.

**N**

**LOST LAKE**

0.5 MILE

**27**

LOST LAKE TRL.

HUCKLEBERRY
MTN. TRL.

**FS 13**

Portland

FEET

7000

6500

6000

5500

5000

4500

4000

3500

3000

1.3          2.7          4.0          5.3

MILES

Western red cedar on the
Old-Growth Trail of Lost Lake

then choose a little beach off the trail to sit on a log and find some peace while you eat. Keep an eye out for signs identifying tree species.

After just less than a mile, you'll come to a marshy area where the trail becomes a boardwalk. After another mile, the Huckleberry Mountain Trail (#617) leads right 2.5 miles to an intersection with the Pacific Crest Trail. During its 900-foot climb, this trail passes Devils Pulpit and Preachers Peak—but not, according to the map, Huckleberry Mountain. Go figure. Just past the Huckleberry Mountain Trail, veer right from the Lakeshore Trail onto the Old Growth Trail (#657). To reach it, after you veer right the first time, stay left as you approach a group of buildings. This will put you onto a road; the Old Growth Trail begins 100 yards ahead on a boardwalk and immediately passes between two of the largest cedars you are ever likely to see. They're both in the neighborhood of 12 feet thick.

This trail is a great one for the kids because it's not too long and includes educational signs explaining the roles in a forest's life of nurse logs, the forest canopy, the weather, pileated woodpeckers, and other animals. Some of these trees are hundreds of years old and more than 200 feet tall. When the boardwalk runs out, go another 0.3 miles, follow a trail through the campground down to the lake, and turn right to get back to your car.

To climb Lost Lake Butte for a view of, as the resort's hiking map puts it, "pretty near everything worth seeing," start in the General Store parking area. Walk back up the road and, at the turnoff for the main exit, look for a sign and a trail heading into the woods. You'll come to an unsigned trail intersection; turn right and uphill here. A hundred yards later, you'll cross another road and aim for a sign that says "Lost Lake Butte Trailhead." It can get confusing in here, but when in doubt, keep going uphill. It's a steady climb of 1,300 feet in 2 miles to an old fire lookout. Mount Hood, of course, is the dominant view to the south, but you can also see as far north as Mount Rainier (but not Mount Baker, as the resort map says). Then just come back down the way you went up and get yourself a cool drink in the store as a reward for all your effort. Constant access to refreshments is one of the great things about Lost Lake.

For more information, call the Lost Lake Resort office at (541) 386-6366.

# MACLEAY TRAIL

## KEY AT-A-GLANCE INFORMATION

**LENGTH:** 2.2 miles to Macleay Park; 4.5 miles to Pittock Mansion

**CONFIGURATION:** Out-and-back

**DIFFICULTY:** Easy to Macleay Park and the Audubon Society; moderate to Pittock Mansion

**SCENERY:** Quiet woods, predatory birds (in cages), three must-see trees

**EXPOSURE:** Shady

**TRAFFIC:** Light use on the trail but moderate on weekends; heavy at the mansion

**TRAIL SURFACE:** Packed dirt with some gravel

**HIKING TIME:** 1 hour to the Audubon Society; 2.5 hours for the whole thing

**SEASON:** Year-round

**ACCESS:** No fees or permits needed.

**MAPS:** USGS Portland

**FACILITIES:** Water and toilets at trailhead and Audubon Society; water at mansion

## IN BRIEF

If you just take the easier trip to the Audubon Society, you'll get some quiet time in the woods, including two monumental trees, and close-up views of (caged) wildlife. If you put in a little more effort, you'll get that and some history with a great view—and another monumental tree. And it's all right in the middle of town!

## DESCRIPTION

If the headquarters of the Forest Park Ivy Removal Project is open, it's worth a look inside. It has cleared hundreds of acres and saved thousands of trees in Forest Park from invasive English ivy, which creates "ivy deserts" where no native plants can survive. In this building the crews house some of their "trophies," ivy roots bigger than you can imagine such things being. Gawk, get some water, and head up the trail.

What you're walking up here is Balch Creek, named for the man who once owned this land—also the first man in Portland to be tried and hung for murder. Small as it is, the creek was the original water supply for the city of Portland. As astounding as that may seem, consider that in

## DIRECTIONS

From downtown Portland, drive west on Burnside Street and turn right on NW 23rd Avenue. Proceed 23 blocks and turn left on Thurman Street. Go six blocks to NW 28th Avenue and turn right. Go one block, turn left on NW Upshur, and follow it three blocks to the trailhead at the end of the road. This trailhead can also be reached via Tri-Met. From downtown, take the #15 bus (NW 23rd Avenue), but make sure it's headed for Thurman Street and not Montgomery Park. Get off at Thurman and 28th, walk one more block, and descend a flight of steps at the side of the bridge. Driving time is 15 minutes.

Montgomery Park

N.W. Vaughn

28 N.W. Upshur

Balch Creek

N.W. 28th

N.W. 27th

N.W. Thurman

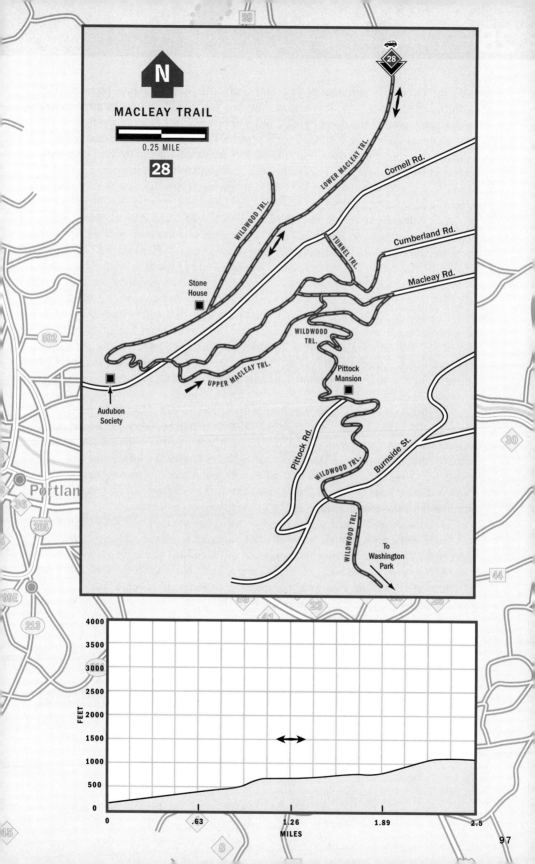

MACLEAY TRAIL

0.25 MILE

28

1987 the Oregon Department of Fish and Game discovered a native population of cutthroat trout living in it. It is one of only two year-round streams in all of Forest Park. Check some of the deeper pools, and you just may see some of the fish.

Keep an eye out, at 0.4 miles, for a Douglas fir on your left that is marked with a plaque as a Portland Heritage Tree, one of 235 such trees around town to be forever protected from the saw. This one happens to be the tallest tree in the city of Portland, at 241 feet, and is thought to be the tallest in any major American city. (A 255-footer in Seattle blew down in 1993.)

At a half mile, you'll intersect the 30-mile Wildwood Trail at an old stone building that was a rest room until the early 1960s when a storm destroyed its pipes by uprooting numerous trees. Stay straight (upstream) on the Wildwood Trail, and after a half mile you'll come to Macleay Park. Whether you're headed for Pittock Mansion or not, turn right here and walk 100 yards to the Portland Audubon Society. They rehabilitate injured owls and hawks here, birds you can view in cages for no charge; they also have an extensive collection of mounted animals and an excellent gift shop plus bookstore. Three loop trails explore sanctuaries from here; free maps of those and all of Forest Park are available at the gift shop. Particularly worth visiting is a shelter overlooking a pond, just below the headquarters. You can impress your friends by telling them that the massive sequoia beside the parking lot is actually less than 100 years old. They grow quickly at first.

To just do a 2.8-mile hike, head back to the car. To add another 2.4 miles (and just over 400 feet in elevation), stay on the Wildwood Trail by walking along the parking lot of Macleay Park, crossing sometimes-busy Cornell Road in a crosswalk, and re-entering the forest. After 100 yards, turn right on Upper Macleay Trail. This trail climbs for about 0.2 miles, then flattens out. At half a mile, check out the cool pattern on the wooden bench. Just past that, rejoin the Wildwood Trail, turning right and uphill for the final 0.6 miles to the Pittock Mansion parking lot.

The home (see "Nearby Activities" below) is to your left. Wander out to the front yard, with roses and the view of city and mountains, and admire yet another spectacular tree: a European white birch that offers enough shade for a small town.

If you were on the bus, you don't have to walk back down the trail. You can, instead, walk down the road from the mansion to Burnside Street, about 0.3 miles away, cross over it (quickly), and take the #20 (Burnside) bus to downtown. You can also continue on the Wildwood Trail for one mile (and down 300 feet) to connect with the Washington Park/Hoyt Arboretum hike (see page 195).

For more information, contact the Portland Parks and Recreation office at (503) 823-7529.

### ▶ NEARBY ACTIVITIES

Pittock Mansion, built in 1914 by the owner/publisher of the *Oregonian* and founder of the Portland Rose Festival, is open for tours daily from noon to 4 p.m. Cost is $4.50.

# MARQUAM TRAIL TO COUNCIL CREST

## ▶ IN BRIEF

A lesson in what makes Portland great, this pleasant trail through a wooded canyon just minutes from downtown leads to the highest point in town, where you can take in a view of four volcanoes.

## ▶ DESCRIPTION

Council Crest got its name in 1898 when a group of visiting ministers met there after a two-hour wagon drive. They assumed local natives must have held many a council there. In the early and mid-twentieth century you could ride a trolley to the top and visit an amusement park. Today you can get there by car or bus, but the best way is to walk up the Marquam Trail through a wooded canyon in which it's easy to forget you're in a city of more than a million people.

At the trailhead shelter, there are two signs leading you to the Marquam Trail. If you got a brochure and feel like adding the Nature Trail, take the path on the left that says 0.7 miles, instead of the one on the right that says 0.4 miles. This leads you 0.3 miles up the creek to a junction where you turn right and enter the Nature Trail. Numbered signs along the way point out various aspects of the local flora and fauna (corresponding with the

## ▶ DIRECTIONS

From downtown Portland, drive south on Broadway Avenue, and after it crosses I-405, take the second right onto SW 6th Avenue, following the blue **H** signs leading to the hospital. (Don't take the right with the sign COUNCIL CREST.) Stay straight through three lights in the next half mile, eventually passing two large concrete water towers on your right. Here, when the road cuts back to the left, turn right into a parking lot. You can also take Tri-Met bus #8 (Sam Jackson) to the third light, Sam Jackson and Terwilliger, and walk 200 yards to the trailhead. Driving time is 5 minutes.

## ⓘ KEY AT-A-GLANCE INFORMATION

**LENGTH:** 3.7 miles

**CONFIGURATION:** Out-and-back with a side loop

**DIFFICULTY:** Easy on the Nature Trail; moderate to Council Crest

**SCENERY:** Through the woods, past some impressive homes, and then a sweeping vista on top

**EXPOSURE:** Shady all the way up, open on top

**TRAFFIC:** Heavy on weekends and workday evenings but light otherwise

**TRAIL SURFACE:** Packed dirt and gravel

**HIKING TIME:** 2 hours

**SEASON:** Year-round

**ACCESS:** No fees or permits needed.

**MAPS:** USGS Portland; guides to the Nature Trail are available at the trailhead.

**FACILITIES:** Water at the trailhead and at Council Crest

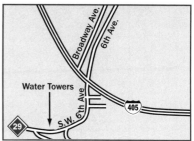

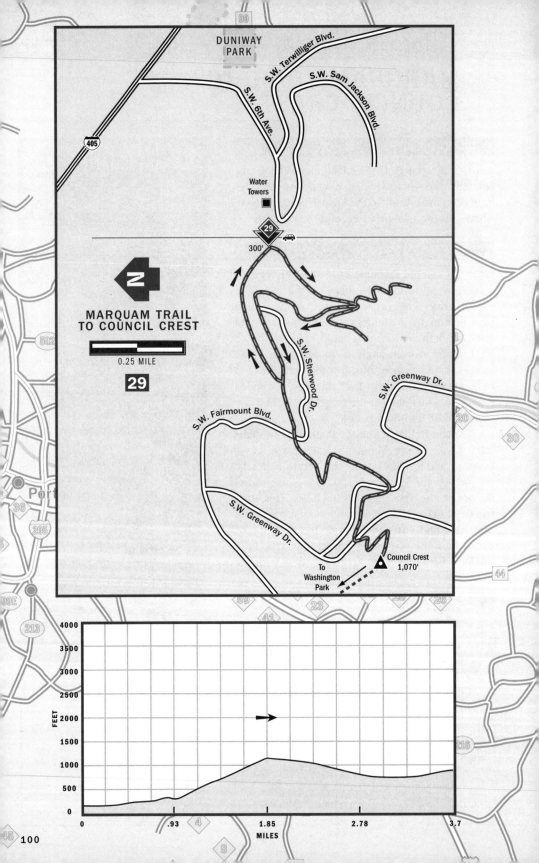

DUNIWAY PARK

S.W. Terwilliger Blvd.

S.W. Sam Jackson Blvd.

S.W. 6th Ave.

405

99

Water Towers

29

300'

MARQUAM TRAIL
TO COUNCIL CREST

0.25 MILE

29

S.W. Sherwood Dr.

S.W. Greenway Dr.

S.W. Fairmount Blvd.

S.W. Greenway Dr.

Council Crest
1,070'

To
Washington
Park

Port

502

36

205

99E

213

45

FEET

4000
3500
3000
2500
2000
1500
1000
500
0

0    .93  4   1.85        2.78        3.7
MILES

brochure) as you traverse back to the right on a flat 0.4-mile cutoff to the Marquam Trail, which leads to Council Crest.

At this junction, if you don't feel like going up the hill, stay right and you'll be back at the car in 0.4 miles (this is the right-hand trail you skipped at the trailhead). But for the best view in town, turn left and follow the trail up Marquam Gulch. You don't really need a map for this one, because you'll be following Council Crest signs at several junctions. The first is a right turn after 0.2 miles; the second is a left turn 0.6 miles later. At this point you'll start going uphill a bit. Just before you cross a road at the one-mile mark, keep your eyes peeled for an extremely cool treehouse on your left. Oh, to be a kid in a neighborhood like this!

After crossing yet another road, in an area planted decades ago with May-blooming rhododendrons, you'll come into the wide, open area atop Council Crest, where couples come to snuggle and kids come to throw the Frisbee. Take a moment on the two benches in front of you to admire the view of Mount Hood and the dates of the people the benches were dedicated to: they both made it to age 98 and died within a year of each other.

Now, go up to the stone circle at the top of the park. Plaques up there point out each of the four volcanoes and give a native name for them. Also to the east you can see into the Columbia River Gorge. The view to the west goes out to Beaverton and, on a clear day, the Coast Range. But for an odd, secret treat, find the small metal disc in the middle of this stone enclosure, then stand on it and say, "Portland rocks." Almost creepy, isn't it?

You can connect this trail to the Washington Park hike, if you're up for something a little longer. As you start back down the trail, take a left just after you enter the trees, turning to the northwest. This trail will traverse the hill for a few minutes, then turn downhill and to the left, eventually reaching the intersection of Southwest Talbot and Southwest Fairmount. Walk down Talbot about 0.3 miles to the intersection with Southwest Patton. Cross Patton, then turn right onto it, and in 200 feet you'll see a trail heading down the hill to the left. Follow it one mile down through the forest until you reach an access road along US 26. Walk left 50 yards, cross the bridge over the expressway, then look on the left for a trail going up the hill, into the trees again. This will lead you through a meadow, behind the World Forestry Center, and eventually (in 0.2 miles or so) to an intersection with the Wildwood Trail. (This is also the end of the Marquam Trail.) Turn right on the Wildwood Trail, and in 0.1 mile you'll be at the parking lot; across that is the MAX station, where you can catch a train back to town.

To just go back from Council Crest, head back down the trail, following signs for Marquam Shelter, and after 1.3 miles, when you get to a junction pointing left 0.4 miles to Marquam Park, take it. That's the shorter route back to the car that you skipped earlier in favor of the Nature Trail.

For more information, contact the Portland Parks and Recreation office at (503) 823-7529.

▶ **NEARBY ACTIVITIES**

While driving to the trailhead, you may have noticed a place that looks like a circus tent; that's the The Carnival, a longtime favorite with locals for its no-nonsense burgers, hot dogs, and ice cream.

# McCALL NATURE PRESERVE

## KEY AT-A-GLANCE INFORMATION

**LENGTH:** McCall Point Trail is 3 miles long; Plateau Loop is 2.2 miles.

**CONFIGURATION:** Out-and-back to McCall Point; balloon to plateau

**DIFFICULTY:** McCall Point is moderate due to the climb; Plateau is easy.

**SCENERY:** Wildflowers, the Columbia River below, oak trees

**EXPOSURE:** Wide open most of the time

**TRAFFIC:** Moderate when the flowers are out but light otherwise

**TRAIL SURFACE:** Packed dirt

**HIKING TIME:** 1.5 hours to McCall Point; 1 hour for Plateau Trail

**SEASON:** McCall Point open May through November; Plateau Trail open year-round

**ACCESS:** No fees or permits needed.

**MAPS:** USGS Lyle; map at the trailhead

**FACILITIES:** None

## ▶ IN BRIEF

McCall Nature Preserve is in a different world from most of the hikes in this book. It's a glimpse into eastern Oregon, a land of wide-open vistas, grass blowing in the nearly constant wind, and semi-arid forests of oaks and ponderosa pine. It also has views of the Columbia from barren cliff tops, panoramic vistas of Mounts Adams and Hood, and more than 300 species of plants, some of them unique to the Columbia River Gorge.

## ▶ DESCRIPTION

Okay, so this one is more than 60 miles from Portland, even as the crow flies. But it's truly worth the extra bit of driving, especially in the spring and early summer. At those times of the year, there is a kind of rain shroud that exists somewhere between Cascade Locks and Hood River; while it's still pouring in Portland, places like the McCall Preserve are bathed in sunlight and draped in a few dozen different kinds of wildflowers all blooming at once.

Consider wearing long pants here; there are ticks, poison oak, and rattlesnakes in the area.

Start with the McCall Point Trail first and get your exercise out of the way. The trail, which climbs about 1,000 feet in 1.5 miles, starts out nearly flat and on an old jeep road, winding through the kind of open space that is so rare in

## ▶ DIRECTIONS

From Portland on I-84, drive 62 miles east of I-205 and take Exit 69/Mosier. Turn right and follow the Historic Columbia River Highway (US 30) through Mosier for 6.5 miles to the Rowena Crest Viewpoint. The McCall Point Trail begins at a sign at the end of the stone wall. The river-view loop begins across the highway with a set of steps leading over a fence. Driving time is 1 hour and 15 minutes.

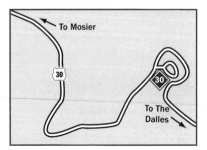

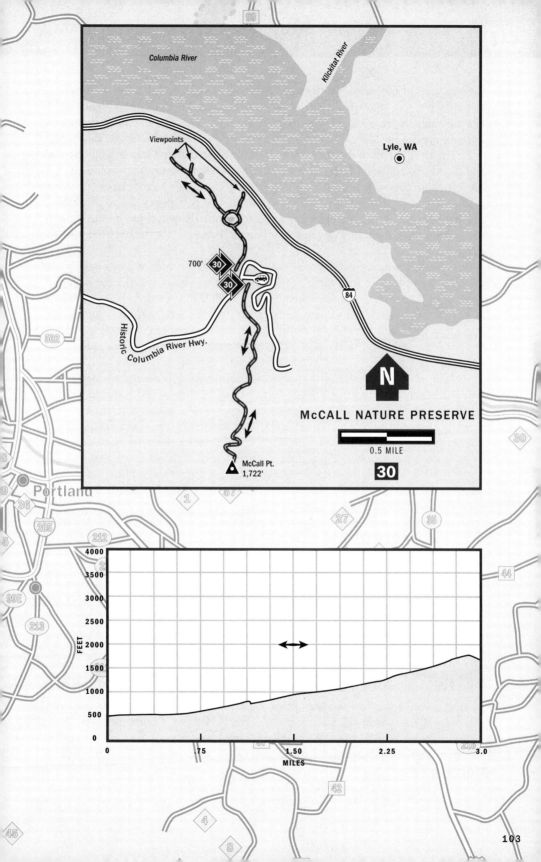

Columbia River

Klickitat River

Lyle, WA

Viewpoints

700' 30

30

Historic Columbia River Hwy.

84

N

McCALL NATURE PRESERVE

0.5 MILE

30

McCall Pt.
1,722'

Portland

4000
3500
3000
2500
2000
1500
1000
500
0

FEET

↔

0    .75    1.50    2.25    3.0
MILES

western parts of the state. The trees you eventually encounter are oaks, most of them Oregon white oak, and some as much as 800 years old. The trail turns slightly uphill when it gains the edge of the ridge, with ever more impressive views out to the east. Keep an eye out for Mount Adams as its summit comes into view across the river.

The second half of the trail is just plain steep, and after a rain it might be slick and muddy, so add solid boots to your clothing list. But soon enough you'll come to McCall Point, an open hilltop with a sprawling view from Mount Hood to Mount Adams; you're actually about halfway between the two peaks, each of which is roughly 35 miles away. Looking west, you can see into the gorge; just to the left of it, the high peak with the towers on top is Mount Defiance, the highest point in the gorge.

Now, you summit hounds out there might stand at McCall Point and notice there's still some more trail going south, through a notch, and then climbing again. I walked about a mile down (and then up) that trail, through some very peaceful oak stands, but technically speaking it didn't go anywhere special before it got pinched between a fence and the edge of a cliff. So my advice is to have yourself a picnic at McCall Point and don't worry about that other trail, unless you're just jonesing for more exercise.

Back at the highway, use the steps over the fence to begin the riverview loop. This wide, easy path (which actually drops 100 feet in elevation) goes out through flower and grass country to loop around a pond. Early in the year, there will be numerous other little ponds and wet areas, each supporting their own microhabitats. The small canyon below you on your left is called Rowena Dell.

When a sign reading TRAIL indicates a right turn, you'll notice another trail that keeps going straight out into the grasslands. There is another pond out there among the trees, as well as other viewpoints out over the river. But the most dramatic view is on the official trail to your right. After that trail has gone past the pond it turns right again, but a small trail to the left leads to the top of a cliff that is not for the acrophobes among us. It's a sheer drop of 500 feet from where you stand (without a railing, so keep an eye on the kids) down to the railroad tracks and the river. The town across the river is Lyle, Washington, which lies on a gravel bar left behind by catastrophic floods that ripped down the Columbia more than 10,000 years ago.

To return to the trailhead, simply follow the trail back around the pond and turn left (uphill) at the sign.

For more information, call the Columbia River Gorge National Scenic Area office at (541) 386-2333, or the Nature Conservancy at (503) 230-1221.

## ▶ NEARBY ACTIVITIES

As long as you're this far east, keep going to The Dalles and visit the Columbia Gorge Discovery Center, the official interpretive center for the Columbia River Gorge National Scenic Area. Its displays range from a working model of the Columbia before and after the Dalles Dam to a Living History Center with presentations on the life of Oregon Trail pioneers.

# McNEIL POINT

## ▶ IN BRIEF

You don't have to do this whole trail to make it worthwhile; it passes through a cathedral forest to wildflower meadows and alpine ponds, then gets up close and personal with Mount Hood. But if you do go all the way up, you can see the trickle that is the source of the Sandy River and hear glaciers pop and rumble.

## ▶ DESCRIPTION

This is a honey of a hike! You start out on the Top Spur Trail, which climbs gradually for half a mile to a veritable highway interchange of trails. First you'll reach the Pacific Crest Trail (PCT); turn right on it. In 100 feet you'll get to the Timberline Trail, a trail to Bald Mountain (marked with a sign reading VIEWPOINT), and another trail leading down 2.2 miles to the Ramona Falls Trail (see page 129).

To simply head for McNeil Point, follow the Timberline Trail (#600) uphill and to the left. But it's well worth it to see the magnificent view from the open side (not actually the top) of Bald Mountain, a mere 0.4 miles past the VIEWPOINT sign, also on the PCT. Head out there to take in the sweeping view of Mount Hood and the Muddy Fork of the Sandy River. Then either come back the same way or keep going and look for a faint cutoff trail that goes over the ridge to your left, just before the PCT goes back into the woods. The

## ▶ KEY AT-A-GLANCE INFORMATION

**LENGTH:** 9.2 miles

**CONFIGURATION:** Out-and-back

**DIFFICULTY:** Easy to Bald Mountain viewpoint; hard to McNeil Point

**SCENERY:** Old-growth forest, meadows, rugged mountainside

**EXPOSURE:** Shady with a few open spots

**TRAFFIC:** Moderate use on August weekends but light otherwise

**TRAIL SURFACE:** Packed dirt with roots, a few small stream crossings, some rocks and snow

**HIKING TIME:** 5.5 hours

**SEASON:** July–October

**ACCESS:** Northwest Forest Pass required

**MAPS:** Mount Hood Wilderness

**FACILITIES:** None at trailhead; there's water on the trail, but it must be treated.

## ▶ DIRECTIONS

From Portland on US 26, drive 36 miles east of I-205 to Zigzag and turn left onto Lolo Pass Road at the Zigzag Store. Go 10.6 miles to Lolo Pass and turn right onto paved FS 1828, which is the first right at the pass. Go 3.1 miles and turn left onto gravel FS 118, following a sign for Top Spur Trail. The trailhead is 1.2 miles ahead on the right. Driving time is 1 hour and 20 minutes.

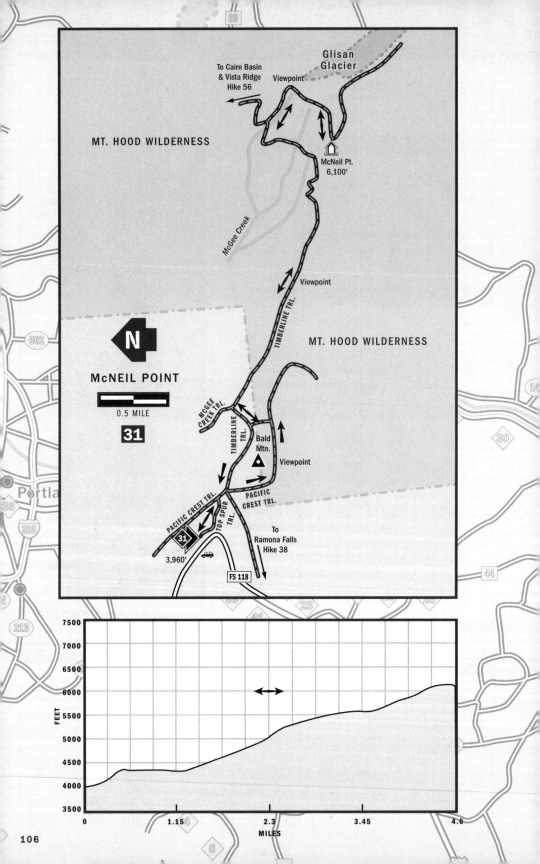

Glisan
Glacier

To Cairn Basin
& Vista Ridge
Hike 56

Viewpoint

MT. HOOD WILDERNESS

McNeil Pt.
6,100'

McGee Creek

Viewpoint

TIMBERLINE TRL.

MT. HOOD WILDERNESS

N

McNEIL POINT

0.5 MILE

**31**

MCGEE CREEK TRL.

TIMBERLINE TRL.

Bald
Mtn.

Viewpoint

PACIFIC CREST TRL.

PACIFIC
CREST TRL.

TOP SPUR TRL.

**31**

3,960'

To
Ramona Falls
Hike 38

FS 118

FEET

7500
7000
6500
6000
5500
5000
4500
4000
3500

0          1.15          2.3          3.45          4.6
MILES

Portla

cutoff goes about 100 yards over the ridge and back to the Timberline Trail; turn right for McNeil Point.

This stretch of the Timberline Trail is in a true cathedral forest—the tall, straight trees, mostly hemlocks, have no branches in their lower portions, creating a forest scene that's both open and lofty. Adding to the pleasure are the many huckleberry bushes that make up the ground cover, whose juicy morsels are ripe in late August. You'll hardly notice that you've started climbing in earnest.

On the Timberline Trail, at the first big view of Mount Hood you come to (you'll have gone 2.3 miles), look for the large, unnamed waterfall across the valley on Hood's flank. At 3.3 miles, you'll cross a fork of McGee Creek and, if it's August, be in the land of wildflowers. Lupines, daisies, pasque flowers, lilies, and butterflies will welcome you to the high country. Just a bit farther are a couple of ponds, which make ideal places to stop for lunch. You can skip and frolic in this area and call it a day, or keep going to the higher country.

At about 3.6 miles, just after the Mazama Trail has come in from the left, you'll reach a tiny stream flowing out of a flower-filled bowl with a snowfield at the top. If you just want more meadows without more climbing, stay on the main trail as it swings to the left, negotiate a somewhat sketchy stream crossing, and connect with the outer reaches of the Vista Ridge hike for Cairn Basin and Eden Park. If you're set on McNeil Point, turn right (up the tiny creek) and follow the trail among the flowers.

About 0.3 miles up, the trail reaches the top of a windswept little ridge and then turns up it, eventually crossing a rock slide and then (in most years) a snowfield. Be careful on both these terrains; although they aren't steep, remember that even big rocks move and even packed snow is slippery. The trail keeps going up the ridge face, crossing more small patches of snow. At a junction near the top, go right for the easiest route or left to stay higher and try your skills at glissading down a small snowfield.

One mile from the turnoff at the creek, you'll reach the 1930s-era stone shelter at McNeil Point. From here the view is stupendous: Mount Hood looming above you, the valley of the Muddy Fork of the Sandy stretching out below you, the other Cascade volcanoes

Mount Hood and the Sandy River
headwaters from Bald Mountain

beyond. As you look at Mount Hood, the sprawling glacier on your right is the Sandy Glacier and the trickle coming out the bottom of it is the beginning of the Sandy River, which flows into the Columbia all the way down at Troutdale.

Also, as you look at Mount Hood, you'll notice some more trail going up above you, into the Really High Country. It's not on any maps, but if you follow it you will (A) soon run out of breath as you approach 7,000 feet in elevation with virtually no switchbacks, and (B) find yourself on a narrow, rocky ridge between the Sandy (on your right) and Glisan (on your left) Glaciers.

I sat up there one day listening to the glaciers pop and moan as they slid slowly but relentlessly down the face of the mountain. You might even see massive boulders tumbling down the slope; you can certainly pick out their trails on the snow. At all costs, be careful up there, and most definitely resist the temptation to hop onto the snow.

You may hear or see reports of another, more direct trail between McNeil Point and the Timberline Trail, connecting with the latter at a point west of the ponds. The word from many hikers is to avoid that trail. It's steep, rocky, brutal, and unnecessary. The one described here is the only reasonable way to go.

No matter what the weather is when you start, bring warm clothing if you're going to McNeil Point. It's above the tree line, and weather changes quickly up there. For more information, contact the Mount Hood Visitor Information Center at (503) 622-7674.

## ▶ NEARBY ACTIVITIES

On the way back on US 26, check out the Oregon Candy Farm. It's not, unfortu-nately, the mini-world of candy cane barns and sugar-water streams it sounds like, but it is a store with a heck of a selection of candies and chocolates. Go ahead: you deserve it after going to the high country.

# MIRROR LAKE

## ▶ IN BRIEF

You can go a short way on this hike and join the weekend throngs at a lovely little lake that has a great view of Mount Hood. You can also put in a little more effort and leave the vast majority of the crowds behind to claim an even better view at the top of, believe it or not, Tom, Dick, and Harry Mountain.

## ▶ DESCRIPTION

When you come around the corner on US 26 and see 75 cars parked on the side of the road, it's not a fair or something: It's the Mirror Lake trailhead. Think about starting early or going on a weekday so you'll have a decent chance for some quiet time. You'll see that the interest in this trail is well justified.

The lower portions of the trail have some rhododendrons that will bloom pink in June, and the upper portions are cool and shady, keeping you from warming up too much as you head up the hill. But it isn't even much of a hill, gaining 800 feet in 1.4 well-graded miles. Just below the lake, you'll come to the outlet creek and a trail junction. You can go either way to loop 0.4 miles around the lake, but if you're headed up the ridge, go right. The lake itself is a beauty. The beaches are on the right side, the campsites are on the left, and the view of Mount Hood you're looking for is at the far end, on the boardwalk in a marshy area.

To get to the top of Tom, Dick, and Harry Mountain, walk to the far right side of the lake (as you face it when you arrive) and follow a trail that

## ▶ DIRECTIONS

From Portland on US 26, drive 45 miles east of I-205 and park at the trailhead on the right. It's half a mile past the historic marker for the Laurel Hill Chute on the right. Driving time is 1 hour and 5 minutes.

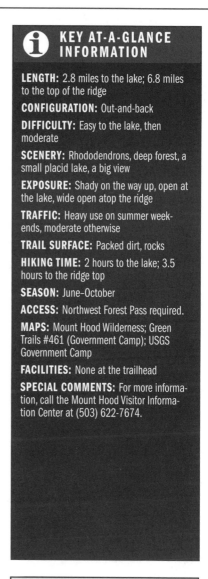

## ⓘ KEY AT-A-GLANCE INFORMATION

**LENGTH:** 2.8 miles to the lake; 6.8 miles to the top of the ridge

**CONFIGURATION:** Out-and-back

**DIFFICULTY:** Easy to the lake, then moderate

**SCENERY:** Rhododendrons, deep forest, a small placid lake, a big view

**EXPOSURE:** Shady on the way up, open at the lake, wide open atop the ridge

**TRAFFIC:** Heavy use on summer weekends, moderate otherwise

**TRAIL SURFACE:** Packed dirt, rocks

**HIKING TIME:** 2 hours to the lake; 3.5 hours to the ridge top

**SEASON:** June–October

**ACCESS:** Northwest Forest Pass required.

**MAPS:** Mount Hood Wilderness; Green Trails #461 (Government Camp); USGS Government Camp

**FACILITIES:** None at the trailhead

**SPECIAL COMMENTS:** For more information, call the Mount Hood Visitor Information Center at (503) 622-7674.

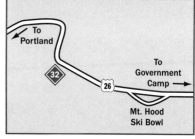

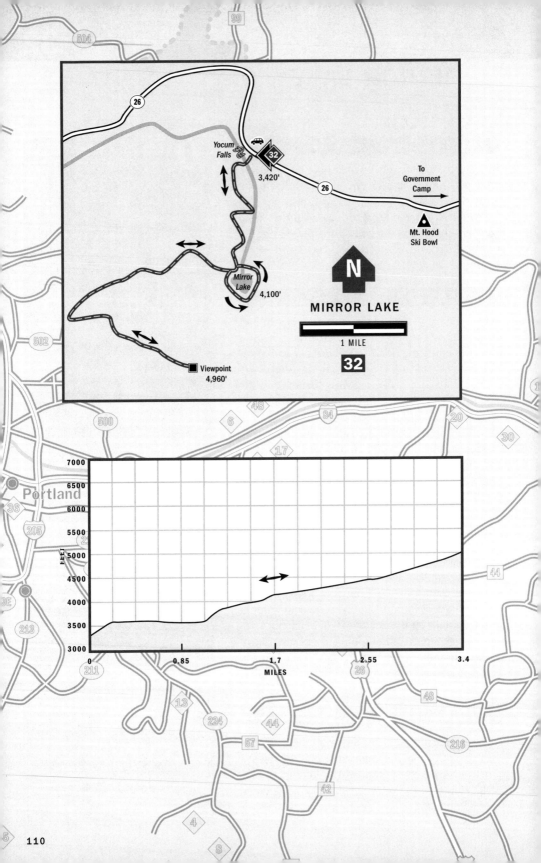

26

Yocum
Falls

🚗

32

3,420'

26

To
Government
Camp

▲
Mt. Hood
Ski Bowl

Mirror
Lake

4,100'

**N**

**MIRROR LAKE**

1 MILE

**32**

■ Viewpoint
4,960'

FEET

7000
6500
6000
5500
5000
4500
4000
3500
3000

0      0.85      1.7      2.55      3.4
MILES

goes right and slowly climbs the face of the ridge. The place you're headed for is actually right above you, but you have to walk almost two miles to get there. As for the name, it indicates the three peaks on the ridge—not, as some would suggest, because every Tom, Dick, and Harry hikes this trail.

The trail is really just two long switchbacks, each one almost a mile long. It's time to turn left when you get to some very odd large piles of rocks, which no one has ever been able to explain. The forest opens up a little more here and, owing to the elevation, just might get you a little winded. When you get to a rocky area (neither steep nor dangerous) you're almost there.

The view from on top of this ridge is really something, considering how close you still are to the car. For starters, look how pitifully small Mirror Lake is—and how far down there. It never ceases to amaze me how quickly one gains elevation hiking. Right in front of you, looming across the highway, is Mount Hood in all its glory. Mount Adams is actually blocked by it. To the left is Mount St. Helens. What looks like a shoulder on St. Helens is in fact Mount Rainier, some 100 miles to the north.

In case you're still feeling energetic, resist the temptation to explore the other two peaks on this ridge—Tom and Dick, as it were. They're off limits because they are home to protected peregrine falcons.

Although this trail is open as early as the first of June, it will often have patches of snow on it until the end of that month, because it is shady and faces north.

## ▶ NEARBY ACTIVITIES

The easternmost peak of Tom, Dick, and Harry Mountain is the summit of Mount Hood Ski Bowl, which in the summer is like a constant carnival. You can bungee jump, ride the Alpine Slide, play mini-golf, drive go-karts, take a trip in a helicopter, or ride the chairlift to the top of the hill and hike or mountain bike down. The entrance is one mile east on US 26.

# MOUNT HEBO

**LENGTH:** 8 miles from Hebo Lake to South Lake

**CONFIGURATION:** One-way with a shuttle, or out-and-back

**DIFFICULTY:** Moderate

**SCENERY:** Quiet forest, meadows, wildlife, and sweeping views from mountaintop meadows.

**EXPOSURE:** A few stretches out in the open, but nothing dangerous at all.

**TRAFFIC:** Light

**TRAIL SURFACE:** Packed dirt, muddy in spring

**HIKING TIME:** 5 hours

**SEASON:** Year-round, but there could be snow in winter.

**ACCESS:** Northwest Forest Pass required.

**MAPS:** Siuslaw National Forest; USGS Hebo covers the area, but this trail isn't on it.

**FACILITIES:** Water and toilets at Hebo Lake Campground

## ▶ IN BRIEF

Mount Hebo is a long, narrow mountain topped by meadows with a 360-degree view of mountains and ocean. There are few sights in the Coast Range to equal it.

## ▶ DESCRIPTION

If you start at the Hebo Lake Camground, you'll see a big informative sign that says this trail is called the Pioneer-Indian Trail. Truly, it should be called the Indian-Pioneer Trail, since all the pioneers did was follow an old Indian trail over the mountain. They were looking for another way from Tillamook to the Willamette Valley in the 1850s, when travel through the Coast Range was heinous.

According to one account, the name Hebo came from this party, one of whom said the mountain was so high it should be called Mount Heave Ho, since it was heaved up above its surroundings.

## ▶ DIRECTIONS

From Portland on US 26, drive 20 miles west of I-405 and turn left on OR 6, following a sign for Tillamook. Drive 51 miles to Tillamook and turn left (south) onto US 101. Travel 19 miles to the tiny town of Hebo and turn left (south) onto OR 22. Go a quarter-mile and turn left onto FS 14. The Hebo Lake Campground is 4.6 miles ahead on the right. Driving time is 1 hour and 40 minutes. To start at the far end, or stash a car for a shuttle, keep going on FS 14 to South Lake. Past the Hebo Lake turnoff, stay right at the radio towers at 3.3 miles, and at 5.3 miles stay right again, this time leaving the pavement (if you miss this turn, you'll quickly come to the end of the road). At 6.2 miles, stay on FS 14 to the right, and at 6.8 miles you'll pass tiny North Lake on the left. Stay left at 7.1 miles, and at 7.6 miles turn right onto FS 1428, where a sign says "narrow road." South Lake is 0.2 miles ahead on the left.

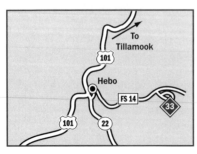

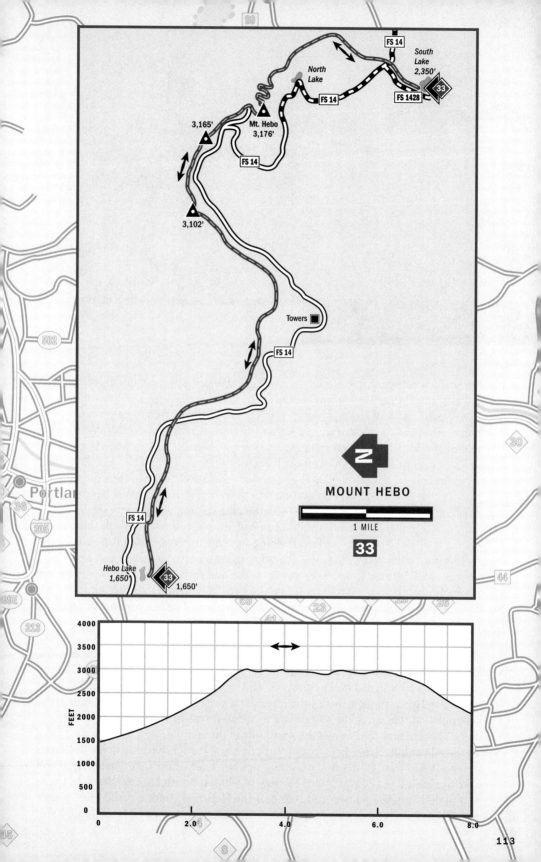

North Lake

FS 14

South Lake
2,350'

FS 14

FS 1428

33

3,165'

Mt. Hebo
3,176'

FS 14

3,102'

Towers

N

MOUNT HEBO

1 MILE

33

FS 14

Hebo Lake
1,650'

33

1,650'

4000
3500
3000
2500
2000
1500
1000
500
0

FEET

0    2.0    4.0    6.0    8.0

Portland

Chillin' out on top of Mount Hebo

Those nutty pioneers; it's too bad the name got changed. It's more fun to holler, "Who wants to hike Heave Ho?"

Starting from the campground, you'll climb gradually through a young forest—much of it planted in the early 1950s—with more signs scattered through it, these referring to local plants and animals. Speaking of animals, I encountered several elk in here once, so stay quiet and on the lookout.

Around 1.5 miles out, you'll pass a nice meadow on the left, then the trail will climb a little more. Just after the second time you cross the road, you're basically done climbing and you're on the summit—although the summit is really three miles long.

You'll pass through about another mile of forest—you're actually ducking under a cluster of radio towers—before popping out into the open. You'll find the view worthwhile. It stretches from the Cascades to the coast. See if you can spot Cape Lookout and Tillamook Bay. Keep going on the trail through the meadows, traveling northeast. Just before it ducks back into the trees, note that a trail goes off to the left to some more little peaks. Any of these places makes a fine rest and picnic area; my friends and I even added a nap to the mix.

If you've used one car, turn around here and you'll have about an eight-mile day. If you have a car at South Lake, keep on going. You'll pass through the forest, traverse another meadow and, around six miles out, come to a footbridge followed immediately by a signed trail leading left. This will take you out to the official summit of Mount Hebo, though there isn't much of a view there. There is a Mount Hebo Campground that would be a fine place to spend the night.

The trail now leads along the south side of the summit, with more views, before starting downhill. Heave Ho's height (isn't that fun?) is 3,176 feet, and South Lake is around 2,400 feet. So it's not a severe drop, but I can attest that coming up it will take some wind out of you. Along the way you'll pass North Lake on the right (more of a puddle in late summer) and countless huckleberries, both red and blue. A mile past North Lake, you'll cross FS 14, and a half mile past that you'll be at South Lake.

# MOUNT MITCHELL

## ▶ IN BRIEF

Mount Mitchell is a moderate climb that builds suspense by hiding its amazing view until the last few steps. Not that it isn't nice on the way up— especially when you get to the meadows higher up—but the peek-a-boo view of Mount St. Helens from the top is simply extraordinary.

## ▶ DESCRIPTION

When you start this hike, you might wonder why you chose it. Take my word for it, though. The recently cut forest in the beginning will give way, and there will be views later. After the first 0.3 miles (which you may have driven), you'll climb pretty steeply, up 1,200 feet in about 0.9 miles; then you'll start to circle around to the southern side of the mountain. The next 0.7 miles only gains a little more than 300 feet, during which time things will start to open up a bit and you'll get a view off to the south, across North Siouxon Creek to an unnamed 3,300-foot peak.

Just past two miles, the trail turns right and heads uphill, out into the meadows of bear grass and wildflowers. You'll see the summit now, but

## ▶ DIRECTIONS

From Portland on I-5, drive 21 miles north of the Columbia River and take Exit 21/Woodland. Turn right onto WA 503 (Lewis River Road) and travel 29 miles to Cougar. Three miles past Cougar, at a sign saying END 503, turn right onto an unmarked road Take it 0.3 miles, and turn left onto FS 10. And the big red DANGER sign refers to the creek below, not the road. Take FS 10 for 4 miles (note that it turns right at 1.6 miles) and park on the shoulder where a dirt track goes into the woods on the right. If you've got clearance on your vehicle, you can drive another 0.3 miles up this road (stay left where it splits), but if you have any doubts, it isn't worth it. Driving time is 1 hour and 10 minutes.

## ❶ KEY AT-A-GLANCE INFORMATION

**LENGTH:** 5.4 miles

**CONFIGURATION:** Out-and-back

**DIFFICULTY:** Moderate

**SCENERY:** Not much on the way up (it's all second-growth forest) but meadows up top and a big view of Mount St. Helens and Mount Adams

**EXPOSURE:** Shady on the way up, then open on top

**TRAFFIC:** Use is light all the time.

**TRAIL SURFACE:** Packed dirt on the way up, some rock at the top

**HIKING TIME:** 3 hours

**SEASON:** June–October

**ACCESS:** No fees or permits needed

**MAPS:** USGS Mount Mitchell

**FACILITIES:** None at the trailhead; no water on the trail; public rest room in Cougar

**SPECIAL COMMENTS:** For more information, contact the Mount St. Helens National Volcanic Monument at (360) 247-3900.

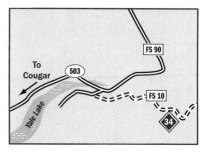

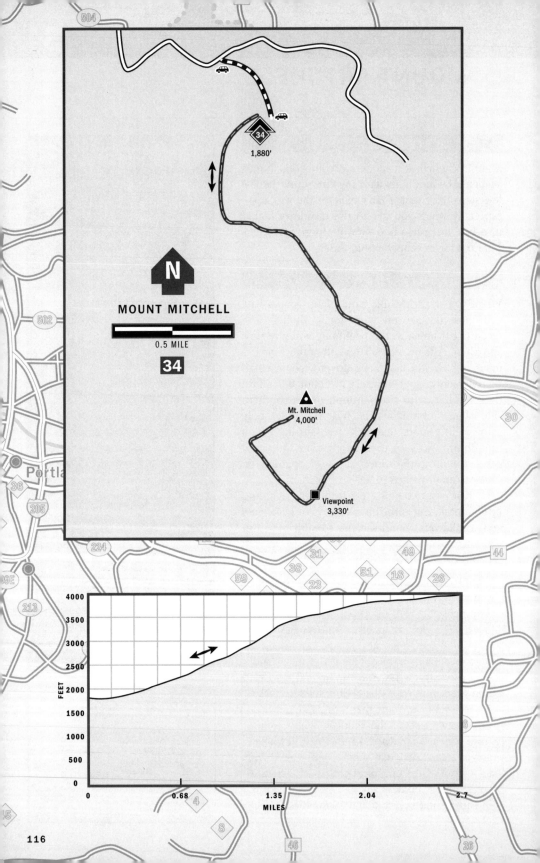

**MOUNT MITCHELL**

N

0.5 MILE

**34**

34
1,880'

Mt. Mitchell
4,000'

Viewpoint
3,330'

Mount Saint Helens and Swift Reservoir
from the top of Mount Mitchell

what's so intriguing about this hike is that you still can't see anything of the real view you'll get from up there. The trail eventually gets onto some rock, just below the summit, but it's no problem keeping your footing.

You might have some problems keeping your breath, however, when you get to the top and look out over the Swift Reservoir to Mount St. Helens, just 12 miles away. From here, it's easy to see the patterns of mudflows that resulted from the 1980 eruption. One of these went from the high slopes of the mountain, down Lava Canyon, and into the reservoir. Look around for more impressive views: To your right is Mount Adams; between Mount Adams and Mount St. Helens is Mount Rainier; and behind you is Mount Hood.

Didn't see all this coming, did you?

# NEAHKAHNIE MOUNTAIN

## KEY AT-A-GLANCE INFORMATION

**LENGTH:** 3, 4, or 7.2 miles

**CONFIGURATION:** Out-and-back

**DIFFICULTY:** Moderate/hard

**SCENERY:** A secluded beach, lookouts over the sea, old-growth forest.

**EXPOSURE:** Shady all the way up

**TRAFFIC:** Use is heavy all summer, especially on weekends, but moderate otherwise.

**TRAIL SURFACE:** Gravel, packed dirt with some roots, muddy in sections, rocks on top

**HIKING TIME:** 2 hours for the short options; 4 hours if you start at the beach

**SEASON:** Year-round, but beware of nasty weather and muddy trails in winter and spring.

**ACCESS:** No fees or permits needed.

**MAPS:** USGS Arch Cape and Nehalem

**FACILITIES:** Rest room at northern trailhead

**SPECIAL COMMENTS:** For more information, call the Oregon State Parks office at (800) 551-6949.

### IN BRIEF

One of the classic views on the Oregon coast is from the top of this 1,600-foot peak, which juts straight above the sea.

### DESCRIPTION

Perhaps all these trailheads have you confused; don't be. It's really very simple: Neahkahnie Mountain has a killer view, from 1,600 feet above the ocean, and you have two options for how to get there: the express and the local. The express is a 3-mile round-trip from the southernmost trailhead; it gains 850 feet. The local is the scenic option, starting at the beach and offering more to see on the way up. It gains 1,600 feet in 3.6 miles.

First, the "express." From the trailhead, you'll switchback up through open areas filled with tasty red thimbleberries in late summer to a junction with a road that leads left to some radio towers. Cross the road and follow the trail. You'll climb gradually for another 0.3 miles, pass to the north of (and below) the radio towers, and then in another 0.3 miles come to the summit. It's a little rocky scramble, but nothing intense.

There are actually three routes up the last little bit to the summit. The best is the first one

### DIRECTIONS

From Portland on US 26, travel 74 miles west of I-405 and turn south on US 101. The campground trailhead (where you'd park to go to the beach) is 14 miles ahead on the right. It's the third of three lots in succession on US 101. The middle trailhead for Neahkahnie Mountain is 0.9 miles farther up US 101 on the right before the viewpoint. For the southernmost trailhead, drive 1 mile past the Middle trailhead and turn left onto a gravel road by a brown hiker sign. The trailhead is 0.4 miles up on the left. Driving time is 1 hour and 35 minutes.

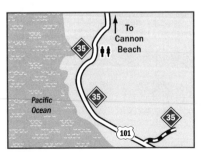

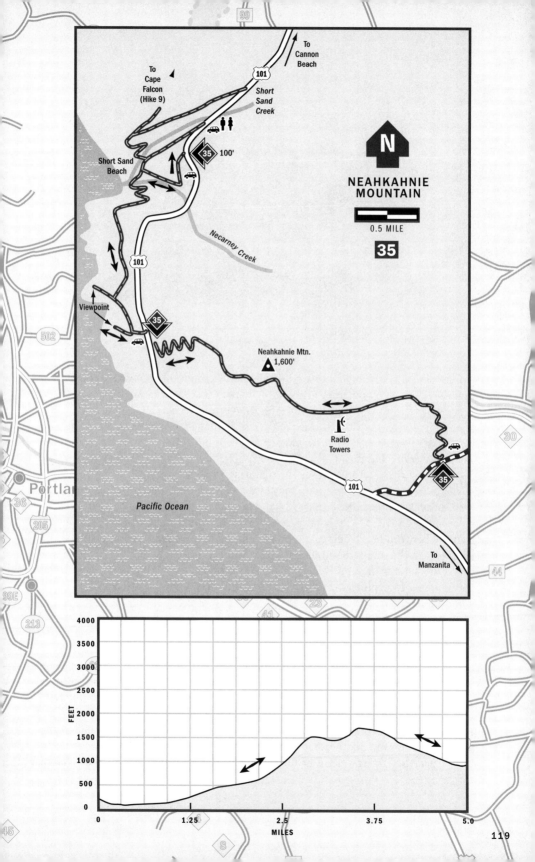

NEAHKAHNIE
MOUNTAIN

0.5 MILE

35

To Cannon Beach

To Cape Falcon (Hike 9)

101

Short Sand Creek

35 100'

Short Sand Beach

Necarney Creek

101

Viewpoint

35

Neahkahnie Mtn. 1,600'

Radio Towers

101

35

Pacific Ocean

Portland

To Manzanita

FEET

4000
3500
3000
2500
2000
1500
1000
500
0

0       1.25       2.5       3.75       5.0

MILES

you come to when hiking up this south-side trail. Right in the spot where you pop out
into the open, after you cross to the west side of the ridgeline, you'll see a little trail
heading up and to your right. You might also notice that the same trail continues to
your left, skirting the ridge to the south. You can follow this little scramble on your
way back, if you'd like; just be aware that there are thorns at the start, one little
exposed section, and then half a mile of easy going to the towers. Walk down the road
0.1 mile past them, and you'll see the trail where you came up.

For the "local," the one with the stops along the way, start at the parking lot for
the Oswald West State Park campground. Walk down the trail, among some awesome
sitka spruces, toward Short Sand Beach. In 0.1 mile you'll come to a junction offering
a choice between beach and campground; choose beach, unless you'd like to use the
rest room in the campground. In another 0.1 mile, turn left at another junction, this
time crossing a wonderful, bouncy suspension bridge over Necarney Creek. Take a
few minutes to explore the lovely beach, which has some pretty decent tidepools
around to the left.

Now, back on the trail to Neahkahnie Mountain, you'll climb up a ridge covered
with massive sitka spruces. About 0.2 miles up the trail you'll actually go through one
of them.

When you get to the top of the ridge, you may notice there are some more
western hemlocks around. These trees and Douglas firs are the only ones you'll find
from sea level to higher elevations in the Cascades. When the walk-through tree is 0.3
miles behind you, look for a large western red cedar just by the trail on the left, and
just beyond that two ridiculously large sitka spruces, with foot-thick branches that
have turned upward and become trees in their own right. If you think they can't get
any bigger, the largest spruce of the hike, with several trunks, is 0.2 miles farther
along.

When you pop out into the open, in a meadow more than 200 feet above the sea, you'll have come 1.3 miles since leaving your car. Just ahead you'll see a trail splitting off to the right; it leads to a cliff-top ocean viewpoint among the trees. Just before you reach the shoulder of US 101, you'll see another trail just like it. The second one is the one to take. And don't wander around in these meadows. I know a guy who fell into a 15-foot hole here and had to be pulled out with a rope.

When you reach US 101, cross it carefully, and start into the woods at a trail sign which, for some reason, reads NEAHKAHNIE MOUNTAIN: 1.5 MILES. Ignore that—it's two miles to the summit. You'll climb in the open for 0.6 miles before going back into the trees.

At this point, you're at about 1,000 feet above sea level. You'll keep climbing gradually after this, and then if the trail seems to be dipping downward, don't worry. You're just traversing around to the far side of the mountain, where the view is. When you come to a junction where two large trees fell, stay to the right. Eventually you'll be back into the open and see a small trail heading up to the left; that's the summit.

From the top of Neahkahnie, you can see all the way south to Cape Meares; look for Three Arch Rocks offshore there. If it's a really clear day, you might make out Cape Lookout south of Cape Meares. The beach town seemingly at your feet is Manzanita, and the body of water beyond it is Nehalem Bay. During the invasion-scare days of World War II, the Coast Guard had a lookout up here, while soldiers patrolled the beaches on horseback and blimps from Tillamook cruised offshore.

If you chose to do a one-way hike with a car shuttle and you started at the beach, time your arrival on the summit for just before sundown. It's quite a show from up there, and even at dusk it's no problem getting to your car at the southernmost trailhead.

# OAKS BOTTOM

## KEY AT-A-GLANCE INFORMATION

**LENGTH:** 3 miles

**CONFIGURATION:** Loop

**DIFFICULTY:** Easy

**SCENERY:** Wildlife, woods, water, and even an amusement park

**EXPOSURE:** Shady for the most part, but occasionally in the open

**TRAFFIC:** Heavy use on weekends, moderate otherwise

**TRAIL SURFACE:** Packed dirt and gravel

**HIKING TIME:** 2 hours, but only because you'll want to birdwatch

**SEASON:** Year-round, but it will get muddy in winter and spring.

**ACCESS:** No fees or permits needed.

**MAPS:** USGS Lake Oswego; there's also a map on a sign at the trailhead.

**FACILITIES:** Water at the trailhead; rest rooms and water along the way

**SPECIAL COMMENTS:** For more information, call the Portland Parks and Recreation office at (503) 823-2223.

## IN BRIEF

The heart of this trail is essentially a viewing platform around the edge of a watery wildlife preserve. It's home to dozens of bird species, especially in spring and fall, and it couldn't be more conveniently located.

## DESCRIPTION

It is so easy, when living in a city, to think that we are "here" and nature is out "there" somewhere, in the hills or on the coast. Occasionally you'll be walking down the street and see some Canada geese fly overhead, and you'll remember that nature is actually all around us. Whenever you need a reminder, just go down to Oaks Bottom.

Oaks Bottom is 160 acres of wildlife habitat just a few miles from downtown. It supports some 140 species of birds at various times of the year, especially in the spring and fall migration seasons. At any time of year you can expect to see herons and ducks, and if you're lucky, you might catch a glimpse of beavers, deer, cormorants, woodpeckers, ospreys, kingfishers, or bald eagles.

There are actually three trailheads for Oaks Bottom, but the one described above is the most convenient and is closest to the best parts of the park. From that trailhead, walk downhill on a moderate grade. At 0.1 mile, you'll see a wide trail

## DIRECTIONS

From downtown Portland, go south on Broadway Avenue and follow signs for the Ross Island Bridge (US 26 East). After crossing the bridge, turn right at the first light (Milwaukie Avenue). Go south 1.1 mile on Milwaukie and park in the signed trailhead on the right, just past Mitchell Street. You can also take Tri-Met's #19 Woodstock bus from downtown to the trailhead. Driving time is 10 minutes.

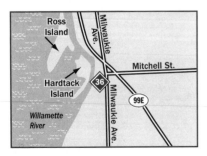

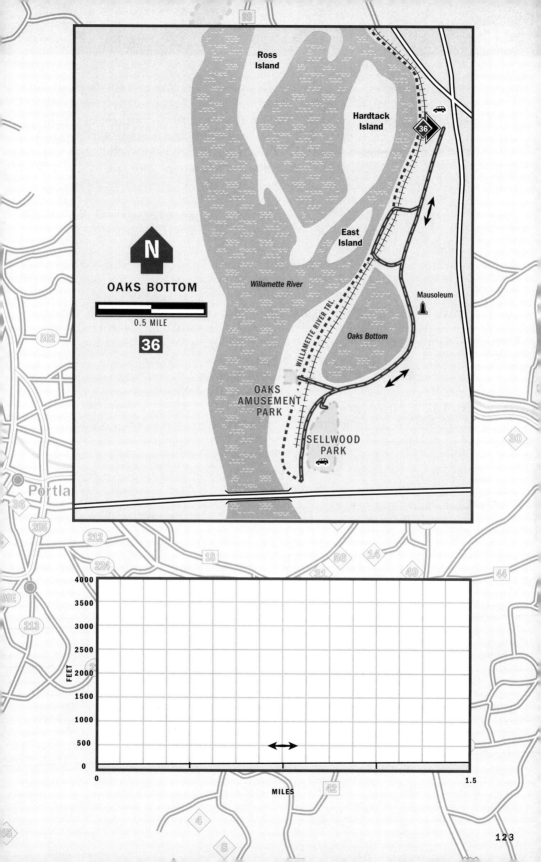

**Ross Island**

**Hardtack Island**

**East Island**

*Willamette River*

**N**

**OAKS BOTTOM**

0.5 MILE

**36**

WILLAMETTE RIVER TRL.

*Oaks Bottom*

Mausoleum

**OAKS AMUSEMENT PARK**

**SELLWOOD PARK**

| FEET | |
|---|---|
| 4000 | |
| 3500 | |
| 3000 | |
| 2500 | |
| 2000 | |
| 1500 | |
| 1000 | |
| 500 | |
| 0 | |

0

1.5

**MILES**

going into an open area to the right. This is a series of meadows between the main trail and the railroad tracks—actually landfill from before this was a city park. Explore them in search of birds, or spread out a blanket for a picnic. Alternatively, stay straight on the trail, cross under the power lines and over the railroad tracks, and connect with a system of small trails in the woods beyond. There are several viewpoints of an amazingly quiet stretch of the Willamette River, one of which is just above a large drainpipe with comforting warning signs of raw sewage overflow. It is highly recommended that you do not get in this stretch of the river.

Back on the main trail, you'll reach a fork at 0.3 miles. The trail to the right also leads to the railroad tracks and to the woodsy trails beyond, as well as to a collection of NO TRESPASSING signs telling you not to venture along the tracks to the left. This also connects to the Willamette River Trail (see page 201). Staying left at the fork, you'll pass through an area that was the subject of an ivy-removal project in 2000. English ivy, not native to the Pacific Northwest, has taken over many of Portland's parks, creating "ivy deserts" where no native plants can grow. So the city went in, removed ivy from this section, and planted native conifers, especially western red cedar, in an attempt to re-establish the native plants. You can judge for yourself how it worked.

The trail crosses a bridge and begins to skirt a marsh/meadow area (depending on the time of year) of alder, blackberry, dogwoods, and reed grass—and oaks, of course. After a few minutes you'll come to Oaks Bottom proper, a large pond that was part of the Willamette River before the construction of the railroad cut it off from the main river in the late nineteenth century. What is now the park was used as a dumping ground for asphalt and other construction materials. But the area was purchased by the city in 1969 and turned into a wildlife reclamation area. The pond is best viewed in spring and late fall, when the maximum amount of water is present—both in the pond and on the trail, by the way. Wear sturdy boots and bring binoculars. At all times of the year, look for great blue herons standing still in the water, awaiting a meal, and in the summer, Canada geese swooping in for a landing on their way north or south.

When the trail reaches the end of the lake, one branch cuts off to the right and heads for Oaks Amusement Park (see "Nearby Activities" below). Another continues straight ahead to a trailhead at the southern end of the park. A third, the smallest one, climbs a small hill to the left to Sellwood Park, where there are water fountains and rest rooms. At this point, you've seen the best of the park, so you might as well head back. Consider crossing the railroad tracks and exploring those woods, or just go back on the main trail and look for more birds.

Remember to be thankful for your little reminder that Mother Nature isn't always that far away.

## ▶ NEARBY ACTIVITIES

If you hear the screams of children coming from across the pond, don't call 911 on your cell phone; it's just Oaks Amusement Park in continuous operation since 1905. They've got all the midway thrill rides, the Northwest's oldest skating rink, and a kids' area, Acorn Acres, that opened in 1999.

# OPAL CREEK

## IN BRIEF

Opal Creek's history can be traced from ancient times to a modern-day legislative showdown, but its value can hardly be measured. It is an almost completely preserved sample of what the Northwest used to be, a place that hasn't been logged and where the water runs clear. It's the largest such area in the state that's at a low elevation. You don't even have to work hard to appreciate it.

## DESCRIPTION

For thousands of years, the Santiam Indians had their summer camp at the confluence of what we now call Opal Creek and Battle Ax Creek. Other tribes would come here to trade such items as fish from the Pacific Ocean and obsidian from east of the Cascades. In the 1850s, pioneers arrived and started mining for silver and gold. Not much of either was found, but there were enough other minerals to keep mining alive here until the early 1980s. A mining town was built at the confluence in the 1920s, and it came to be known as Jawbone Flats; according to legend, while the men were out mining, the women were back there "jawboning." A sawmill was also built nearby, but it burned in the 1940s. In 1992 the mining company donated 4,000 acres of land to the nonprofit group Friends of Opal Creek, with the desire that

## KEY AT-A-GLANCE INFORMATION

**LENGTH:** 7 miles round-trip to Opal Pool; 12 miles round-trip to Cedar Flats; 13 miles to see it all

**CONFIGURATION:** Out-and-back

**DIFFICULTY:** Easy/moderate

**SCENERY:** Virgin forest and clear-water pools

**EXPOSURE:** Shady

**TRAFFIC:** Use is heavy on summer weekends but moderate otherwise.

**TRAIL SURFACE:** Gravel road for 3.2 miles; otherwise packed dirt, roots, rocks

**HIKING TIME:** 2.5 hours to Opal Pool; 5 hours to Cedar Flats; 6 hours to see it all

**SEASON:** March–mid-November

**ACCESS:** Northwest Forest Pass required.

**MAPS:** USGS Battle Ax; Green Trails #524

**FACILITIES:** Outhouses at the trailhead in summer; outhouses along the trail and at Jawbone Flats

**SPECIAL COMMENTS:** For information, call (503) 897-2921, or go to www.opalcreek.org. You can also call the Detroit Ranger District office at (503) 854-3366.

## DIRECTIONS

From Portland on I-5, drive 35 miles south of I-205 and take Exit 253/Stayton/Detroit Lake. Turn left (east) onto OR 22 and follow it 22.5 miles, and then turn left onto Little North Santiam Road, following a sign for Elkhorn. In just over 15 miles, the pavement will end; beware that beyond this there are some serious potholes. Stay left at two junctions; the trailhead is at the end of the road, 5.6 miles after you leave the pavement. Driving time is 1 hour and 40 minutes.

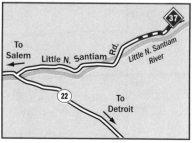

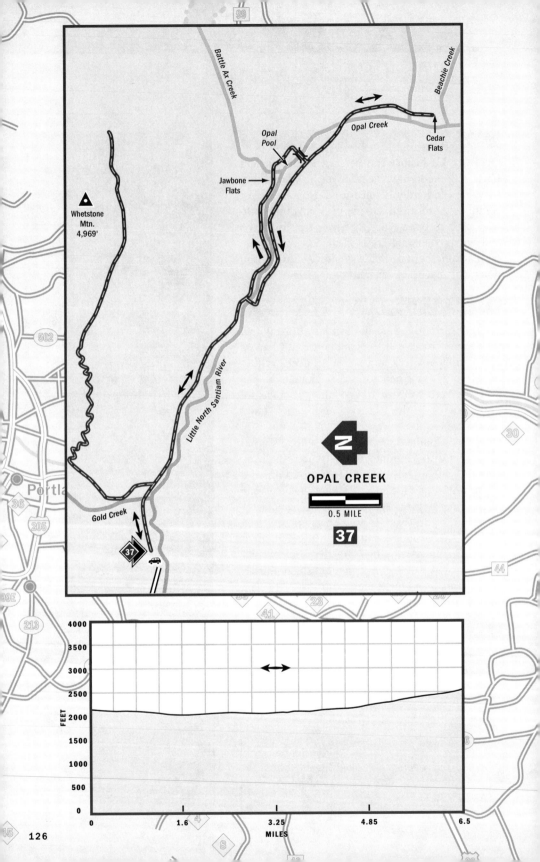

Battle Ax Creek

Beachie Creek

Opal Pool

Opal Creek

Jawbone Flats

Cedar Flats

Whetstone Mtn. 4,969'

Little North Santiam River

OPAL CREEK

0.5 MILE

37

Gold Creek

37

FEET

4000
3500
3000
2500
2000
1500
1000
500
0

0    1.6    3.25    4.85    6.5

MILES

it be preserved. Meanwhile, the Forest Service announced plans to log 15,000 acres of the Little North Santiam Valley.

This is when Opal Creek became world-famous; a massive effort was launched to save it from the saw. National TV crews visited, a book was written, and the fight went all the way to the U.S. Congress, where in 1998 the 35,000-acre Opal Creek Wilderness and Scenic Recreation Area was finally established. Today Friends of Opal Creek operates an educational camp at Jawbone Flats, and a Y-shaped system of easy trails brings visitors into the magical land of what used to be.

From the gate, you'll start by walking slightly downhill on an old road. Most of the big trees are still ahead, but there is a Douglas fir on the right (a side trail leads to it at about 0.2 miles) that is thought to be between 700 and 1,000 years old. There's a rustic outhouse at 0.3 miles, just before a crossing of Gold Creek on a high bridge; 0.1 mile past that the Whetstone Mountain Trail appears on the left. This 3.5-mile trail climbs almost 3,000 feet to a superb view. About 0.2

The road to Jawbone Flats after a snowfall

miles past that trail, you'll cross over a series of half bridges; keep an eye out for an old mining shaft on the left just past them. It's not recommended that you go in there.

The most impressive forest along the road occurs around the one-mile mark, where a host of Douglas firs are in the six-foot-thick range. At a wide spot in the road around 1.7 miles out, look for a trail to the right, leading 100 yards to a rocky viewpoint. At 1.9 miles, look for a tiny waterfall on the left, flowing through a cedar tree. For what it's worth, I took my 2003 Christmas card picture at this waterfall.

At two miles, you'll see on the right a trail leading into an area filled with old mining equipment and the burned-out remains of the sawmill's steel and masonry boiler. Behind the one building still there is a trail leading 100 feet to a falls; it's known as either Sawmill Falls or the Waterfall of the Children, depending on who you ask. This falls is the end of the road for a winter run of steelhead from the ocean. Look for a log stuck on the rocks high up on the left. That should give you an idea how high the water gets here.

Just past the sawmill site, you'll come to a fork. Straight ahead on the road there's a river access point on the right at 0.2 miles, then Jawbone Flats in 1.2 miles. Here, you'll find several cabins from the 1920s and 1930s, and two new ones built after a fire in 1999. (They were both built largely from wood cut and milled right on the site.) To reach local highlight Opal Pool from here, go straight through the camp on the road, following signs through a right-hand turn and past a collection of old vehicles that includes a U.S. Navy fire truck. The pool is 0.1 mile past the cars.

A long-anticipated bridge over Opal Creek is in place just above Opal Pool, enabling hikers to do a loop by crossing over to the Opal Creek Trail.

Back at the first fork in the road, a right turn will take you across a bridge and then left onto the Opal Creek Trail proper. Several side trails will lead left to the Little North Santiam; then after one mile a sign will lead to you to Opal Pool on the left. In summer you will often see people jumping off the rocks into the amazingly clear pool. You're now looking at Opal Creek itself, probably the clearest water you could ever see and the best bet in Oregon for a stream you could drink out of. I have probably ingested two gallons of Opal Creek and never gotten sick; take that for what it's worth and make your own decisions.

Another mile up the trail, a bridge offers a glimpse down into the crystal-clear waters; there's also a great little rock pool on the far side that is a safe place for a quick dip. Another mile up, the trail more or less ends at Cedar Flats, where Beachie Creek flows into Opal Creek and three 1,000-year-old cedars frame the trail.

I say "more or less ends" because the trail beyond there, to Franklin Grove, is not maintained and is not worth the effort. The reason it isn't maintained is that the Forest Service plans to relocate the trail and build a new, four-mile section up to Opal Lake. There are also plans to connect the Opal Creek Trail with the Little North Santiam Trail, which currently ends several miles down that river. None of that work had begun when this book was written, but one day you'll be able to hike from the Elkhorn recreation area (back on Little North Santiam Road) to Opal Lake, some 17 miles one-way. Call the Ranger District office at (503) 854-3366 for an update.

## ▶ NEARBY ACTIVITIES

A mile back on OR 22, you may have noticed the Gingerbread House. It will be on your left as you head home. Stop in there for some fresh, warm gingerbread after the hike, and your day will be complete.

# RAMONA FALLS

## ▶ IN BRIEF

This trail is immensely popular, and it's no wonder. It's a fairly easy hike to a uniquely beautiful falls, with plenty of room for a picnic when you get there. There's even a side trip available for a sweeping view of Mount Hood.

## ▶ DESCRIPTION

From the massive trailhead parking lot, the trail is essentially flat for a little over one mile, at which point there's a junction. Either way leads to the falls; the left follows a creek, is shadier, and is probably a better way to go up. Going that way, you'll reach another junction in half a mile; stay right for the falls, or go left for a 4.4-mile round-trip diversion to Bald Mountain, with its majestic view of the northwest side of Mount Hood, including the headwaters of the Sandy River. Just be warned: It's a 1,700-foot climb, and it's more easily reached as part of the McNeil Point hike (see page 105).

Heading toward Ramona Falls, you'll soon see 100-foot cliffs across the creek that have a vaguely pinkish hue. That's basalt, and the reason it's pink is that it's recently exposed due to rockfall from the face of the cliffs. As basalt weathers,

### ⓘ KEY AT-A-GLANCE INFORMATION

**LENGTH:** 7.1 miles

**CONFIGURATION:** Balloon

**DIFFICULTY:** Easy

**SCENERY:** A pleasant stream, soothing woods, and a one-of-a-kind waterfall

**EXPOSURE:** In the woods all the way, with occasional open spots

**TRAFFIC:** Heavy use, especially on summer weekends

**TRAIL SURFACE:** Packed dirt

**HIKING TIME:** 3 hours

**SEASON:** May–October

**ACCESS:** Northwest Forest Pass required.

**MAPS:** Mount Hood Wilderness; Green Trails #461 (Government Camp); USGS Bull Run Lake

**FACILITIES:** None at the trailhead, but a campground with water and toilets is less than a mile away.

**SPECIAL COMMENTS:** For more information, contact the Mount Hood Visitor Information Center at (503) 622-7674.

## ▶ DIRECTIONS

From Portland on US 26, drive 36 miles east of I-205 to Zigzag. Turn left onto Lolo Pass Road at the Zigzag Store and proceed four miles before turning right onto paved FS 1825, which is not marked; it's the first road after a parking area on the right. Cross the river, and after a mile on FS 1825, stay right at a fork. A little more than one mile later, stay left at another fork; the trailhead is a few hundred yards ahead. Going right at the last fork would take you 0.3 miles to Lost Creek Campground, where water and toilets are available. Driving time is 1 hour.

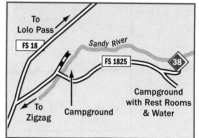

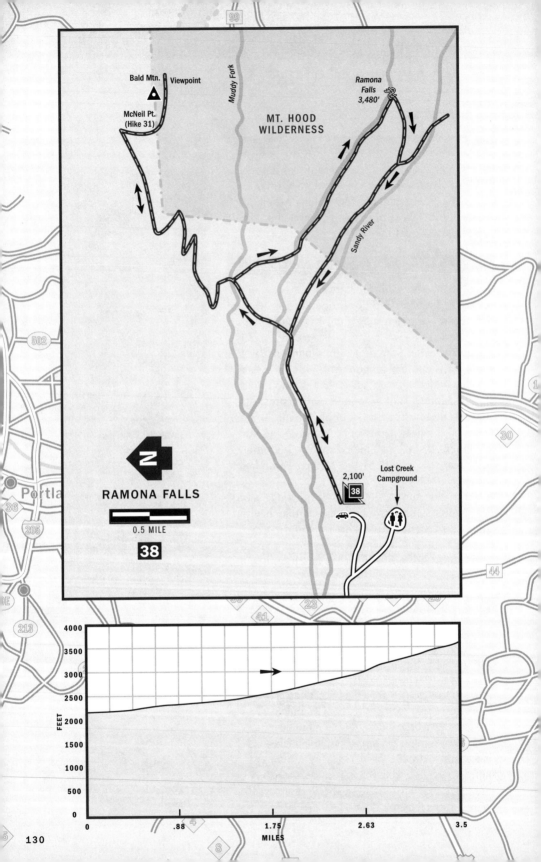

Bald Mtn. Viewpoint

McNeil Pt.
(Hike 31)

Muddy Fork

MT. HOOD
WILDERNESS

Ramona
Falls
3,480'

Sandy River

N

RAMONA FALLS

0.5 MILE

**38**

2,100'

**38**

Lost Creek
Campground

FEET

4000
3500
3000
2500
2000
1500
1000
500
0

0          .88          1.75          2.63          3.5
                    MILES

it gets darker. The creek itself is a lovely little mountain stream with pools safe enough for kids to play in (so you might want to come back this way). When you catch a brief glimpse of Hood through the trees ahead—and the trail turns uphill a bit and starts to seem a wee bit tedious—you're almost there.

Ramona Falls is a perfect example of how a tiny stream can make a heck of a waterfall. The best comparison for these falls is to one of those pyramids of champagne glasses; as the water cascades over broken columns of basalt, it spreads out into a 120-foot extravaganza of water that emits a cool, misty spray into the open area in front of it. No wonder so many people come here with kids and dogs and picnic supplies! Just beware of the gray jays that haunt the area; they'll take food right out of your hands if you're not careful.

There's a nice story, by the way, behind the naming of Ramona Falls. In 1933 a Forest Service employee came across the falls while scouting the area for a trail; at the time, he was courting a girl and named the falls in her honor. One would like to think he won fair Ramona's hand in marriage.

To complete the loop back to the parking lot, keep going past the falls and turn right down the trail. This route is a little more open, has a lot more rhododendrons, and traverses the edge of the Sandy River Gorge on its way back to the first trail junction. From there, turn left and walk just over one mile back to your car.

## ▶ NEARBY ACTIVITIES

The Zigzag Store at US 26 and FS 18 is still in its original 1916 building. It was originally a market and then, in 1917, the Zigzag post office. It's also conveniently located for a cool drink after the hike.

# SADDLE MOUNTAIN

## IN BRIEF

The highest point in northwest Oregon, Saddle Mountain is also one of the most popular hiking trails in the state. It goes through flower-filled meadows unparalleled in this part of the state and has a view on top that stretches from the ocean to the mouth of the Columbia River to the Cascades.

## DESCRIPTION

Saddle Mountain just doesn't seem to belong in its surroundings. It's the highest point in this part of the state, but the other hills around it aren't even close. It doesn't even look like them, with its two-headed, rocky summit of "pillow lava," which looks like that because it erupted underwater, millions of years ago when this area was the sea floor. Then, when you get on top of it, you might think you're on Mount Hood, with the far-away views and the wildflowers all over. Of course, with the crowds on summer weekends, you might think you're in Forest Park right after 5 p.m. on a weekday. Whatever—it's a great hike, so start early in the morning and get there ahead of everybody else.

When you get out of your car, you might be a little intimidated as you look up at the mountain. You might even see some speck-sized people up there. The good news is, you'll be up there soon enough; the bad news is, that's not the summit.

Things start out mellow, in a young forest filled with big, old stumps—relics of logging in the 1920s and fires in the 1930s. After 0.2 miles, you'll see a side trail to the right, which leads 0.1 mile to a great view of Saddle Mountain—the only

## DIRECTIONS

From Portland on US 26, travel 66 miles west of I-405 and turn right at a sign for Saddle Mountain State Park. The trailhead is seven miles ahead, at the end of the road. Driving time is 1 hour and 25 minutes.

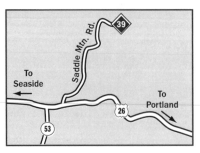

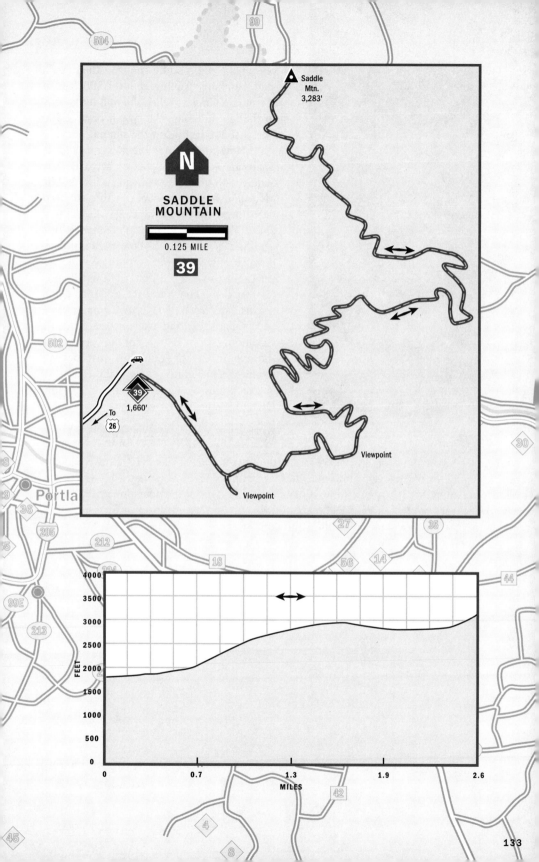

Saddle
Mtn.
3,283'

N

SADDLE
MOUNTAIN

0.125 MILE

39

39
1,660'

To
26

Viewpoint

Viewpoint

4000
3500
3000
2500
2000
1500
1000
500
0

FEET

0          0.7          1.3          1.9          2.6
MILES

Upper slopes of Saddle Mountain after a spring snow shower

one in the park, oddly enough. Then you'll start climbing, gaining about 1,100 feet in the next 1.4 miles. When the trail turns back to the left and stays flat, you'll be at 2,900 feet, just 300 feet below the summit.

Now you're out in the flower meadows. There are several rare species here, like the Saddle Mountain saxifrage and Saddle Mountain bittercress—species that survived here during the last Ice Age. Stay on the trail and on the footbridges, and remember it's against the rules to pick flowers. You'll drop down briefly and cross the saddle—this is the point you can see from the car, which is now very small on your left—and then climb the last, steep scramble to the summit.

On a clear day, you can see from the volcanoes of the Cascades to the Pacific, and the mouth of the Columbia just beyond Astoria to the north. On a really clear day, you can make out the mountains of the Olympic Peninsula beyond that.

### ▶ NEARBY ACTIVITIES

A few miles before the turnoff from US 26, no doubt you noticed Camp 18. How could you not? It might look like a logging museum, and it is, but it's also a restaurant with a famously filling Sunday buffet. It's served from 10 a.m. to 2 p.m., and it includes prime rib! As one newspaper story put it, at Camp 18 "you can throw on one serious feedbag." It's not a bad way to prepare for an assault on Saddle Mountain.

# SALMON BUTTE

▶ **IN BRIEF**

This easy-to-get-to trail is a mellow climb through old-growth forest and giant rhododendrons to a viewpoint that takes in Mount Hood, Mount Jefferson, and the heart of the Salmon-Huckleberry Wilderness.

▶ **DESCRIPTION**

This trail is so well graded, you'll hardly notice you're going uphill, except for occasional views down the valley or up toward the peak. Other trails might climb similar elevation in half the distance, but they'll leave you more tired. So this is a perfect way to get on top of something without spending the whole day or wearing yourself out.

The trail starts out through an area that was clear-cut 30 years ago, so there's not much in the way of old trees, but soon enough you get into the hemlocks and moss-draped Douglas firs—and some seriously large rhododendrons that will bloom in late June. At 1.3 miles, you'll come to an area at the end of a ridge with a view to the top of the butte. Just under two miles up, a trail to the right at a switchback leads to a steep, wildflower-filled meadow with a perfect rock for a photo opportunity. Around three miles up, you'll come to another open area loaded with rhodies and a

▶ **DIRECTIONS**

From Portland on US 26, drive 36 miles east of I-205 and turn right onto Salmon River Road, which is 0.1 mile before the Zigzag Store on the left. Stay straight on this road for 6.5 miles; you'll come to a small parking area on the left and a very small road entering the trees on the right. If you have any concerns about the clearance on your car, park on the left and walk up the last 100 yards of the rough road to the trailhead. Driving time is 1 hour and 5 minutes.

ℹ **KEY AT-A-GLANCE INFORMATION**

**LENGTH:** 8.6 miles

**CONFIGURATION:** Out-and-back

**DIFFICULTY:** Moderate

**SCENERY:** Pleasant forest on the way up, panoramic view on top

**EXPOSURE:** Shady with occasional open spots, then wide open on top

**TRAFFIC:** Moderate on weekends, light otherwise

**TRAIL SURFACE:** Packed dirt, some rocks at the top

**HIKING TIME:** 4 hours

**SEASON:** June–October

**ACCESS:** Northwest Forest Pass required.

**MAPS:** Salmon-Huckleberry Wilderness

**FACILITIES:** None at the trailhead

**SPECIAL COMMENTS:** June is the best time for this hike; that's when the rhododendrons are in bloom. For more information, call the Mount Hood Visitor Information Center at (503) 622-7674.

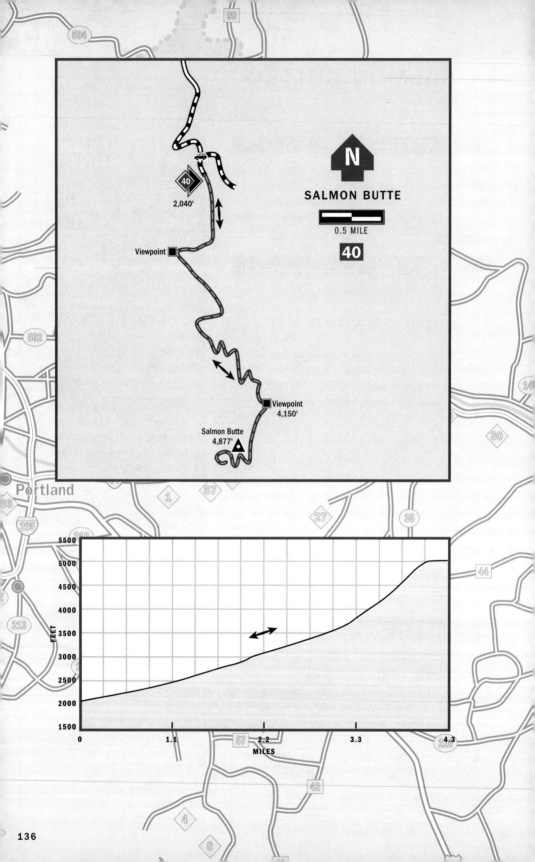

SALMON BUTTE

40

0.5 MILE

40

2,040'

Viewpoint

Viewpoint
4,150'

Salmon Butte
4,877'

view to the left of the sweeping Salmon River Valley. You'll now have climbed 2,100 of the 2,800 feet in your hike.

Near the top, the trail dead ends into an old road that once served a lookout tower; turn right and follow the road to the top, which is reached by a rocky scramble of about 100 feet. From here you're looking south and east, with Mount Hood 15 miles to your left, Mount Jefferson 35 miles to your right, and Mounts Adams and Rainier off on the horizon. In front of you is the Salmon-Huckleberry Wilderness; what a difference a lack of clear-cuts makes, eh? While you're on top, look around for old pieces of glass and metal that are part of the burned-down lookout tower. Then cruise back down the same gentle grade you came up.

▶ **NEARBY ACTIVITIES**

The Mount Hood Brewing Company in Government Camp (ten miles east on US 26) serves good pizza and generally has about six of the brewery's beers on tap, with cool names like Cloud Cap Amber and Ice Axe IPA.

# SALMON RIVER

## KEY AT-A-GLANCE INFORMATION

**LENGTH:** The lower section is 5.2 miles round-trip; the middle section is 7.2 miles round-trip.

**CONFIGURATION:** Out-and-back

**DIFFICULTY:** Easy/moderate

**SCENERY:** Old-growth forest; spawning salmon in the spring and fall

**EXPOSURE:** Shady

**TRAFFIC:** Use is heavy all summer long and extremely heavy on weekends.

**TRAIL SURFACE:** Packed dirt with rocks and roots

**HIKING TIME:** 2 hours for the lower loop; 3.5 hours for the upper

**SEASON:** Year-round

**ACCESS:** Northwest Forest Pass required.

**MAPS:** USFS Salmon-Huckleberry Wilderness

**FACILITIES:** None at trailheads; water and toilets at Green Canyon campground

**SPECIAL COMMENTS:** For more information, you can contact the Mount Hood Visitor Information Center at (503) 622-7674.

## IN BRIEF

The Salmon River, which starts on the slopes of Timberline Ski Area, is the only river in the Lower 48 states to be classified as a Wild and Scenic River from its headwaters to its mouth. There are three sections of trail along it, two of which are described here. They are extremely easy to get to, and in the fall they host spawning salmon. The uppermost section, accessed by a different road, is less interesting than these, tougher to find, and not worth the effort. Its only advantage is that nobody hikes it.

## DESCRIPTION

Start with the lower, easier section. From the roadside parking area (the first one you came to while driving in), you'll start out downhill through a beautiful forest of Douglas firs and Western red cedars. You'll be close to the river after 0.1 mile and stay there most of the rest of the way. After two little footbridges over side creeks, you'll come to the first of several trails leading down to the river. You will pass two more small bridges, and in 0.3 miles you'll come to a campsite with a log that sticks out over the river. It's perfectly sturdy, but be sure of your balance before you go out on it.

The best thing about this trail, other than its convenience and the river itself, is the nature of the old-growth forest. Look for "nurse" logs, which have fallen and are now the home of new

## DIRECTIONS

From Portland on US 26, drive 36 miles east of I-205 and turn right onto Salmon River Road, which is 0.1 mile before the Zigzag Store on the left. Stay straight on this road for 2.7 miles to the lower trailhead (just beyond the Mount Hood National Forest sign), or for 4.9 miles to the upper trailhead, at a bridge over the river. Driving time is 1 hour.

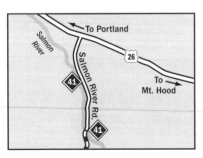

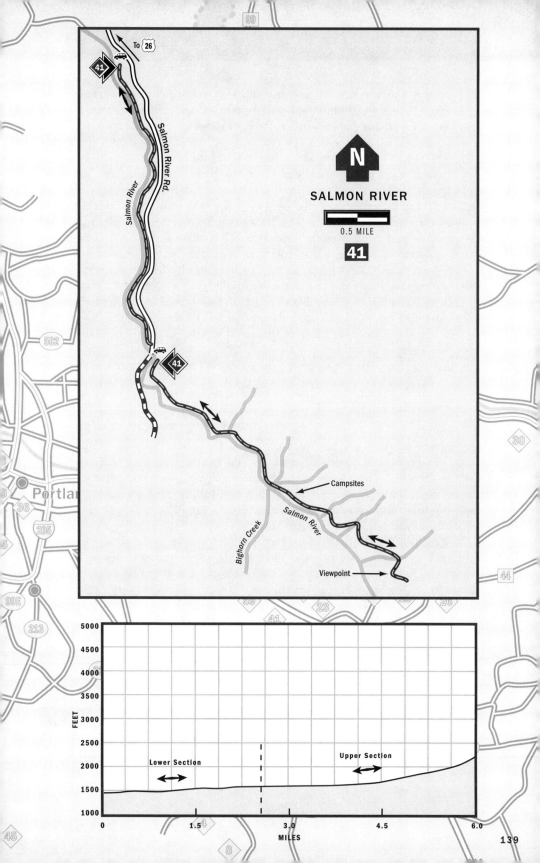

To 26

41

N

SALMON RIVER

0.5 MILE

41

Salmon River Rd.

Salmon River

41

Campsites

Bighorn Creek

Salmon River

Viewpoint

FEET

5000
4500
4000
3500
3000
2500
2000
1500
1000

Lower Section

Upper Section

0          1.5          3.0          4.5          6.0

MILES

Portland

139

trees. Just past the campsite with the suspended log, you'll go up a set of steps, at the top of which there's an absolutely massive Western red cedar; you can't miss it, as it's right next to the trail and about ten feet thick. At about the one-mile mark, look for a hollowed-out cedar stump with a new tree growing from it; just past it is the biggest Douglas fir (about eight feet thick) on this stretch of the river.

At about the 1.5-mile mark, you'll come to the first of two sections where the trail joins the road for a brief time. On this first one, you want to take the second trail back into the woods; the first trail is used by anglers and leads to the river. About 50 yards off the road, look for three large trees—two firs and a cedar—almost bonded together. Just past here, where a downed tree lies along the bank, I came across several spawning salmon on a late September hike. They were in the shallows just a few feet from shore. The fish will actually go several miles farther upstream; if you hike the upper section of this trail in the fall, you'll get more chances to see them.

There are two more highlights to this trail. One is a cedar tree so large that a hollowed-out area in its base is big enough to be called a cave. The other is a "nurse" log, cut into three pieces for trail-construction purposes, which is now host to no fewer than eight cedar saplings.

Just after a second section on the roadside, you'll drop back into the woods for another brief spell before emerging at the upper trailhead, where the road crosses the river.

Now, for the upper section. From the trailhead, walk upstream through a forest of Douglas fir. Just less than a half mile up, you'll pass a deep pool where fishermen often gather. A little while past this, when you get another view of the river from about 40 feet above it, look (in September and October) for dark shapes swirling about in the pools. Those are salmon; the black-gray ones are Chinook, and the less often seen gold ones are Cohos. Consider that they have spent their lives in the ocean and have swum all the way up the Columbia River some 75 miles, about 41 miles up the Sandy, then about 20 miles up the Salmon.

At the two-mile mark, a series of campsites on the right offer yet more chances to get close to the river and look for fish. After this, you'll embark on just about your only climb of the day, picking up about 600 feet in 1.6 miles to an overlook of the Salmon River Canyon. After you pop out into the open, make sure you go as far as the rock outcrop for the best view. Just be very careful around here, and don't try any of the trails going down toward the river. You might go down farther and faster than you ever intended.

That scenic view is your recommended turnaround, as you're now 3.6 miles from the upper trailhead, but the trail actually goes another 10.8 miles upstream to a road near Trillium Lake. But at this point you've seen the best of it, so head back.

▶ **NEARBY ACTIVITIES**

Start your day with breakfast at the Zigzag Inn, 0.1 mile east of Salmon River Road on US 26. They do good things with French toast there.

# SALMONBERRY RIVER

## ▶ IN BRIEF

Have you ever wanted to wander off down the railroad tracks? This is your chance. The Port of Tillamook Bay allows hiking access on this (still active) 16-mile section through a roadless canyon in the Coast Range.

## ▶ DESCRIPTION

First things first: Yes, there are still trains going through here, roughly one per day. But official railroad policy is that (A) hikers are welcome, except during fire season, and (B) trains are required to blow their whistles all the way through the canyon. The grade and the curves also keep the trains slow, so you'll have plenty of time to get out of the way. I speak from experience: You will hear a train coming! Some of the smaller maintenance vehicles are quieter, but they also stop a whole lot quicker.

## ▶ DIRECTIONS

For the upper trailhead at Cochran, from Portland on US 26, drive 37 miles west of I-405 to Timber Junction and turn left onto Timber Road, following a sign for Timber. Go 3 miles to Timber and turn right onto Cochran Road. The pavement will end in a half mile; stay right at a junction in 3.7 miles, then left at 6.2 miles and left again at 6.3 miles, this time leaving Cochran Road and following a sign for Standard Grade Road. Park 0.1 mile ahead, where the road crosses the tracks. Driving time is 1 hour.

For the lower trailhead at Salmonberry, stay on US 26 for 17 more miles and turn left onto Lower Nehalem Road, following a sign for Lower Nehalem River. Go a half mile and turn left at a stop sign, then continue 12 miles to where the road crosses the tracks. There's parking on the left. Driving time is 1 hour and 30 minutes.

## ❶ KEY AT-A-GLANCE INFORMATION

**LENGTH:** Up to 16 miles with a shuttle

**CONFIGURATION:** One-way or out-and-back

**DIFFICULTY:** Easy

**SCENERY:** Remote forested canyon, mountain stream, high bridges, tunnels, and railroad tracks

**EXPOSURE:** One very high trestle, several tunnels, possibly a train or two

**TRAFFIC:** Light

**TRAIL SURFACE:** Railroad tracks, gravel

**HIKING TIME:** 7 hours to do the whole thing

**SEASON:** Access is typically closed from early July to mid-October because of fire season; call the railroad for details; possible snow in winter.

**ACCESS:** No passes required.

**MAPS:** USGS Rogers Peak and Cook Creek.

**FACILITIES:** None at either trailhead; there's water on the trail, but it would have to be treated.

**SPECIAL COMMENTS:** Bring a flashlight, since at times you'll be going through tunnels. There's only one real long tunnel, which you're required to go around on a trail, but it gets dark in the others, and footing can be tricky.

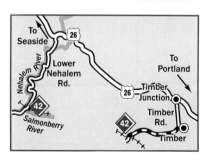

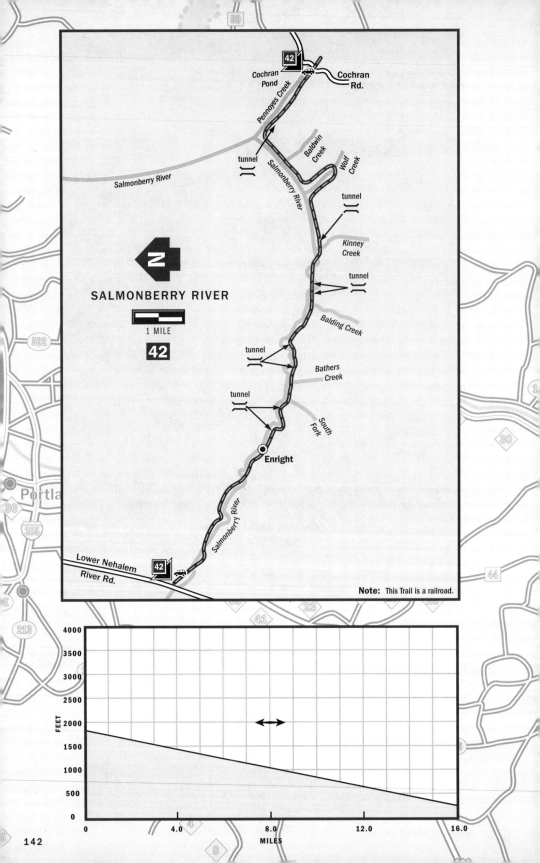

SALMONBERRY RIVER

1 MILE

42

Cochran Pond

Cochran Rd.

Pennoyes Creek

tunnel

Salmonberry River

Baldwin Creek

Wolf Creek

tunnel

Kinney Creek

tunnel

Balding Creek

tunnel

Bathers Creek

tunnel

South Fork

Enright

Salmonberry River

Lower Nehalem River Rd.

42

**Note:** This Trail is a railroad.

Portla

8

4.0   8.0   12.0   16.0

MILES

FEET

4000
3500
3000
2500
2000
1500
1000
500
0

Now, with all the warnings aside, this is a unique hiking experience. Come in the spring or early summer for lush greenery and roaring water, or in October for fall colors and migrating salmon. Either way, you're likely to have the place to yourself, since I've never encountered anybody (or another guidebook) that knows about this place.

I'll describe the way I like to do it, which is one-way from Cochran to Salmonberry, with a car or a friend waiting at the other end. It's 16 miles, downhill, and such a mellow grade (about 100 feet per mile) you'll hardly notice the elevation change.

From the crossing at Cochran, head off to your right, following the pair of tracks down the hill. In 0.1 mile you'll see Cochran Pond on the right, and by this time you will have figured out something about walking on a railroad: unless you're 5-foot-1 or 6-foot-9, walking on the ties is awkward. They're too short to step on each one and too far apart to step on every other one. The good news is that for 90 percent of the walk, there's enough dirt and/or gravel between them that

Bridge over the Salmonberry River

the surface is flat. Just be careful that you don't twist anything, and know that in many places you'll have gravel or even a slight trail to walk on beside the tracks. Besides, walking down the tracks is just so . . . Woody Guthrie.

About a mile down, you'll encounter the first of many small tunnels. They're all short enough that a train won't sneak up on you while you're in there, so just give a listen and then head on through. Just past this one is the first trestle. The second tunnel leads onto the highest trestle of the hike, a good 100 feet above Baldwin Creek. For the next several miles it's just more of the same—tunnels and trestles and ties and trees. Watch for herons along the river and old train equipment along the tracks, and enjoy the solitude.

Around 7 miles out (exact mileage is tough to figure) you'll encounter a 1925 steel bridge, and less than a mile later you'll come to the long tunnel that you're not to go through. The reason is that it's about 500 feet long and has a curve to it, so if a vehicle was coming, you might not know it. On the downhill end of this tunnel, there's a sign showing the way to the trail, but on the uphill end you'll just have to scramble through some brush on the right side, actually following an old railroad track, until the trail becomes a little clearer. Just hug the hillside, and you'll be back on the tracks in a few minutes; you might even enjoy the brief spell of walking on actual ground.

A few miles later you'll come to—surprise!—the "town" of Enright, apparently only two houses. It was actually a train station with a post office in the early 1920s, and it has no road access. There's an old water tower at the downhill end of it. If you're headed downhill, you're about two-thirds of the way done here.

A couple miles beyond Enright, you'll come to another steel bridge, this one over a long deep pool. Officially, I can't recommend anybody jump off the bridge and into this deep, inviting pool, but the thought did occur to me. The water is quite refreshing. While I was contemplating the leap on an October afternoon, I noticed a large fish swimming around down there. On closer inspection, I found about a half-dozen chinook salmon in the pool, mostly on the downstream side of the bridge. I watched for half an hour as they swam in circles, chased each other, and splashed around. One of them must have been 30 inches long.

At this point, you're only about two miles from Salmonberry, so you may start to see other people. When I hiked the whole stretch on an October Saturday, I encountered only two hunters and two fishermen the whole day. A half-mile or so below the salmon pool, look for a cable crossing the river; it leads to a house over there in the woods. Can you imagine living there?

When you start to see houses—the "town" of Salmonberry—across the river to your left, you're about a half-mile from the road, and walking on something other than railroad tracks will probably sound pretty nice. But if you're looking to relax a little, there's a nice little section of beach on the far side of the Nehalem River. Just keep going on the tracks across the Nehalem, then scramble down to the right and follow a faint trail though a batch of snowberry bushes to a sandy little nap spot. It's probably underwater in spring and summer, but I had a pleasant October lie-down there after my walk. And here's an interesting thing about the Nehalem River: it actually starts just on the other side of Cochran, flows through Timber, then travels some 100 miles in a great northern loop through four counties to get to this point, which is only 16 miles from where it started. Go figure.

## ▶ NEARBY ACTIVITIES

If you want to see this canyon for a whole lot less effort, you can actually ride a train through it. The Port operates tourist trains with open-air cars and a barbecue at Cochran during summer and fall. They also have a line that runs up and down the coast between Tillamook and Wheeler. Call (503) 842-8206 or visit www.potb.org for more information.

# SAUVIE ISLAND

## ▶ IN BRIEF

Two casual strolls on the edge of the city offer a glimpse into the local world of wildlife—and back into the past. Both of them are easy to reach and easy to do, and there's plenty of other stuff to do on the island while you're out there.

## ▶ DESCRIPTION

First, let's go to Oak Island, which is actually a peninsula in a lake on an island in a river.

Some hikes are in the wilderness, some are walks through history, some are educational, some offer a distant view. This one feels like just being out in the country. You'll even skirt a couple of crops! The whole scene might remind you of

## ▶ DIRECTIONS

From Portland on US 30, drive 10 miles west of I-405 and turn right to cross the Sauvie Island Bridge. The Sauvie Island Market (where you buy your parking pass) is on your left, 0.1 mile beyond the far end of the bridge. Go 2 more miles and turn right on Reeder Road.

For Oak Island: After 1.3 miles on Reeder Road, turn left onto Oak Island Road—although since Reeder goes off to the right here, it's more like keeping straight. After 1.9 miles you'll leave the pavement, and .8 mile later you'll cross a dike. At the bottom of the dike, go straight; the trailhead is .4 mile ahead at the end of the road. Driving time is 25 minutes.

For Warrior Rock: After 10 miles on Reeder Road, you'll leave the pavement and come to a series of parking areas for Welton Beach, just over the dike to your right. Past that is parking for Collins Beach, which happens to be clothing-optional but is blocked from the road by forest. At 2.3 miles after you left the pavement, the road ends at the parking area for Warrior Rock. Driving time is 40 minutes.

## ℹ KEY AT-A-GLANCE INFORMATION

**LENGTH:** 3 miles for Oak Island, 7 for Warrior Rock

**CONFIGURATION:** Oak Island is a loop; Warrior Rock is out-and-back.

**DIFFICULTY:** Easy

**SCENERY:** Lakeshore, woods, meadows, beaches, and birds

**EXPOSURE:** Oak Island is mostly open; Warrior Rock is mostly in the woods.

**SOLITUDE:** Use is moderate on summer weekends, light otherwise

**FACILITIES:** There's an outhouse at each trailhead; the nearest water is at the Sauvie Island Market

**TRAIL SURFACE:** Packed dirt and grass, some beach

**HIKING TIME:** 1 hour for Oak Island, 3 hours for Warrior Rock

**SEASON:** Oak Island is open April 16 to September 30; Warrior Rock is year-round.

**ELEVATION:** 100 feet all around

**ACCESS:** A parking pass is required for all of Sauvie Island. A day pass is $3 (annual pass is $11) and can be bought at the Sauvie Island Market.

**MAPS:** USGS St Helens; a free hiking map can also be obtained at the Sauvie Island Market.

**SPECIAL COMMENTS:** For more information call Sauvie Island Information Center, (503) 621-3488.

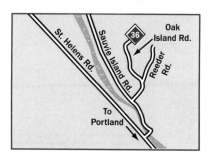

**145**

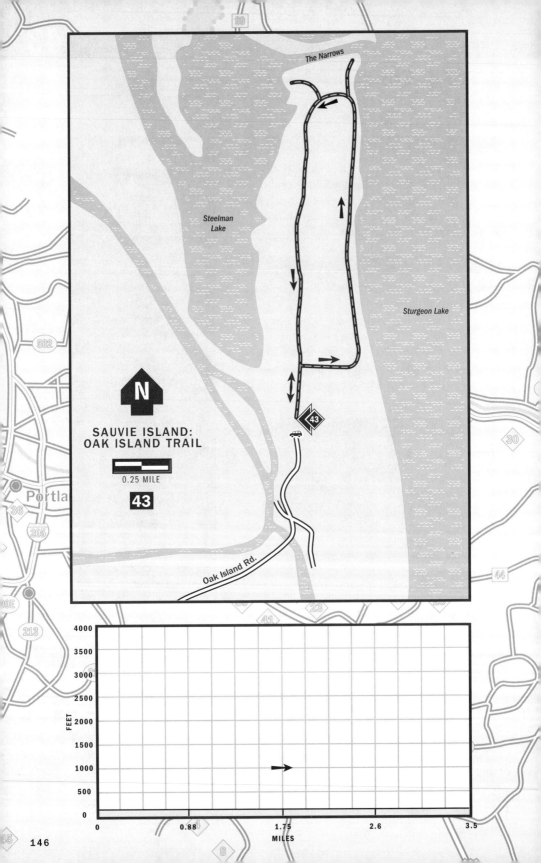

The Narrows

Steelman
Lake

Sturgeon Lake

N

SAUVIE ISLAND:
OAK ISLAND TRAIL

0.25 MILE

43

Oak Island Rd.

| FEET | | |
|---|---|---|
| 4000 | | |
| 3500 | | |
| 3000 | | |
| 2500 | | |
| 2000 | | |
| 1500 | | |
| 1000 | | |
| 500 | | |
| 0 | | |

0        0.88        1.75        2.6        3.5
MILES

visiting your country grandparents. But even the crops are part of a plan by the Oregon Department of Fish and Wildlife to manage waterfowl in this area—and waterfowl is what Oak Island is all about.

Sauvie Island (named for a French-Canadian employee of the Hudson's Bay Company) has, for thousands of years, been a resting place for migratory birds. At the peak of the fall migration, some 150,000 ducks and geese are here. Several thousand sandhill cranes come, as well. In all, some 250 species of birds spend some amount of time on the island each year, including bald eagles by the score in the winter. So if you were to go to Oak Island in the middle of a summer day, you might wonder what the big deal is. But if you come in the spring, or early on a summer day when the animals haven't hidden from the heat yet, you just might see a whole different world. And in fact, even though the bulk of the migratory birds are gone when the trail is open, there are numerous songbirds here, as well as ducks, geese, and even bald eagles who spend the whole summer.

From the trailhead, you walk a few minutes on the mowed roadway/trail to a junction. Along the way, be sure to grab a guide from the box; it corresponds to several signs around the trail. Go either way you wish, or strike off into the grassy meadows or woods. If you stay on the trail, going right will take you to a view of Sturgeon Lake, which at some times of the year might be a long way off because it's so shallow. Turn left here, and in 0.9 miles, when the signed trail turns left, follow another trail to the right 200 yards to The Narrows, a—you guessed it—slim body of water that connects Sturgeon Lake to the east with Steelman Lake to the west.

Continuing on the loop trail, you'll head back to the left and walk along a plowed area; Fish and Wildlife actually farms some 1,000 acres of its land on Sauvie Island as part of a cycle that brings alfalfa, corn, millet, and other foods to migratory birds in the winter and cattle in the summer.

And now for the other stroll—Warrior Rock.

In the fall of 1805 Lewis and Clark's Corps of Discovery floated down the Columbia River and managed to miss the Willamette River entirely. It wasn't that they were fools; it's just that the Willamette's entry was blocked from view by the forested wetland which is now called Sauvie Island. While much of it has long since been diked, and some is now farmed, about half of it is managed by the Oregon Department of Fish and Wildlife.

Lewis and Clark, while exploring the island that was the summer and fall home of the Multnomah Indians, actually camped on the beach that is just beyond the parking area. If for some reason you would like to skip the beach entirely, walk over a low point in the fence at the southern end of the parking lot, then walk through the pasture, parallel to the river, to the trees. You'll find the road there.

To start on the beach, follow the trail out onto it and stroll along, considering what it must have looked like in 1805, but also how quiet it is today. Look, also, for animal tracks leading from the woods to the water; raccoons, deer, and fox are all common here. But those critters mostly move around at night, and if the hunters and fishermen aren't out, you may have the place to yourselves.

If it's late summer or early fall when the river is low, you can make it almost the whole three miles to the lighthouse just staying on the beach. Otherwise, go as far as you want, and then look for a place to head up into the woods. Once up on the bluff, you will encounter a trail that once served as a service road to the lighthouse. Follow it through a world of blackberries, oak, alder, and maple. After about 2.5 miles, at a point where the trail is right at the top of the bluff, look to the right for an old shipwreck on the beach. Just a few minutes later, you'll come to a large meadow; stay right for 0.2 miles to the lighthouse.

Warrior Rock got its name when members of a 1792 English expedition up the Columbia (the party that named the river for their ship and Mount Hood for the head of the English navy) found themselves surrounded on this rock by dozens of native warriors. They made peace and lived to tell the tale. The lighthouse was maintained by the U.S. Coast Guard to warn ships of the rock. And speaking of ships, there's a decent chance you'll see an ocean-going vessel, making its way roughly 70 river miles from Portland to the Pacific Ocean at Astoria.

A hundred yards up the sandy beach to the left, somebody cut a perfect little bench into a large piece of driftwood; hopefully, the river will not have reclaimed it before you get there. A few minutes beyond that, at the northwestern tip of Sauvie Island, you'll come to old pilings which no one can seem to explain. Leading theories are it was a fish processing plant, a boatworks, or a loading dock for shipping milk from island dairies. Whatever it was, it offers a viewpoint of the town of Saint Helens, Oregon, which was founded in 1845—and in case you're wondering why the town and the nearby mountain are called Saint Helens, well, the same English sailors who named Hood and the Columbia named Mount St. Helens for the English ambassador to Spain at the time, a certain Baron Saint Helens. His real name was Fitzherbert; thank goodness they chose his official name.

Nothing like some useless trivia to think about while you're walking back to the car. And speaking of which, if you stay on the trail all the way, you'll come to the cow pasture above the beach where you started. Just walk across it—careful where you step—to the fenced parking area and step over the low portion of the fence to your right, next to the hunters' check-in stand.

And, for the record, Lewis and Clark saw the Willamette on the way home, in the spring of 1806. Clark stood on a bluff where the University of Portland is today.

## ▶ NEARBY ACTIVITIES

Many of the farms on Sauvie Island are "you-pick-em" operations, with treats like berries, flowers, pumpkins, and corn. One of them, on Reeder Road, even has a corn maze (or a maize maze). You can't miss it. Stop and get a little something for dinner on your way home, if you don't get lost. Also, the 1856 Bybee–Howell House, the oldest home in Multnomah County, is now a museum including farm implements from the old days. It's open weekends from June 3 through September 3.

# SERENE LAKE

## IN BRIEF

Several lakes, a flower-filled meadow, late-summer huckleberries, and some dramatic views await on this remote and little-known loop hike, which is just one of several options in the area. You can visit mountain lakes here with just over a mile of walking.

## DESCRIPTION

The recommended loop here is just one of several options from the trailhead. You could, for example, take Trail #700 down 1.3 miles to Shellrock Lake, and then another mile to Hideaway Lake. To access that one, walk to the uphill end of the parking area and follow an old road 100 feet, then follow the trail down to the lake.

But our loop is the most popular one in the area, because it takes in several lakes and a variety of scenery. Just bring mosquito repellant if you're here in the early summer.

From the trailhead, take the Serene Lake Trail (#512)—and ignore the mileage listed on these signs. They don't even agree with each other! Note, for example, that the sign here says

## KEY AT-A-GLANCE INFORMATION

**LENGTH:** 7.7 miles to do the whole thing

**CONFIGURATION:** Loop

**DIFFICULTY:** Moderate

**SCENERY:** Lakes, a meadow, forest, panoramic views

**EXPOSURE:** Shady most of the way, with a few open spots

**SOLITUDE:** Use is moderate on summer weekends, light otherwise.

**TRAIL SURFACE:** Packed dirt with roots and rocks

**HIKING TIME:** 5 hours

**SEASON:** June–October

**ELEVATION:** 4,600' at the trailhead, 3,940' at the lowest point

**ACCESS:** Northwest Forest Pass required.

**MAPS:** Green Trails # 492 (Fish Creek Mount) and #493 (High Rock)

**FACILITIES:** None at the trailhead; water on the trail should be treated.

**SPECIAL COMMENTS:** For more information, call Clackamas Ranger District, (503) 630-4256.

## DIRECTIONS

From Portland on OR 224, travel 44 miles southeast of I-205, through the town of Estacada, to the ranger station at Ripplebrook. Half a mile past the ranger station, turn left onto FS 57. Follow FS 57 for 7.6 miles, and turn left onto FS 58. After 7 miles, turn left, following a sign for High Rock, then 0.1 mile later, turn left onto FS 4610. Take that 1.3 miles and a left onto FS 4610-240, which is marked simply "240." The last 4.4 miles of the drive to this trailhead are narrow and pretty rough, so if your car is low to the ground, think about going someplace else. The trailhead is at the end of the road. Driving time is 1 hour and 40 minutes.

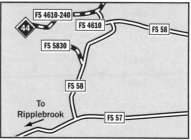

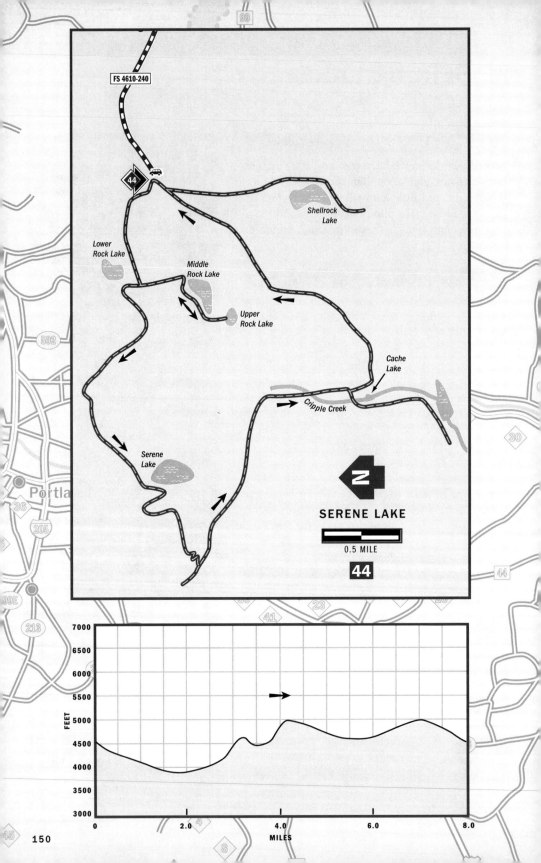

FS 4610-240

44

Shellrock
Lake

Lower
Rock Lake

Middle
Rock Lake

Upper Rock Lake

Cache
Lake

Cripple Creek

Serene
Lake

N

SERENE LAKE

0.5 MILE

44

Portla

FEET

7000
6500
6000
5500
5000
4500
4000
3500
3000

0        2.0        4.0        6.0        8.0

MILES

ROCK LAKES 0.5 MILES. When you get to the first trail junction (which is in 0.8 miles), notice that the sign now says it's a mile back to the trailhead and another quarter-mile to Lower Rock Lake. So ignore the signs.

From this junction, go left a couple hundred yards to Middle Rock Lake. From the campsite there, turn right, cross the creek, walk to the far end of the lake, then up the hill a short ways to Upper Rock Lake, the smallest of the three. That trail gets a little brushy and can be tough to follow in early summer. If you keep going around Middle Rock Lake to the left, you'll get to a nice rock where the water is deep just off shore— an excellent place to jump in.

Back at the main trail (in other words, had you not turned left for Middle Rock Lake) go another 0.2 miles and you'll come to a trail leading right to Lower Rock Lake. All these lakes are stocked with trout, by the way, so if you're into fishing, get a license and bring your rod. If you've got small kids, or you feel done for the day, go back to the car now, and you will have done around two miles. But for an even nicer lake, and then some, keep going.

You'll put in another half mile going downhill, then turn up for most of a mile to gain the top of a ridge, thick with bear grass. Just over the top of the hill (and three miles from the trailhead) you'll come to Serene Lake, which is nothing short of lovely. Fishermen pull 15-inch trout from its deep, cold, green water. The same boulders, grassy shallows, downed trees, and thickly vegetated shoreline that hide the fish also make for outstanding scenery for humans.

If you're camping, there are several excellent spots, one at the trail junction on the right side, one at the far end on a point that sticks out into the lake, and another on the left side. There's also a huge boulder about 100 yards along the shoreline from the trail junction, it's an awesome spot to jump into the (very cold) lake. There's a decent trail all the way around the lake, but you'll have to cross a couple of rock slides to make the circuit.

Beyond Serene Lake, the trail climbs about 500 feet in 0.8 miles to the top of a ridge and a junction with the Grouse Point Trail (#517). Turn left here, and at the top of the hill look for an open area to the left. There's no trail to it, but there's a cliff over there with a sublime view back down to Serene Lake, as well as of Mounts Saint Helens, Rainier, Adams, and Hood. The two bare peaks to the right are the Signal Buttes. Also, as you look north towards Hood, you're seeing an area of about eight miles as the crow flies with only one road and two trails to break it up.

Back on the trail, there's another (lesser) view from a one-acre clearcut, which was put in for helicopters to drop off firefighters.

Then you'll drop down quickly to Cache Meadow.

When you get to flower-filled Cache Meadow, you'll find an intersection. Turn left and go 200 yards to the remains of an old shelter that recently burned; just don't go stomping around in the meadow, as the flowers are very fragile.

To complete the loop, just keep going past the shelter for 300 yards, turn left onto Trail 517, and take it uphill one mile until you come to an abandoned fire road. Turn right again, and in a mile you'll be back at the car. Just keep an eye out, in the clear areas along the road, for a view back to Mount Jefferson. That makes this a five-volcano day!

# SILVER FALLS STATE PARK

## KEY AT-A-GLANCE INFORMATION

**LENGTH:** Up to 7.5 miles

**CONFIGURATION:** Loop

**DIFFICULTY:** Easy

**SCENERY:** Every type of waterfall in a forested canyon

**EXPOSURE:** Shady all the way

**TRAFFIC:** Use is heavy all spring and summer; otherwise, it's moderate or light.

**TRAIL SURFACE:** Pavement, gravel, and packed dirt; some falls are wheelchair-accessible.

**HIKING TIME:** 3 hours to hike the whole thing

**SEASON:** Year-round, but wet in winter and spring with occasional snow

**ACCESS:** $3 day-use fee per vehicle

**MAPS:** USGS Drake Crossing; free maps are available in the South Falls Lodge at the trailhead.

**FACILITIES:** Water, rest rooms, snack bar, and gift shop at the trailhead

**SPECIAL COMMENTS:** Dogs, even on a leash, are not allowed on the Canyon Trail. For more information, contact the Silver Falls State Park office at (503) 873-8681.

## IN BRIEF

If it's waterfalls you're after—especially the chance to get behind them—this is the hike of your dreams. It's an easy loop that's known as the Trail of Ten Falls. There are also shorter loops available, all of which take in views of one or more waterfalls.

## DESCRIPTION

This is the crown jewel of the Oregon State Parks system; it's also the most visited park in the state. Unless it's a rainy weekday in the winter, you probably won't be close to alone here, but it hardly matters. It's one of the finest walks around, especially if you're into waterfalls. By the way, Silver Creek was named not for its color but for a pioneer who settled here in the 1840s. He was known as "Silver" Smith because it was said he brought a bushel of silver dollars with him from back east.

At the trailhead, be sure to visit the South Falls Lodge, built of native stone and wood by the Civilian Conservation Corps (CCC) in 1941. You can warm yourself by two massive fireplaces, enjoy photos of the park and some of the tools used by the CCC, and take advantage of that most modern of conveniences, a snack bar with an espresso stand.

## DIRECTIONS

From Portland on I-5, drive 17 miles south of I-205 and take Exit 271/Woodburn. Turn left and follow OR 214 for 14 miles to Silverton. Note that you'll be turning right at 2.7 miles, then left at 3.9 miles. Both intersections have signs, but they could still be missed. In Silverton, follow signs for Silver Falls State Park, staying on OR 214 for 15 more miles. After entering the park, continue on OR 214 for 2.3 miles and park on the right at the South Falls parking area. Driving time is 1 hour and 15 minutes.

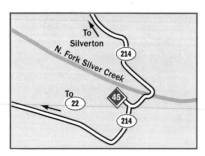

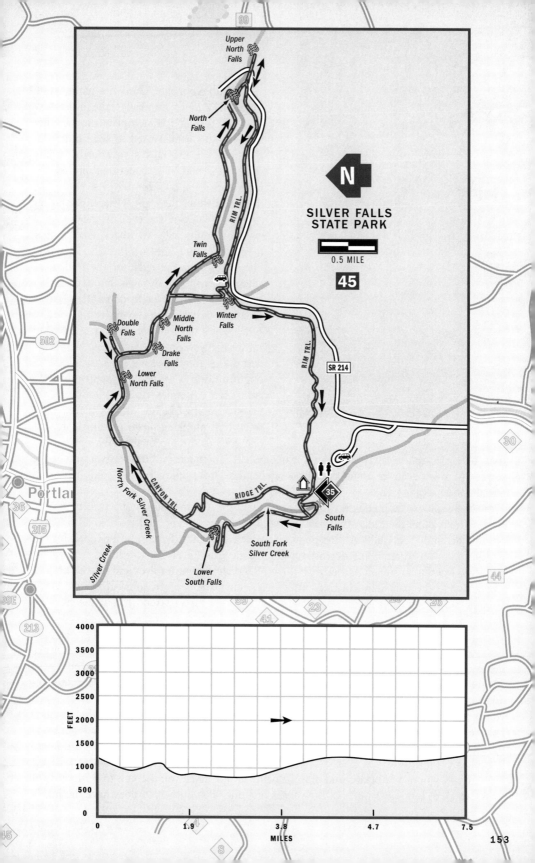

Upper North
Falls

North
Falls

RIM TRL.

Twin
Falls

N

SILVER FALLS
STATE PARK

0.5 MILE

45

Double
Falls

Middle
North
Falls

Winter
Falls

RIM TRL.

Drake
Falls

SR 214

Lower
North Falls

Portland

CANYON TRL.

RIDGE TRL.

35

North Fork Silver Creek

South
Falls

Silver Creek

South Fork
Silver Creek

Lower
South Falls

FEET

4000
3500
3000
2500
2000
1500
1000
500
0

0          1.9          3.8          4.7          7.5

MILES

Lower South Falls in Silver Fallls State Park

With your hot drink in hand, walk toward 177-foot South Falls, take in the view from the top, and contemplate the fact that in the 1920s a man used to send old automobiles over the falls as a Fourth of July stunt. It's said that fishermen pulled car parts out of the pool for decades. Now, take the trail behind the sign. (*Note*: this is as far as your dogs can go, even if they're on a leash.) The trail will switchback down for 0.2 miles, then go behind South Falls. The cave-like setting was created over the millennia, when water seeped through the rocks above, froze and expanded, and then cracked away the rocks that now lie at your feet.

When the trail comes to a bridge 100 yards later, you can cross it and make it a day with a 0.4-mile loop. It's the first of several opportunities to cut the loop short. But keep going for 0.8 miles to see 93-foot Lower South Falls. Just before you get there, you'll see a trail plunging down to the right; that one goes to the top of the falls, but beware that there's no rail to keep you from a fearsome fall. The main trail descends a number of steps, often wet even in summer, and passes behind Lower South Falls, a combination of curtain and cascade falls.

In 0.3 miles you'll come to your second chance to cut the loop short. Turn right, and it's one mile along the Ridge Trail back to the lodge; stay straight, and it's 1 mile to Lower North Falls, a 30-foot slide. At this point you've left the South Fork of Silver Creek for the North Fork; the two combine downstream of you to form Silver Creek—this is why you're suddenly walking upstream, rather than down. Keep an eye out for deer and beaver, both of which live in the park. Human tree-cutters left their mark, too; on some of the big cedar stumps you can still make out springboard slots, where loggers stood to cut the trees by hand.

Just past Lower North Falls, make sure to go left for a 0.1-mile side trip to see Double Falls, at 178 feet. Its shallow splash pool, which you can get in if you'd like, almost always hosts a rainbow when the sun is out. Back on the main trail, in the next 0.6 miles you'll pass 27-foot Drake Falls (named for a photographer whose images were instrumental in the creation of the park), and 103-foot Middle North Falls, which you can also go behind. When you get to the bridge (the halfway point for the full loop), you can turn right for one last chance to cut the loop short. Take this trail for half a mile to Winter Falls, and then continue past it, turn right onto the Rim Trail for 1.6 miles back to the lodge, and your day is done at 5.1 miles.

If you ignore the bridge and stay straight, in 0.3 miles you'll come to 31-foot Twin Falls, which at low water times of the year is just one falls, but which does have the hike's best picnic spot, right at the creek's edge. After another 0.9 miles (look for the rocks in the creek with ferns growing on top!), you come to North Falls, which you'll see coming for a while before you get there and which is probably the most spectacular falls in the park. Once again, the trail takes you behind the falls. Back there, look for the columns in the rock overhead, left when lava cooled around trees and then the trees rotted—15 million years ago!

After that, you have the only climb of any significance, up some steps to gain a couple hundred feet or so, then along a railing with another view back down to North Falls. When you get to the Rim Trail on the right, go ahead and put in the 0.4-mile loop to Upper North Falls, a seldom-visited 65-foot drop in an area with ample opportunity to wander around on the rocks.

On the Rim Trail's 2.5-mile trip back to the lodge, you'll pass by the top of Winter Falls, more of a damp spot in the late summer and fall, and through some pleasant forest where I have encountered deer on three occasions. When you get to the picnic area and road, stay right and you'll be back at the lodge. I recommend another coffee drink.

## ▶ NEARBY ACTIVITIES

Just upstream from the parking area, there's an official swimming area in Silver Creek. The kids should love it, and if it's a hot day, grown-ups could probably use a dip in the creek as well. There are also cabins you can rent for the night.

# SIOUXON CREEK

## KEY AT-A-GLANCE INFORMATION

**LENGTH:** 7.8 miles

**CONFIGURATION:** Out-and-back

**DIFFICULTY:** Moderate, but only because of the distance

**SCENERY:** Old-growth forest, waterfalls, pools in the river

**EXPOSURE:** Shady all the way

**TRAFFIC:** Use is moderate on summer weekends but light otherwise.

**TRAIL SURFACE:** Packed dirt with some rocks and roots

**HIKING TIME:** 3 hours

**SEASON:** Year-round, but muddy in winter and spring with occasional snow

**ACCESS:** Northwest Forest Pass required.

**MAPS:** Green Trails #396 (Lookout Mountain)

**FACILITIES:** None at the trailhead; the water on the trail must be treated

**SPECIAL COMMENTS:** For more information, contact the Mount St. Helens National Volcanic Monument office at (360) 247-3900.

## ▶ IN BRIEF

An easy, pleasant stroll along a mountain stream, with old-growth forest all around and waterfalls up above. What more could you want? Even the kids will like it; with supervision, they could go for a swim.

## ▶ DESCRIPTION

The only thing spectacular about this hike is how easy and scenic it is. There are no panoramic viewpoints, no exotic geological features, and no serious hiking challenges. It's just a beautiful river in a peaceful, lush, tree-filled canyon, with waterfalls all over the place and not too many hikers.

From the trailhead, there are several trails leading into the woods. Just take any of them and turn right when you reach the main trail. You'll walk downhill briefly and cross West Creek on a log bridge. At this point, Siouxon Creek will be far below you so getting to it isn't worth the effort; that chance will come later. At 0.9 miles you'll see, on the right, the Horseshoe Ridge Trail. Ignore it. After 1.4 miles the trail crosses Horseshoe Creek (so named because it drains a horseshoe-shaped ridge, of which you're crossing the open mouth).

## ▶ DIRECTIONS

From Portland on I-205, drive five miles north of the Columbia River and take Exit 30/Orchards. Turn right onto WA 500, which turns into WA 503 in 0.9 miles (follow signs for Battle Ground). Stay on WA 503 for 25 miles, passing through the town of Amboy. Just past the Mount St. Helens National Volcanic Monument headquarters, turn right onto NE Healy Road. Go nine miles (note that Healy turns into FS 54 at 2.4 miles), then turn left (uphill) on FS 57. After 1.2 miles on FS 57, turn left onto FS 5701. The trailhead is 3.6 miles ahead, at the end of the road. Driving time is 1 hour and 15 minutes.

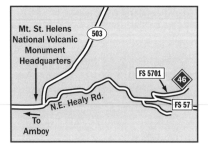

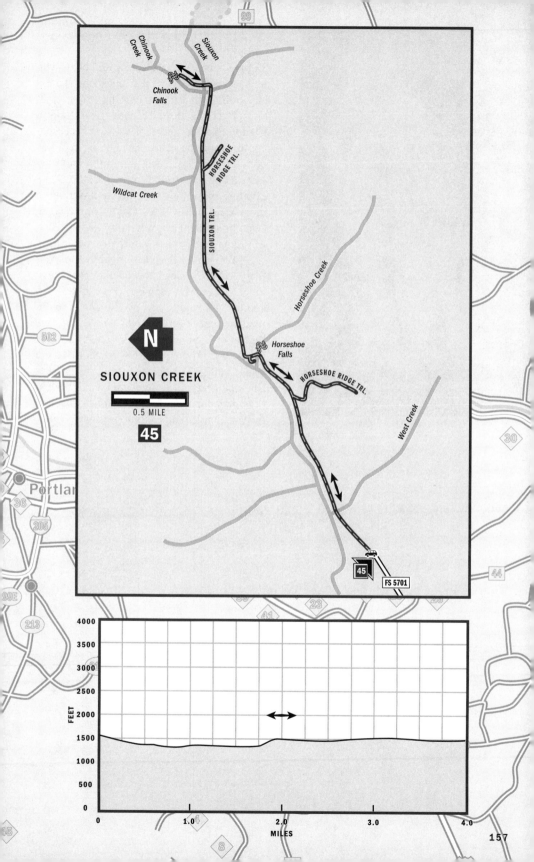

Chinook
Creek

Siouxon
Creek

Chinook
Falls

HORSESHOE
RIDGE TRL.

Wildcat Creek

SIOUXON TRL.

Horseshoe Creek

Horseshoe
Falls

HORSESHOE RIDGE TRL.

West Creek

**N**

**SIOUXON CREEK**

0.5 MILE

**45**

**45**   FS 5701

Portland

4000

3500

3000

2500

2000

1500

1000

500

0

FEET

0   1.0   2.0   3.0   4.0

MILES

Chinook Falls at the upper end of the Siouxon Creek hike

There will be a waterfall above and below you here; to get a view of the lower one, take a side trail to the left just after the bridge.

Over the next 0.3 miles you'll climb slightly to a viewpoint of Siouxon Falls that could almost be called a really big rapid as opposed to a classic falls. Then the trail traverses along flat ground for half a mile, some 200 feet above the creek, before dropping to its side for half a mile. This is where some swimming might happen—just know that it would be brief, unless you're part polar bear.

When a trail comes in from the right (the second appearance of the Horseshoe Ridge Trail), you've gone three miles. Go another 0.7 miles and you'll come to an unnamed creek on the right and a nice new bridge over Siouxon Creek, which at this point flows through a narrow gorge. Cross the bridge and go 0.3 miles to beautiful, 50-foot Chinook Creek Falls. Sit down here or back at the bridge for a snack, and then head back to the car. Simple but beautiful, wasn't it?

# SOUTH FORK TOUTLE RIVER

## ▶ IN BRIEF

Without driving all the way around to the other side of Mount St. Helens, this is the most dramatic view you can get of the results of that mountain's 1980 eruption. A major mudflow went all the way down the Toutle (*toodle*) River to the Columbia, where shipping was stopped for days while the debris was dredged out. This hike will show you the South Fork of that river, where the mudflow was half a mile wide, as well as a glimpse of the majesty that the eruption destroyed.

## ▶ DESCRIPTION

First, an important note. As of the summer of 2003, the last 3.7 miles of the road to this trailhead were closed due to a landslide. The Forest Service had the intention, but no schedule, to rebuild it. So call ahead for the latest information. If it hasn't been rebuilt, you can still do this hike, but it will be six roundtrip miles longer, because you'll have to park at the Blue Lake trailhead and walk three miles down the Toutle Trail to the junction mentioned below, the one that's 0.6 miles from the trailhead at the end of FS 8123. From the Blue Lake trailhead, just stay left on the Toutle Trail. If the road is open, ignore this paragraph and proceed as described below.

## ▶ DIRECTIONS

From Portland on I-5, drive 21 miles north of the Columbia River and take Exit 21/Woodland. Turn right onto WA 503 (Lewis River Road) and travel 28 miles; then turn left onto FS 8100, between mileposts 35 and 36, following a sign for Kalama recreation area. Travel 11.5 miles on FS 8100, and then stay straight at a junction, which puts you on FS 8123. The trailhead is at the end of FS 8123, 6.4 miles ahead. Driving time is 1 hour and 25 minutes.

## ⓘ KEY AT-A-GLANCE INFORMATION

**LENGTH:** 7 miles

**CONFIGURATION:** Loop

**DIFFICULTY:** Hard

**SCENERY:** Old-growth forest, waterfalls in canyons, flower-filled meadows

**EXPOSURE:** Most of the hike is shady until the end when you'll be out in the open.

**TRAFFIC:** Use is moderate on summer weekends but light otherwise.

**TRAIL SURFACE:** Packed dirt with rocks and roots in most places; some areas are just rock.

**HIKING TIME:** 4 hours

**SEASON:** June–October

**ACCESS:** Northwest Forest Pass required.

**MAPS:** USFS Mount St. Helens National Monument

**FACILITIES:** None at trailhead; the water on the trail must be treated.

**SPECIAL COMMENTS:** For more information, contact the Mount St. Helens National Volcanic Monument office at (360) 247-3900.

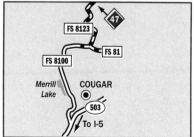

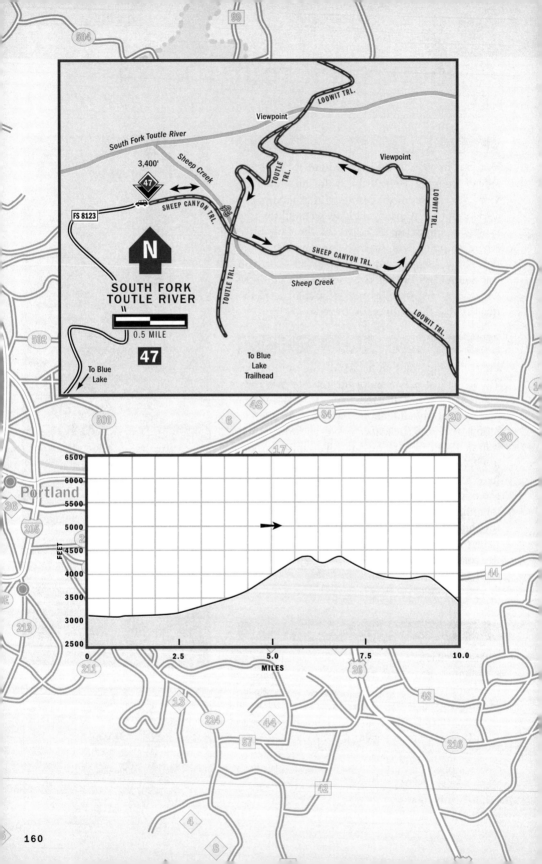

South Fork Toutle River

LOOWIT TRL.

Viewpoint

Viewpoint

South Fork Toutle River

3,400'

Sheep Creek

47

TOUTLE TRL.

LOOWIT TRL.

FS 8123

SHEEP CANYON TRL.

SHEEP CANYON TRL.

Sheep Creek

LOOWIT TRL.

N

TOUTLE TRL.

SOUTH FORK
TOUTLE RIVER

0.5 MILE

47

To Blue
Lake

To Blue
Lake
Trailhead

FEET

6500
6000
5500
5000
4500
4000
3500
3000
2500

0        2.5        5.0        7.5        10.0

MILES

From the trailhead at the end of FS 8123, things will be easy for the first 0.6 miles, giving you a chance to get warmed up. After that, you get to a rock cairn, marking a trail junction. To the left the trail leads across a bridge that spans Sheep Canyon; that's the way you'll be coming back. For the loop, keep going straight and start climbing gradually through a lovely forest. Just after some neat cliffs appear on the right, look for a triple-trunked fir tree to the right of the trail.

After 2.2 miles (1.6 since the junction) you'll come to an intersection with the Loowit Trail, which goes all the way around Mount St. Helens. Turn left here and climb just a little more, through a wonderful subalpine area of firs and hemlocks. In August the place will be ablaze with flowers, especially blue lupine.

Soon you'll drop down and traverse an ash-filled ravine with a pond below you. Keep an eye out among the trees down there for deer or elk. After a little more climbing you'll find yourself at the top of a cliff looking out over the canyon of the South Fork Toutle River. The river, some 800 feet below you, is in the process of recarving its way through the mudflow. The contrast between your side of the canyon and the other side, well within the blast zone, couldn't be more stark.

The trail will now turn downhill, descending Crescent Ridge, for 1.5 miles to a junction with the Toutle Trail. Go to the right here, exploring around the edge of the mini-gorge the river has cut into the mudflow. Then go back to the Toutle Trail and follow it for 1.5 miles through old-growth forest. You'll climb over a small ridge, but the reward is a field of huckleberries at the bridge over Sheep Canyon. Cross that bridge, turn right at the junction, and you're 0.6 miles from the car.

## ▶ NEARBY ACTIVITIES

If you'd like to see what this eruption was all about, go see the award-winning 28-minute film on the giant screen at Castle Rock, Washington. Castle Rock is at Exit 48 on I-5, 27 miles north of Woodland. You can't miss the theater.

# TABLE MOUNTAIN

## KEY AT-A-GLANCE INFORMATION

**LENGTH:** 8.6 miles

**CONFIGURATION:** Out-and-back

**DIFFICULTY:** Hard

**SCENERY:** 5 volcanoes and the whole gorge from the top

**EXPOSURE:** Shady, then open rock at the top

**TRAFFIC:** Use is moderate on summer weekends but light otherwise.

**TRAIL SURFACE:** Grass, packed dirt with rocks

**HIKING TIME:** 5 hours

**SEASON:** Year-round, but it occasionally gets snowfall on top.

**ACCESS:** No fees or permits needed.

**MAPS:** USGS Bonneville Dam

**FACILITIES:** The trailhead for the longer hike has toilets; the other one doesn't. Neither trailhead has water. Water along the way must be treated.

**SPECIAL COMMENTS:** For more information, call the Columbia River Gorge National Scenic Area office at (541) 386-2333.

## IN BRIEF

This tough climb has a great reward on top: one of the best panoramas in the whole Columbia River Gorge, including a bird's-eye view of the Bonneville Dam, from a lunch spot atop 800-foot cliffs.

## DESCRIPTION

The first part of this hike might leave you wondering why you chose it. Walking under power lines isn't the most thrilling outdoors experience to be had. But this route to Table Mountain's spectacular summit is shorter and much less crowded than the one on the Pacific Crest Trail (PCT), so hang in there. Just step over the cable and follow the grassy road—really just a mowed clearing—under the power lines. After 0.2 miles, turn left (still following the power lines) and cross a brushy creek. At the first tower beyond the creek, follow a trail that leads into the woods on the right.

This trail will go a flat 0.2 miles west, cross a tiny creek, and join an old, overgrown logging

## DIRECTIONS

From Portland on I-84, drive 37 miles east of I-205 and take Exit 44/Cascade Locks. As soon as you enter the town, take your first right to get on the Bridge of the Gods, following a sign for Stevenson, Washington. Pay a $1 toll on the bridge, and at the far end, turn left onto WA 14. The North Bonneville Trailhead is located two miles on the right—this is the starting point for the longer hike and also has the only public toilet in the area. To go for the shorter hike, continue another 1.1 mile on WA 14 and turn right, crossing under the railroad tracks. Just beyond the tracks, turn right onto Cascade Drive and travel 1.2 miles, to where the road crosses under power lines next to Greenleaf Slough. The trail begins beyond a cable blocking a grassy road that follows the power lines north. Driving time is 45 minutes.

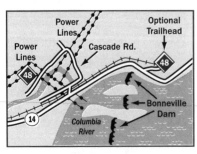

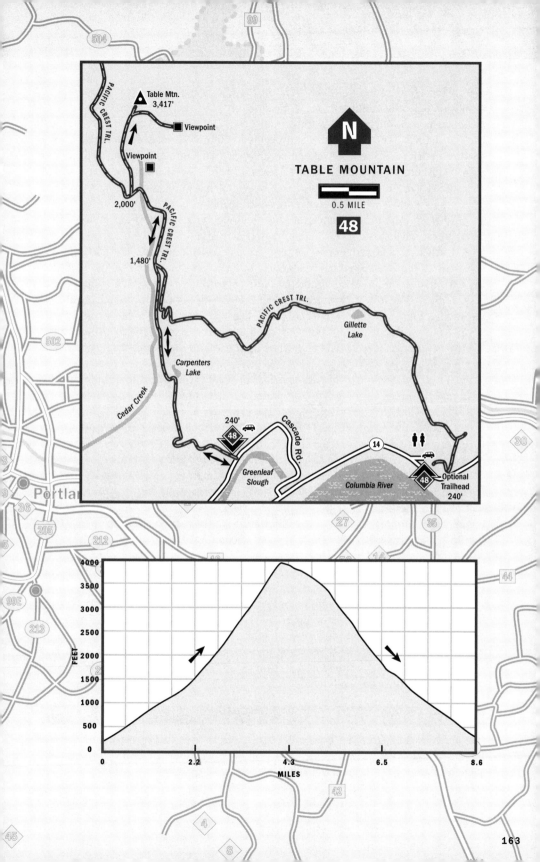

PACIFIC CREST TRL.

△ Table Mtn.
3,417'

■ Viewpoint

Viewpoint
■

2,000'

PACIFIC CREST TRL.

1,480'

**N**

**TABLE MOUNTAIN**

0.5 MILE

**48**

PACIFIC CREST TRL.

Gillette
Lake

Carpenters
Lake

Cedar Creek

240'
**48**

Cascade Rd

14

**48**
Optional
Trailhead
240'

Greenleaf
Slough

Columbia River

Portland

4000
3500
3000
2500
2000
1500
1000
500
0

FEET

0          2.2          4.3          6.5          8.6
MILES

road, which (unlike the trail) is visible on the USGS map. Follow this road slightly uphill for 0.4 miles until you see a meadow on your right. (At the far end of this meadow, though tough to see, is Carpenters Lake.) Now follow the road as it switches back to the left, then right again, and begins to climb the ridge. For one mile you'll parallel Cedar Creek on your left, in an area with far more alders than cedars, and then you'll intersect the PCT. Had you started back at North Bonneville, you would have hiked five (admittedly easy) miles to get to this point; by starting under the power lines, you've cut that distance to about two miles.

Turn left onto the PCT and continue climbing moderately through a more interesting forest. There are a few Douglas firs of decent size, but this whole area has been logged, much of it more than once. After 0.3 miles, a side trail leads left to a campsite; stay right on the PCT. About 0.4 miles later, a trail enters from the right; ignore it.

Around 0.3 miles later, at a large, moss-covered rock on the right, you'll intersect another trail. Turn right onto it and start climbing through the woods. And I do mean climbing: Right now you're at 2,000 feet elevation; in 1.2 miles you'll be at 3,417 feet. You'll start in the woods but soon pop out onto the sometimes-loose rock known as scree. A steep switchback winds up toward the ridge top, then gains it and just keeps going up and up.

When you get to the top, and catch your breath, you'll find that trails actually crisscross the broad summit. Stay to the left for views of Mounts St. Helens, Rainier, and Adams. Go right (toward the Columbia River) for a spectacular view that ranges from Dog Mountain and Mount Defiance to Mount Hood, looking right up the Eagle Creek drainage. Beware that the final portions of this trail literally take you a foot away from a drop of hundreds of feet, and there's no protection.

Those cliffs are part of Table Mountain's fascinating geological history. As you look out toward the Columbia, you can start to make out the fact that the southern half of Table Mountain actually slid into the river, leaving behind the cliffs and narrowing the Columbia to just a couple hundred yards at the most (at the point where the Bridge of the Gods crosses). This slide, encompassing an area of more than 10 square miles, occurred about 700 years ago—basically yesterday in geologic time. It created first a natural dam that blocked the river, then the Cascades of the Columbia, which were submerged when the Bonneville Dam went in.

Now look up at Mount Hood. On the left skyline you can see a ridge leading up to a bump just below the snow line. That's Cooper Spur (see page 50). For a real adventure, hike up that one and look for Table Mountain.

You may notice a trail descending the south side of the mountain via an open steep section called Heartbreak Ridge. Don't use it, as it's becoming highly eroded. It's also treacherous and no fun at all.

## ▶ NEARBY ACTIVITIES

Just across WA 14 from the Bonneville North Trailhead is the Visitor Center for the Bonneville Dam, a worthwhile side trip to see the powerhouse and, in spring and fall, salmon migrating up through the fish ladder.

# TAMANAWAS FALLS

## ▶ IN BRIEF

A classic falls in a dramatic setting at the end of an easy, beautiful hike. Tamanawas is a Chinook word for a friendly, guardian spirit, and it's pronounced "ta-MAH-na-was."

## ▶ DESCRIPTION

So many people like this trail that even a flood that wiped out half the bridges on it didn't stop them from going up there. Officially, the trail was closed in the summer of 2000, but Oregonians displayed their typical respect for the government by hiking the "closed" trail in such numbers that the Forest Service acquiesced and put in some helpful additions here and there.

The funny thing about that flood is that the creek that did the damage, Polallie Creek, is spring-fed. I spoke with a ranger who said nobody could figure out how a creek that isn't fed by glaciers could suddenly whip up a flood that actually took out three bridges—two on our trail and one above the falls on the Bluegrass Ridge Trail. She called it a "weird event." Whatever the cause, the Forest Service probably won't rebuild the bridges, so the trail you hike today is what the locals came up with in 2000.

The lower part of the trail was untouched. From the trailhead, walk to your right and cross the East Fork of the Hood River on a one-log bridge with handrails. Note the milky color of this river; that's glacial silt. Ignore a trail going up that stream, and instead contour right, paralleling the

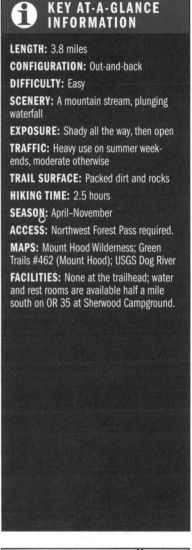

## ⓘ KEY AT-A-GLANCE INFORMATION

**LENGTH:** 3.8 miles

**CONFIGURATION:** Out-and-back

**DIFFICULTY:** Easy

**SCENERY:** A mountain stream, plunging waterfall

**EXPOSURE:** Shady all the way, then open

**TRAFFIC:** Heavy use on summer weekends, moderate otherwise

**TRAIL SURFACE:** Packed dirt and rocks

**HIKING TIME:** 2.5 hours

**SEASON:** April–November

**ACCESS:** Northwest Forest Pass required.

**MAPS:** Mount Hood Wilderness; Green Trails #462 (Mount Hood); USGS Dog River

**FACILITIES:** None at the trailhead; water and rest rooms are available half a mile south on OR 35 at Sherwood Campground.

## ▶ DIRECTIONS

From Portland on US 26, drive 51 miles east of I-205 and turn north on OR 35, following signs for Hood River. After 14 miles on OR 35, and half a mile past the Sherwood Campground, park at the trailhead on the left. Driving time is 1 hour and 30 minutes.

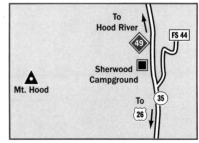

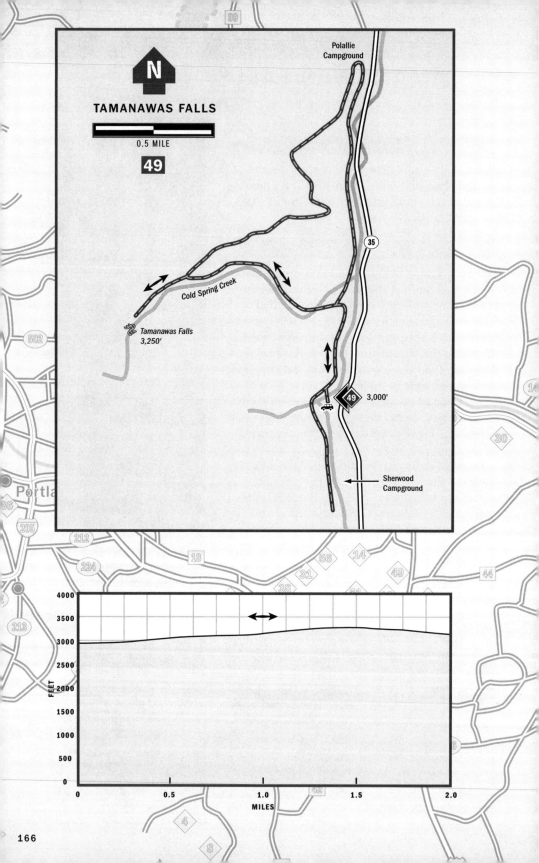

**N**

**TAMANAWAS FALLS**

0.5 MILE

**49**

Polallie
Campground

35

Cold Spring Creek

Tamanawas Falls
3,250'

**49** 3,000'

Sherwood
Campground

Tamanawas Falls in its natural amphitheater

road for 0.6 miles before crossing Cold Spring Creek on another log bridge. This time, ignore the trail that contours right and instead turn upstream.

In less than half a mile, you'll come to a rockslide area and a trail splitting off to the right. The original Tamanawas Falls Trail went left here and crossed the creek on a bridge, but that bridge was wiped out in 2000. The bulk of it was last seen down by the highway. So the new plan was to stay straight and upstream until you're in the face of a larger, older rock slide. It was here that locals made their new way in 2000.

This larger rock slide has been here for a long time; it is, in fact, the reason the trail used to cross the creek for a while. The upper bridge that was wiped out crossed back to your current side of the creek, right at the base of the slide. The way to get across the rocks is to stay high and to the right; there's actually a fairly easy way across it up there. If you look to the far side of the slide, perhaps 150 yards away, you'll see two things: a section of railing that marks the continuation of the trail, and several pieces of bright ribbon on trees, installed by the Forest Service when they realized their "trail closed" note at the trailhead wasn't stopping anybody. Just aim for those markers, and you'll be fine. And when you get there, check out the ruins of the upper bridge lying in the creek. After that, it's about 0.2 miles to the falls.

What makes this falls so special is that even in late summer there's plenty of water coming over it, and also that it's rimmed by basalt walls, much of which are pink because pieces have so recently fallen into the chasm. For this reason, take care if you want to go nearer (or even behind) the falls, as you'll be walking on wet rocks with no official trail and cliffs above you—cliffs that have left ample evidence all around you that pieces of them could come crashing down at any time. These are just little reminders from Mother Nature that we are, after all, visiting her world.

## ▶ NEARBY ACTIVITIES

Travel north on OR 35 and in 7.5 miles turn left and visit the Hutson Museum in Parkdale. It features local history, Indian artifacts, and memorabilia of the early settlers.

# TILLAMOOK HEAD

## KEY AT-A-GLANCE INFORMATION

**LENGTH:** 3 to 10 miles

**CONFIGURATION:** Out-and-back or one-way with a car shuttle

**DIFFICULTY:** Easy/hard

**SCENERY:** Beaches, cliffs above the sea, historic lighthouse

**EXPOSURE:** Mostly in the shade

**TRAFFIC:** Use is heavy all summer, more so on weekends; it's moderate otherwise.

**TRAIL SURFACE:** Packed dirt with roots; year-round mud in some places

**HIKING TIME:** 1 to 5 hours

**SEASON:** Year-round, but muddy in winter

**ACCESS:** To park at Indian Beach or the Ecola Picnic Area, there's a $3 per-vehicle day-use fee.

**MAPS:** USGS Tillamook Head

**FACILITIES:** Trailheads at Ecola State Park and Indian Beach have toilets.

**SPECIAL COMMENTS:** For more information, call the Ecola State Park office at (503) 436-2844.

## IN BRIEF

Hiking options abound among the scenic splendor of Tillamook Head and Ecola State Park. You can sample a beach stroll, dramatic viewpoints, and pieces of history on trail segments, and you're guaranteed to come home amazed. If you make the moderate hike up Tillamook Head, you can even follow in the footsteps of the Lewis and Clark expedition.

## DESCRIPTION

If you were measuring great views per mile of walking, this would be the most efficient area you could visit. Just walking the easy, three-mile round-trip from the picnic area to Indian Beach, you'll get several views of the rock-and-sand-and-water magnificence below. Do as much hiking as you feel up to here, and then kick back on a beach somewhere or stroll around Cannon Beach or Seaside.

First, a little history. On January 7, 1806, William Clark was on his way to see a beached whale the natives had told him about. He and 12 others, including Sacagawea, went over Tillamook Head (he humbly named it "Clark's Mountain") on a trail that forms the basis of the modern-day

## DIRECTIONS

From Portland on US 26, travel 74 miles west of I-405 and turn south on US 101. Go 4 miles and take the first Cannon Beach exit. At the bottom of the hill, turn right, following a sign for Ecola State Park. (*Note:* To avoid paying the $3 fee and to add a couple of viewpoints to your day, park at the "park-and-ride" lot at the bottom of this hill, walk up the state park road 0.9 miles, and take a 1.1-mile trail on the left to the picnic area.) After driving up the road two miles, you'll come to the entrance booth. The picnic area is on the left, and Indian Beach is 1.5 miles to the right. Driving time is 1 hour and 20 minutes.

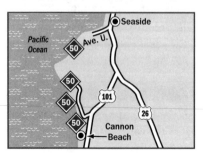

Pacific Ocean

Seaside

**50**

Viewpoint

**N**

TILLAMOOK HEAD

0.5 MILE

**50**

Viewpoint

Indian
Point

Indian
Beach

Ecola
Point

**50**

Pacific Ocean

Park
-N-
Ride

Cannon
Beach

101

4000
3500
3000
2500
2000
1500
1000
500
0

FEET

0          2.5          5.0          7.5          10.0
MILES

Indian Beach in Ecola State Park

path. Clark wrote of the view, "From this point I beheld the grandest and most pleasing prospects which my eyes ever surveyed." He also said the coast had "a most romantic appearance." From his description, it's pretty certain that the exact piece of land he stood on washed into the sea decades ago, but you can still experience pretty much the same view.

And if you're wondering about the name Ecola, it comes from the local Indians' word for whale, not anything to do with the deadly bacteria that sounds similar.

From the Ecola State Park picnic area, take a well-marked trail to the north. In its easy 1.5 miles it never gets far from the view, and at a couple of points it's right at the edge of the cliff—though with fences. When you get to Indian Beach, a favorite with surfers, go left and wander down to the sand for a bit.

The trail north of Indian Beach, tougher than the trail south of it, starts just beyond the rest room. After 100 yards, turn left onto a trail that starts climbing pretty quickly. You'll pass another view or two, but you'll also go through muddy patches. After 1.6 miles you'll come to an old road. Turn left for an ocean view from more than 700 feet up, and also for a World War II–era bunker that housed radar equipment. The lighthouse out there—which no matter what it looks like is a full mile from the coast—was built in 1881 but decommissioned in 1957. It was known as "Terrible Tilly" by the unfortunate souls who used to live out there and maintain the light. Strangely enough, in 1980 it was bought and converted into a columbarium, a repository for the ashes of cremated bodies. The owners make deliveries by helicopter.

Back up the road, turn right to head back to your car, or left for more forest and more views. In one place, not far up on the right, a massive sitka spruce fell over in 1998 but two years later was still being held up by a tree, less than a foot thick, that it just happened to land squarely on top of. Half a mile past the road, and after some switchback climbing, you'll come to a series of viewpoints out to the left, one of which is officially known as Clark's Point of View. Trouble is, a sign marking the spot tends to disappear, presumably tossed into the sea by yahoos.

The official summit of Tillamook Head is 1,130 feet above the sea, and 2.1 miles north of this point. You'll be traveling through mixed forest with the usual views, but my recommendation is to turn back unless you have a car at the Seaside trailhead. At this point, you are 2.1 miles from Indian Beach, 3.6 miles from the picnic area, and 5.6 miles from Cannon Beach. If you did stash a car at Seaside, you're 3.8 miles from there. The trail will continue until the viewless summit, then switchback down for 1.7 miles to the trailhead.

### ▶ NEARBY ACTIVITIES

Seaside is a beachside tourist town. It's worth a stroll, if only to choose between all the fudge, corn dog, and elephant ear outlets on its "Million-Dollar Walk." If you're looking for a little history, there's a model of Lewis and Clark's saltworks (a stove to extract salt from sea water) in Seaside, as well.

# TIMBERLINE LODGE

## KEY AT-A-GLANCE INFORMATION

**LENGTH:** 12.3 miles to Paradise Park; 6 miles to Zigzag Canyon; 2.2 miles to Silcox Hut; 1 mile to White River Canyon

**CONFIGURATION:** Paradise Park, balloon; Zigzag and White River Canyon, out-and-backs; Silcox Hut, loop

**DIFFICULTY:** Easy/hard

**SCENERY:** Meadows filled with flowers, deep canyons, glaciers overhead

**EXPOSURE:** Alternates between shady and open

**TRAFFIC:** Use is heavy all summer long.

**TRAIL SURFACE:** Packed dirt, rock, pavement

**HIKING TIME:** 0.5 to 5 hours

**SEASON:** July–October

**ACCESS:** No fees or permits needed.

**MAPS:** Mount Hood Wilderness; Green Trails #462 (Mount Hood)

**FACILITIES:** The lodge is a full-service hotel.

**SPECIAL COMMENTS:** No matter what the weather looks like, even at the trailhead, carry warm clothing on this hike. Mountain weather changes quickly, and Paradise Park is on a normally windswept ridge. For more information, call the Mount Hood Visitor Information Center at (503) 622-7674.

## IN BRIEF

If you spent just one day in Oregon, you should spend it at Timberline Lodge. If you only go on one hike, you should go to Paradise Park in August or early September. But if you aren't up to a 12-mile loop, options abound at this spectacular mountain palace.

## DESCRIPTION

Timberline Lodge is the greatest man-made thing in Oregon. It was built in 1937 by the Works Progress Administration and dedicated by Pres. Franklin D. Roosevelt the same day he dedicated Bonneville Dam. As astounding as the interior is, it's the setting of the place that requires time to be spent there. Only a few peaks in Oregon are above it, and with few trees around, the views are amazing—especially to the summit of Mount Hood, three miles away and the highest point in the state, and to Mount Jefferson, 45 miles to the south. In August, wildflowers bloom all over the place.

Let's start with the shortest hike, to the White River Canyon overlook. Follow a sign to the right of the lodge, pointing you to the Pacific Crest Trail (PCT). You'll walk uphill a couple hundred yards, perhaps wondering why you're suddenly breathing heavily: there's not as much oxygen up here. At the PCT, turn right (that would be toward Mexico) and walk a half mile to the overlook.

If you'd like to do a one-way hike with a car shuttle, this trail connects (in another half a mile) with the top of the Barlow Pass hike (see page 20).

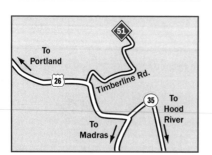

## DIRECTIONS

From Portland on US 26, drive 48 miles east of I-205 and turn left onto well-marked Timberline Road, two miles past Government Camp. Follow Timberline Road six winding miles to the parking lot. Driving time is 1 hour and 20 minutes.

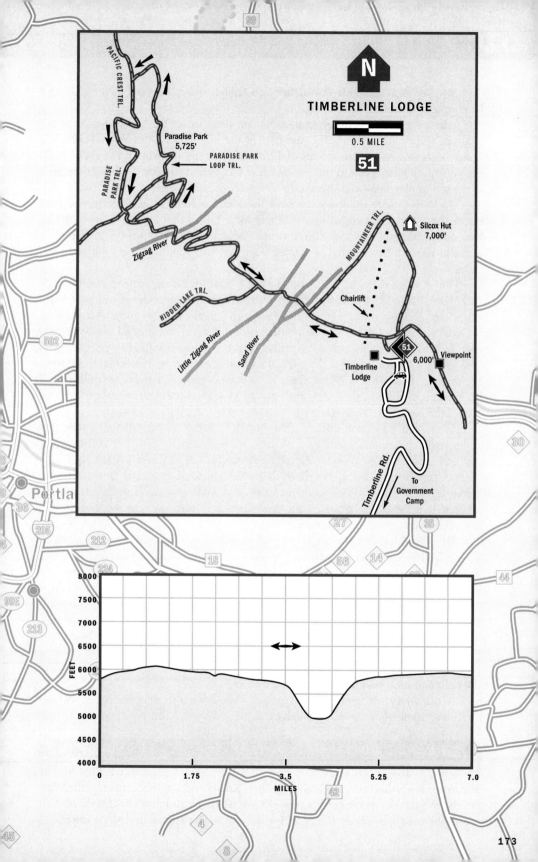

PACIFIC CREST TRL.

Paradise Park
5,725'

PARADISE PARK
LOOP TRL.

PARADISE PARK TRL.

Zigzag River

HIDDEN LAKE TRL.

Little Zigzag River

Sand River

# N

## TIMBERLINE LODGE

0.5 MILE

**51**

MOUNTAINEER TRL.

Silcox Hut
7,000'

Chairlift

Timberline
Lodge

6,000'

**51**

Viewpoint

Timberline Rd.

To
Government
Camp

Portla

FEET

8000
7500
7000
6500
6000
5500
5000
4500
4000

0        1.75        3.5        5.25        7.0

MILES

For our next toughest destination, go straight when you get to the PCT and head uphill 1.1 mile to Silcox Hut.

There seem to be a lot of small trails, but you can see the hut at the top of the chairlift, so just head for it. The last part of the hike is on a dirt road. Timberline Lodge rents this hut out to groups of 12 or more during the winter. For about $100 per person, they take you to the hut by Snow Cat, cook your dinner, then come back in the morning to cook your breakfast.

To loop back to the lodge, go back the way you came or take the service road under the chairlift. Or, for a slightly longer loop, take a trail that goes right (as you look down) from the top of the lift. It drops one mile to the PCT west of the lodge, in forest broken up by flowered meadows. Turn left and you'll be at the lodge in 0.8 miles.

But enough with the preliminaries: Let's head for Zigzag Canyon and Paradise Park. From the lodge, follow the PCT to your left; it will cross under two chairlifts and start descending slowly as it enters the woods. In 0.8 miles, ignore the trail leading up to Silcox Hut. In 1.4 miles, ignore a trail to the left leading to Hidden Lake (it's a nice lake, but it's three miles below you). Just keep on truckin' until, at three miles, you find yourself standing agog at the edge of a massive canyon, with Mount Hood looming to your right. This is Zigzag Canyon. If you've had enough at this point, head back, and you will have done a six-mile out-and-back trip. But for the real prize of this part of the mountain, keep going.

Now, you may have noticed that Paradise Park is actually below Timberline Lodge, making it sound pretty easy. What you need to know, however, is that in the next mile or less, while crossing Zigzag Canyon, you will go down 500 feet and back up 400. Just believe that it's worth it, and press on. You'll cross the Zigzag River on stones (look for the waterfall just upstream), and when you climb to the other side, take the first right (the Paradise Park Loop Trail, 3.7 miles after the lodge) and, yes, keep climbing toward Paradise Park.

This is where things start to get really spectacular. The number and variety of flowers in this area—lupine, daisies, lilies, and those bushy-looking pasque flowers— as well as the plump sweetness of huckleberries in late summer make it a prime destination. After 1 mile, the Paradise Park Trail comes in from the left; you can take it 0.6 miles down to the PCT and shorten your walk by 3.8 miles. But those 3.8 miles are flat and filled with beauty, so keep going. In 1 mile things open up considerably, and in 1.4 miles you'll rejoin the PCT. For British Columbia, turn right; for Timberline Lodge, turn left. In 2.4 miles you'll reach the lower intersection with the Paradise Park Trail. Stay on the PCT as it turns left and starts downhill, and in 0.1 mile stay to the right and drop back into Zigzag Canyon.

From there, just retrace your steps and look forward to all of the coffee and hot chocolate drinks they serve at the lodge.

▶ **NEARBY ACTIVITIES**

Though crowded, spend some time exploring Timberline Lodge. Watch the film The *Builders of Timberline* to hear the story of how artists and artisans came together during the Depression to create this masterwork. Then get to know the details of their accomplishment, especially the Head House with its massive central stone tower.

# TRAPPER CREEK WILDERNESS

## ▶ IN BRIEF

This is like a secret hike. Most people have never heard of it, but everybody who goes there loves it. It's quiet and woodsy with lots of creeks, two waterfalls, and—if you're up for some elevation— a great view from Observation Peak.

## ▶ DESCRIPTION

I can't explain why so few people have heard of Trapper Creek. It's barely an hour from Portland, it's loaded with trails, and it couldn't be any prettier. If you're a fan of the forest and don't mind climbing, this is the place to be. One section of the wilderness was actually set aside in the 1950s as a research area for old-growth Pacific Silver Firs. And up on the ridge, there are huckleberries—the big, blue, juicy kind—everywhere.

The wilderness covers a little over 6,000 acres, and it's basically one U-shaped watershed, drained by Trapper Creek and its many tributaries. It's heavily forested with firs, hemlocks, cedars and pines. Wildflowers are abundant in the spring and early summer, and the animals here include owls, black bears, cougars, and bobcats—though the only sign I've seen of any of those was the sound of an owl and some very fresh, berry-filled

## ▶ DIRECTIONS

From Portland on I-84, drive 37 miles east of I-205 and take Exit 44/Cascade Locks. As soon as you enter the town, make your first right to get on the Bridge of the Gods, following a sign for Stevenson, Washington. Pay the $1 toll, cross the river, and turn right onto WA 14. Go 5.8 miles and turn left, following a sign for Carson, Washington. This is Wind River Road. After 20 miles on this road, stay straight, leaving Wind River Road and following a sign for Government Mineral Springs. Half a mile later, turn right on FS 5401; the trailhead is 0.4 miles ahead, at the end of the road. Driving time is 1 hour and 5 minutes.

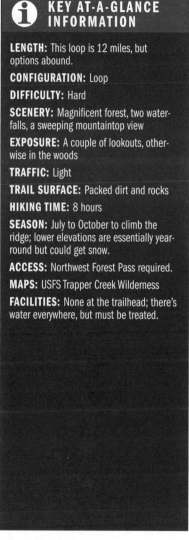

## ⓘ KEY AT-A-GLANCE INFORMATION

**LENGTH:** This loop is 12 miles, but options abound.

**CONFIGURATION:** Loop

**DIFFICULTY:** Hard

**SCENERY:** Magnificent forest, two waterfalls, a sweeping mountaintop view

**EXPOSURE:** A couple of lookouts, otherwise in the woods

**TRAFFIC:** Light

**TRAIL SURFACE:** Packed dirt and rocks

**HIKING TIME:** 8 hours

**SEASON:** July to October to climb the ridge; lower elevations are essentially year-round but could get snow.

**ACCESS:** Northwest Forest Pass required.

**MAPS:** USFS Trapper Creek Wilderness

**FACILITIES:** None at the trailhead; there's water everywhere, but must be treated.

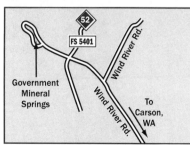

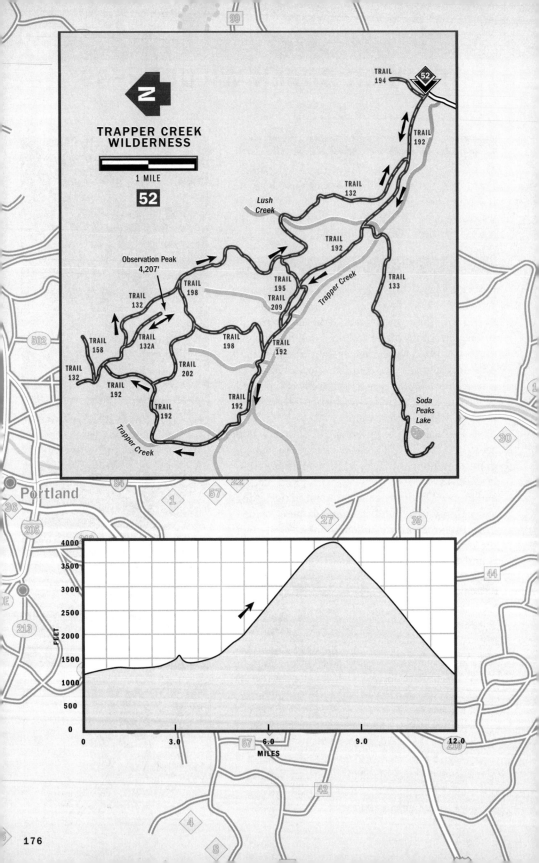

TRAIL
194

TRAIL
52

TRAIL
192

**N**

**TRAPPER CREEK
WILDERNESS**

1 MILE

**52**

TRAIL
132

Lush
Creek

TRAIL
192

TRAIL
195
TRAIL
209

TRAIL
133

Observation Peak
4,207'

TRAIL
198

Trapper Creek

TRAIL
132

TRAIL
132A

TRAIL
158

TRAIL
198

TRAIL
192

TRAIL
132

TRAIL
202

TRAIL
192

TRAIL
192

Soda
Peaks
Lake

TRAIL
192

Trapper Creek

bear scat on the trail. You have virtually nothing to fear from a black bear; if you see one, you'll likely see its rump disappearing into the woods.

To explore this area, you have numerous options; let this challenging 12-mile loop serve as an introduction. From the trailhead, start into the woods on the Trapper Creek Trail, #192, which you'll follow for six miles to its end. Right off the bat you'll intersect the Dry Creek Trail (#194), which runs about four miles north along Dry Creek. Half a mile out on 192, look for a rotting stump in the shape of an hourglass. Look, also, for such forest features as woodpecker holes in snags and new trees growing out of old stumps. In one mile, you'll see the Observation Trail (#132) on the right; we'll be coming down this one later. For now, stay straight on 192, and the forest gets even better as you get deeper into the canyon.

Just under a mile later, you'll cross Lush Creek and encounter trail #133, the Soda Peaks Trail, on the left. This leads to the one lake in the wilderness, Soda Peaks Lake; it's a climb of 2,500 feet in about three miles, and the trail doesn't loop back to this one. So unless you're looking for another hill to climb, stay on #192, Trapper Creek Trail.

About a mile later, barely climbing, you'll come to two trails at once: the Big Slide Trail (#195) and the Deer Way Trail (#209). Each of these, and several other trails in the wilderness, were built and are maintained by the Mazamas, a Portland-based mountaineering club which has adopted this wilderness area. But before you go off on one of their trails, you should know a few things about Mazamas and their trails. For one thing—and I say this as a Mazama—there is an element in that crowd that uses the phrase "get your butt kicked" to mean "have a good time." Some of these trails were designed with that attitude: they're steep scrambles, not too worried about things like switchbacks, and they can be tough to follow. And when a log falls across them, rather than cut the log away (like the Forest Service does), the Mazamas might cut a little notch in the top of it, to help you swing your leg over. So these trails are fun—and the Mazamas' signs are really cool—but they aren't necessarily casual.

The Deer Way Trail is basically an easy cutoff that avoids some elevation for those traveling the Trapper Creek Trail, so if that's your bag, take it. Otherwise, the Trapper Creek Trail dips down, for the first time, to Trapper Creek, then crosses Slump Creek before climbing back up the hill to the west end of the Deer Way Trail. Next, you'll cross the Sunshine Trail (#198), a Mazama masterpiece that goes straight up about 2,000 feet in less than two miles. I've done it; it's a "wonderful" butt-kicking.

There's no need to climb that hill, though, because right after this the Trapper Creek Trail gets pretty serious about climbing, as well. You'll have it easy for another half mile, then put in 1,200 feet in just over a mile. It is broken up for you by a side trip to see Hidden Creek Falls, marked by a Mazama sign, and also by a view from the main trail of 100-foot Trapper Creek Falls.

When you get to a wonderful viewpoint looking back down the forested canyon, you're at 3,200 feet, with the last 1,000 feet spread over two miles to Observation Peak. You'll also be in a dreamland forest. To my mind, there's nothing lovelier than a Northwest forest around 3,000–4,000 feet above sea level. And the crossing, at 3,300 feet, of Trapper Creek in a berry-filled basin is about as nice as it gets.

You'll cross one more Mazama trail, the Rim Trail (#202), before the Trapper Creek Trail deadends into the Observation Trail, #132. Turn right here, then take another right onto #132A in half a mile, and within a half mile of climbing you'll be at Observation Peak. My hiking friend and I encountered two other folks up there—the only people we saw on an August Saturday—and we struggled to come up with the right word for the view. As I recall, we settled on "stupid." Look for Mount Saint Helens and its blast zone to the north; from there around to the right, we have Mount Rainier, the Goat Rocks off on the horizon, and then Mount Adams bigger than life. See if you can spot, well to the right of that, the meadow on top of Dog Mountain—it's rare to see it from this direction—and across from that the radio towers atop Mount Defiance, the highest point in the Columbia River Gorge. Right of that are Mounts Hood and Jefferson, and closer in are the two Soda Peaks, host to the aforementioned lake. Nice, huh?

Getting down from here is simple; just go back down the #132A trail you came up and turn right on the Observation Trail, #132. You can follow this trail 5 miles to its end at the #192, a mile up from the parking lot, or you can test your knees going down a Mazama trail. Just turn right on either the Sunshine Trail (#198) or the much shorter Big Slide Trail (#195), and don't blame me if you have a hard time walking the next day. Either way you go, you'll come to the Trapper Creek Trail, and your car is to the left.

## ▶ NEARBY ACTIVITIES

It's all about springs in this area. When you drive back down FS 5401 on your way out, take a right for Government Mineral Springs and follow signs to Iron Mike Well, which puts out mineral water from an iron pump. Or, when you get back to Carson, go to the Carson Hot Springs Resort, with its 1901 hotel and 1923 bathhouse and cabins. You can soak, get a massage, and then they wrap you in hot towels. And in the fall, their restaurant makes a mean apple crisp. Call (800) 607-3678 for details.

# TRILLIUM LAKE

## ▶ IN BRIEF

A perfect place to take the kids, or just to stretch your legs after driving up from Portland, Trillium Lake is a tiny, friendly lake with a big-time view of Mount Hood. In addition to some short, easy hikes, you can fish, boat, picnic, or just lie around, catch some rays, and feed the ducks.

## ▶ DESCRIPTION

Most outdoorsy Portlanders know Trillium Lake as a cross-country ski area, famed for the terror felt by many beginners on the long hill you drive down from US 26 in the summer. But in the summer the lake is a beautiful, peaceful place to get a little taste of what the Mount Hood area has to offer; and if you've got kids along, they can swim, fish, and paddle in the lake all day long.

To hike around it, start at the day-use area located just before the road crosses the dam at the lake's southern end. Stop here and take the picture of Mount Hood that so many other people have taken. In case you're wondering, that square area of snow high up on the mountain is the Palmer Snowfield, scene of summer-long skiing and snowboarding at Timberline Ski Area. Walk along the road across the dam, perhaps throwing some crumbs to the ducks, and ask the fishermen how they're doing. At the far end of the dam, follow the trail to the right into the woods.

In the first part of the trail you won't be right by the lake because the shore on that side is

## ⓘ KEY AT-A-GLANCE INFORMATION

**LENGTH:** 2 miles

**CONFIGURATION:** Loop

**DIFFICULTY:** Easy

**SCENERY:** Marshes, lake, birds, forest

**EXPOSURE:** Shady except when crossing the dam

**TRAFFIC:** Heavy use all summer long, moderate when school is in session

**TRAIL SURFACE:** Packed dirt, boardwalk, pavement

**HIKING TIME:** 1 hour

**SEASON:** May–November

**ACCESS:** $4 day-use fee per vehicle

**MAPS:** Mount Hood Wilderness; Green Trails #462 (Mount Hood)

**FACILITIES:** Toilets in the day-use area near the dam; water available in the campground

**SPECIAL COMMENTS:** For more information, contact the Mount Hood Visitor Information Center at (503) 622-7674.

## ▶ DIRECTIONS

From Portland on US 26, drive 49 miles east of I-205 and turn right at a sign for Trillium Lake. At the bottom of the hill, stay straight ahead for the day-use areas. The hiking trail, as described here, starts in the second day-use area you come to on the road. Driving time is 1 hour and 10 minutes.

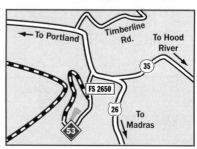

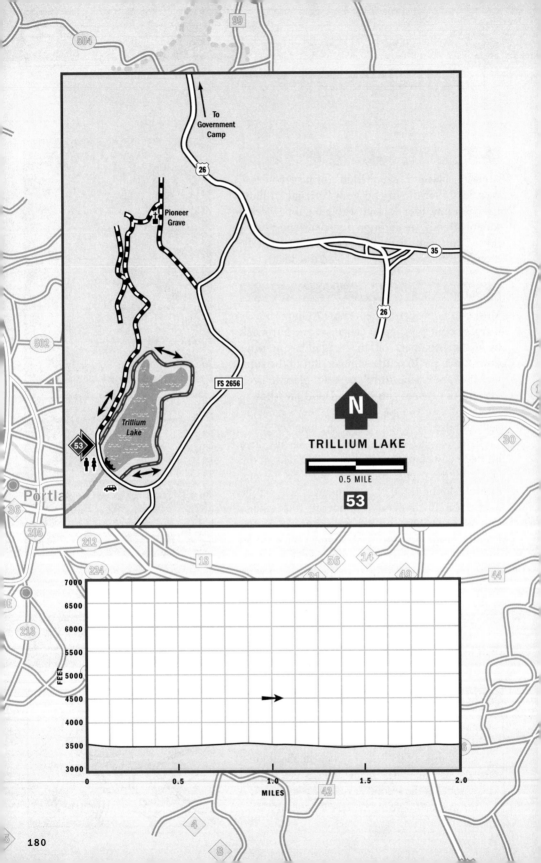

To
Government
Camp

26

Pioneer
Grave

35

26

FS 2656

Trillium
Lake

53

N

TRILLIUM LAKE

0.5 MILE

53

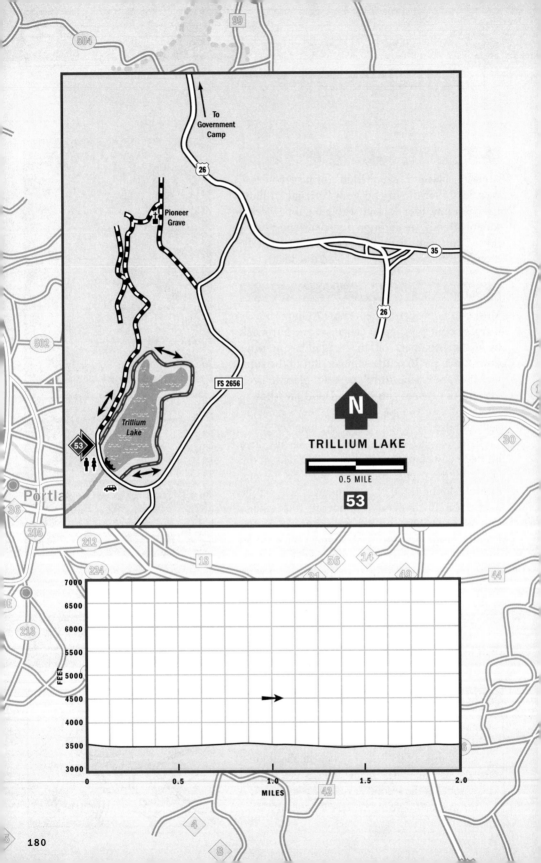

FEET

7000
6500
6000
5500
5000
4500
4000
3500
3000

0        0.5        1.0        1.5        2.0
              MILES

Fishing on Trillium Lake with Mount Hood in the background

marshy and filled with tall grass. So you'll have to enjoy the forest. At 0.6 miles, a short boardwalk goes out to the right for a glimpse of the shoreline. At 0.8 miles, there's a camp-site on the right with access to a relatively private spot on the lakeshore. Beyond this point, the trail becomes a boardwalk through a marshy area thick with vegetation. It will seem like you're swimming through the wildflowers late in the summer.

As you round the northern end of the lake, you'll pass from marsh to meadow, with a view of a corner of the lake that's covered with lilypads. Then, coming back to the more crowded eastern shore, there are numerous beaches for the kids to romp on or the parents to sun themselves on. At 1.8 miles (which is also just 0.2 miles from where you started, going the other way) there's a boat ramp and another parking lot. Just beyond that is a dock you can walk out onto (it has rails, so you don't have to worry about the kids). I was out there late one summer day with the sun setting and a few pink-hued clouds hanging around Mount Hood across the way, and some grown-ups on the dock were talking about the stock market and housing prices. Some people just don't get it.

When you drive out, go around the lake for a piece of Oregon history. Drive across the dam and go one mile on the unpaved road, turn right for half a mile, and then go right again and park immediately on the right near a white picket fence. That's a pioneer-era graveyard. Across the road is Summit Prairie, where Barlow Road travelers rested the day before tack-ling Laurel Hill (see page 80).

▶ **NEARBY ACTIVITIES**

You have to stop at some point at the Huckleberry Inn in Government Camp. They've got huckleberry pies, pancakes, and milkshakes, and serve pretty serious cheeseburgers, too. I love that place.

# TRIPLE FALLS

## KEY AT-A-GLANCE INFORMATION

**LENGTH:** 5 miles

**CONFIGURATION:** Out-and-back

**DIFFICULTY:** Moderate

**SCENERY:** Four waterfalls, a spectacular gorge, a view of the Columbia River

**EXPOSURE:** In the forest all the way

**TRAFFIC:** Moderate use on weekends, light otherwise

**TRAIL SURFACE:** Gravel and packed dirt, roots, rocks

**HIKING TIME:** 2.5 hours to Triple Falls

**SEASON:** Year-round, though it gets muddy during winter and spring

**ACCESS:** No fees or permits needed.

**MAPS:** Trails of the Columbia Gorge; Green Trails #428 (Bridal Veil); USGS Multnomah Falls

**FACILITIES:** None at the trailhead; water and rest rooms are available half a mile east at Ainsworth State Park.

**SPECIAL COMMENTS:** For more information, call the Columbia River Gorge National Scenic Area office at (541) 386-2333.

## IN BRIEF

A unique waterfall lies at the end of this moderate hike, but you don't have to go that far to see some fine Columbia River Gorge scenery. You can, in fact, just drive by the trailhead and admire Horsetail Falls.

## DESCRIPTION

If all you do is slow down while driving by Horsetail Falls, you'll be pleased. If that's all you want to see, you should at least cross the parking area and pick some blackberries over by the railroad tracks; they're ripe in late summer. But the great thing about this trail is that the farther you go, the better it gets, and you never have to work very hard at all.

From Horsetail Falls, follow the gravel trail behind the sign describing some of the animals that live in the area. At 0.2 miles, stay right at a trail junction. A few hundred yards later you'll come around a bend and see Upper Horsetail Falls, also known as Ponytail Falls. A popular turn-around spot because it's so near the car, these falls are also a hit with kids because, with supervision, they can get under them and catch some spray. The falls seem to shoot out of a basalt cliff face, and the area behind them is a grotto through which the trail passes. If you get under them, some smaller streams trickle down onto the heads of hikers and dogs. Just don't get directly under the main stream of water; even this relatively small waterfall is extremely powerful.

To keep going, simply follow the trail as it contours around the gorge wall. It soon comes to

## DIRECTIONS

From Portland on I-84, drive 21 miles east of I-205 to Exit 28 /Bridal Veil. Turn left onto the Historic Columbia River Highway and proceed 5.2 miles to the signed parking area at Horsetail Falls. Driving time is 30 minutes.

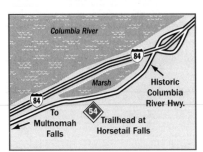

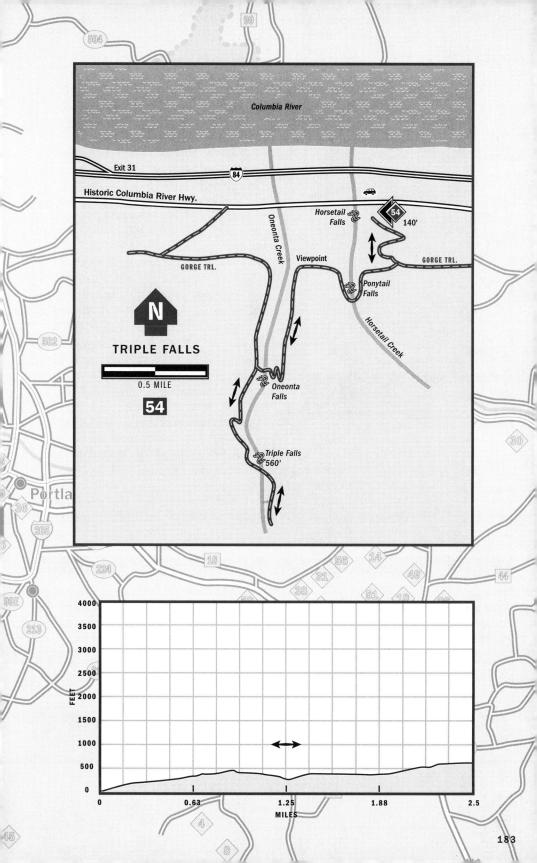

Columbia River

Exit 31

**84**

Historic Columbia River Hwy.

Horsetail Falls

**54** 140'

GORGE TRL.

Oneonta Creek

Viewpoint

GORGE TRL.

Ponytail Falls

**N**

Horsetail Creek

TRIPLE FALLS

0.5 MILE

**54**

Oneonta Falls

Triple Falls 560'

FEET

MILES

Taking a break under Ponytail falls

a brushy area on the right, through which several trails lead out to clifftop viewpoints of the Columbia River. You can make a side loop out there and work your way back to the main trail as it turns away from the river. There's a network of trails in this tiny area, but they all lead to the same place, so you won't get lost.

A mile past Ponytail Falls, after passing underneath a mossy "weeping" rock face, you'll drop down to a bridge over the top of spectacular Oneonta Gorge. A geologic and biological wonder, Oneonta is worth a visit on its own; from here, you're looking down into it from the bridge, with waterfalls above and below you. Just across the bridge (and after a little climbing) is another junction; you can loop back to the highway by going right (you'll have to walk along the road, however, to get back to your car) or you can turn left and head up toward Triple Falls. The trail is rocky in places, and there's a little more elevation gain, but nice views across the way will help keep you moving.

About a mile up you'll see Triple Falls. It's actually just one creek (Oneonta), but it divides into three just before it goes over the edge. So take your pictures from here, and then walk another minute or two to a wooden bridge across the wide stream just above the falls. Across the bridge are some nice rocks for picnicking, and just upstream are some pools the kids can jump in, if you've managed to get them this far.

▶ **NEARBY ACTIVITIES**

Oneonta Gorge is one of the truly amazing sights in the Columbia River Gorge. You can get about a quarter of a mile into it, but not without getting wet. Even in late summer adults will find themselves wading in waist-high water or climbing rocks to avoid it. (I saw one gallant gent carry his girlfriend through this section.) So put on your swimsuit, and some shoes you don't mind soaking, and explore this official U.S. Forest Service Botanical Area.

# TRYON CREEK STATE PARK

Tryon Creek, Oregon's only state park in a major city, is the kind of place you want to come to over and over, just to see what's going on. Are the steelhead in? Are the fall colors hitting? Are the trilliums blooming? Any beavers around?

▶ **DESCRIPTION**

An iron company logged this whole area in the 1880s to provide fuel for their smelter, so what you see today is what's known as second-growth forest. But that shouldn't sound like it's a second-class forest; if nothing else, some of those old tree trunks are amazing! Tryon Creek, a 645-acre park in a ravine between Portland and Lake Oswego, hosts 50 species of birds plus deer, beaver, fox, and a winter steelhead trout run. There have even been sightings of coyote, badger, and bobcat.

There are numerous hiking options that start at the Nature Center, so pick up a free map and pick your own way or call the park for a schedule of ranger-led activities. For our suggested loop, when you come out of the Nature Center, turn left, walk past the Jackson Shelter, and start on the Maple Ridge Trail. As the name implies, this area is home to many vine maples, which put on quite a red and orange show in the fall.

After 0.2 miles, take a right onto the Middle Creek Trail and descend 0.2 miles to cross Tryon Creek at High Bridge. It's worth it to turn right here and explore up the 0.4-mile North Creek

▶ **KEY AT-A-GLANCE INFORMATION**

**LENGTH:** The loop described here is 3 miles; there are 8 miles of hiking trails in the park.

**CONFIGURATION:** Loop

**DIFFICULTY:** Easy

**SCENERY:** A woodsy ravine with a creek

**EXPOSURE:** Shady

**TRAFFIC:** Use can get heavy on weekends, but it's light otherwise.

**TRAIL SURFACE:** Packed dirt and gravel

**HIKING TIME:** 1 hour for this loop

**SEASON:** Year-round

**ACCESS:** No fees or permits needed.

**MAPS:** Free maps are available at the park's Nature Center.

**FACILITIES:** Water and toilets are available at the Nature Center.

**SPECIAL COMMENTS:** For more information, call the Tryon Creek State Park office at (503) 636-9886. The nonprofit Friends of Tryon Creek put on numerous events in the park, from day camps, to nighttime hikes, to classes and lectures. To find out what's going on, call (503) 636-4398.

▶ **DIRECTIONS**

From Portland, drive south on I-5 for three miles and take Exit 297/Terwilliger. Turn right at the end of the ramp, then take the first right onto Terwilliger Boulevard. Stay on Terwilliger for 2.5 miles; the main entrance to the park is on the right. Driving time is 10 minutes.

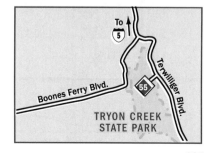

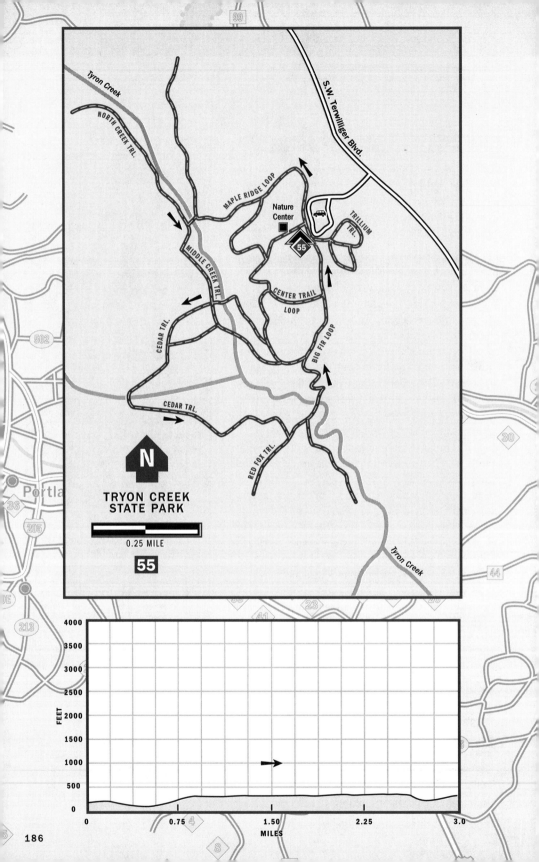

Tyron Creek

S.W. Terwilliger Blvd.

NORTH CREEK TRL.

MAPLE RIDGE LOOP

Nature Center

TRILLIUM TRL.

MIDDLE CREEK TRL.

CEDAR TRL.

CENTER TRAIL LOOP

BIG FIR LOOP

CEDAR TRL.

RED FOX TRL.

Tyron Creek

**N**

**TRYON CREEK STATE PARK**

0.25 MILE

**55**

4000
3500
3000
2500
2000
1500
1000
500
0

FEET

0    0.75    1.50    2.25    3.0
MILES

Portla

Trail, if only for the astonishing fields of impatiens (also known as jewelweed) and a few places to access the creek, one of them a deep pool at a bend. Return to the Middle Creek Trail and follow it 0.2 miles to an intersection with the Cedar Trail. Follow this trail to the right as it crosses a horse trail (careful where you step!) and then climbs briefly into a more open forest. Keep an eye out for a downed cedar trunk on the right that has obviously been explored by many an adventuresome child.

The Cedar Trail crosses the Bunk Bridge, then continues 0.8 miles to a junction with the Red Fox Trail. Turn left here and cross the Red Fox Bridge; if it's winter, keep an eye out for spawning steelhead. Climb briefly to the Old Main Trail, and then turn right and follow it back to the Nature Center.

## ▶ NEARBY ACTIVITIES

The Original Pancake House, founded in 1953, is located not far away at 8601 Southwest 24th Avenue. A third-generation family business that has spawned more than 80 franchises in 22 states, this one won the 1999 James Beard America's Regional Classics Award. Go there, get an apple pancake or a Dutch boy, and know what breakfast can truly be.

# VISTA RIDGE

## KEY AT-A-GLANCE INFORMATION

**LENGTH:** 6 miles to Wy'east Basin; 14 miles to see it all

**CONFIGURATION:** Balloon

**DIFFICULTY:** Moderate; but there's one tricky river crossing.

**SCENERY:** Mountain streams, rocks, glaciers, flowers everywhere

**EXPOSURE:** Shady for a couple of miles, then in and out of meadows

**TRAFFIC:** Moderate use on August weekends, light otherwise

**TRAIL SURFACE:** Packed dirt, roots, rocks

**HIKING TIME:** 3 to 6 hours

**SEASON:** July–October

**ACCESS:** Northwest Forest Pass required.

**MAPS:** Mount Hood Wilderness; Green Trails #462 (Mount Hood)

**FACILITIES:** None at trailhead; the closest are at the Zigzag Store.

**SPECIAL COMMENTS:** For more information, contact the Mount Hood Visitor Information Center at (503) 622-7674.

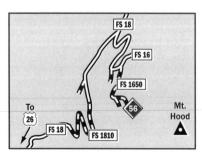

## ▶ IN BRIEF

A short, easy-access trail to several flower-filled bowls at the tree line on Mount Hood, this hike is surprisingly seldom used. That might be because it's a bit of a drive to the trailhead, but rest assured that it's worth it. You can bring the kids for a short picnic outing or stretch out your legs on an all-day affair.

## ▶ DESCRIPTION

Exactly why this hike isn't packed all the time has always been a mystery. All you have to do is climb slightly for a couple of miles through quiet woods and you're in wildflower heaven. The bad news is that the beginning and end of this hike can be tedious; the good news is that when you've gone less than three miles, you're basically done climbing for the day and can choose among four spectacular areas of flowers, meadows, creeks, and mountain views.

From the trailhead, go 0.2 miles to a sign and turn right onto the Vista Ridge Trail (#626). It's not too exciting in here, and it can get buggy, but when you see Mount Adams through the trees to the left, and the trail gets just a bit steeper, you're almost there. At 2.7 miles from the trailhead, you'll arrive at the Timberline Trail (#600),

## ▶ DIRECTIONS

From Portland on US 26, drive 36 miles east of I-205 to Zigzag and turn left onto Lolo Pass Road at the Zigzag Store. Continue 10.6 miles to Lolo Pass and turn right onto unpaved FS 1810, which is the second right at the pass. After 5.5 miles, you'll be back on pavement. In 1.8 more miles, you'll enter FS 18. Go 3.3 miles and make a hairpin right onto FS 16. Go 5.4 miles and turn right onto unpaved but signed FS 1650. Stay left at 2.8 miles; the trailhead is 0.8 miles ahead, at the end of the road. Driving time is 2 hours.

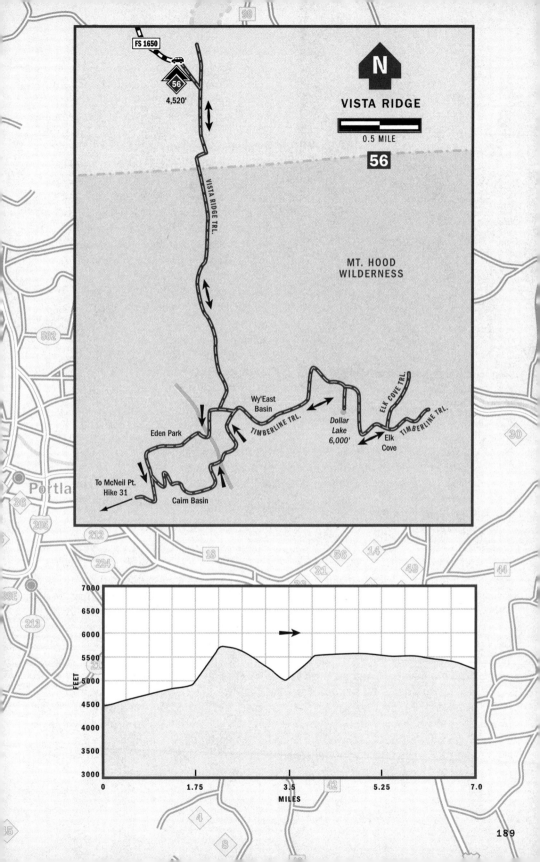

FS 1650

56
4,520'

N

VISTA RIDGE

0.5 MILE

56

MT. HOOD
WILDERNESS

VISTA RIDGE TRL.

Wy'East
Basin

TIMBERLINE TRL.

Dollar
Lake
6,000'

ELK COVE TRL.

Elk
Cove

TIMBERLINE TRL.

Eden Park

To McNeil Pt.
Hike 31

Cairn Basin

7000

6500

6000

5500

5000

4500

4000

3500

3000

FEET

0        1.75        3.5        5.25        7.0

MILES

Timberline Trail on the way to Elk Cove

in an open area with Mount Hood looming right in front of you. Congratulations: you've now climbed the biggest hill of your day—wasn't much, was it? You can go straight ahead for Wy'east Basin and Elk Cove, turn right for Eden Park and Cairn Basin, or go either way and see them all in a big loop.

But let's turn right on the Timberline Trail. You'll briefly plunge downhill and then start contouring around to the left, crossing babbling brooks and admiring more flowers all the time. After one mile of this, you'll cross a larger stream, where logs have usually been placed to make a bridge. A quarter of a mile later, you'll be in Eden Park, which just might be the mountain meadow of your dreams. To preserve the fragile landscape, stay on the trails.

To keep going to Cairn Basin, cross Eden Park and find the trail in the trees as it turns toward Hood. It will climb a small hill, with a view back down to Eden Park, and then pass through a notch and arrive 0.2 miles later in a campsite at Cairn Basin. Here, you can turn right on the Pacific Crest Trail to connect with the McNeil Point hike, which is just 0.3 miles and a tricky river crossing away. Or you can go straight ahead, following a sign for Elk Cove, to complete this loop hike. At the far end of the campsite you'll cross a creek that might be a bit much for the little ones; after that, it's basically a flat mile to Wy'east Basin.

Once there, your car is to your left (go 0.3 miles to the Vista Ridge Trail and turn right) and Elk Cove is to your right. In just a couple minutes on the way to Elk Cove, you'll come to a lovely meadow with a creek and views of Mounts Saint Helens, Rainier, and Adams. Just 1.2 flat miles away, Elk Cove might be the most spectacular of these destinations; it's certainly the largest, and Mount Hood seems to rise out of its far side all at once. Here, you'll find wildflowers throughout August, huckleberries late in the month, and reddish/orange mountain ash in September. I once spoke to a ranger who had seen elk and black bears in Elk Cove. Give either of them their space, and they won't bother you.

As you head back on the Timberline Trail, before you get back to Wy'east Basin, keep an eye out for a side trail leading to Dollar Lake. There's no sign, but it follows a draw uphill in an area of short trees and a tiny stream that's more of a wet spot in the trail. Look for a rocky area uphill of the trail. If you get back as far as the Pinnacle Ridge Trail (#630), you've missed it by about five minutes. Dollar Lake (so named because it's almost perfectly round, like a silver dollar) probably should be called Half-Dollar Lake; you could wade across it in a minute. But it's a quiet, lovely spot to contemplate all the beauty you've seen and say goodbye for now to Mount Hood before heading back to your car.

# WAHKEENA FALLS TO MULTNOMAH FALLS

## ▶ IN BRIEF

Just off I-84 and bookmarked by two beautiful waterfalls, this is the perfect introduction to all that the Columbia River Gorge has to offer, including great scenery, big crowds, and nice, steep climbs.

## ▶ DESCRIPTION

When hiking friends come to visit Oregon, this is where I take them first. They get to see the scenic spectacle that is the Columbia River Gorge, they get to view the highest waterfall in Oregon, they get to see old-growth Douglas firs, and they get their hearts pumping—from excitement and, at times, from effort.

You can hike either way on this trail, and park at either falls; my preference is to park at Multnomah Falls (either on the Historic Columbia River Highway or at the I-84 exit) and begin at Wahkeena Falls. I'll explain why later.

To do this, walk 100 yards down the historic highway to the west of Multnomah Falls Lodge and take the Return Trail (#442), which parallels the road for 0.6 miles to Wahkeena Falls. Along the way you'll pass under an overhanging rock and be cooled off by a mossy, "weeping" rock wall.

Actually several falls in one, Wahkeena Falls encompasses several styles of falls, from sheer drops to cascades to misty sprays. This creek, by

## ▶ DIRECTIONS

To park at Multnomah Falls, take I-84 for 24 miles east of I-205 to Exit 31/Multnomah Falls. Park and walk under the expressway and railroad tracks to the historic lodge. To park at Wahkeena Falls, go 21 miles east on I-84 to Exit 28/Bridal Veil. Turn left onto the Historic Columbia River Highway and proceed two miles to the signed parking area at the falls. Driving time is 25 minutes.

## ⓘ KEY AT-A-GLANCE INFORMATION

**LENGTH:** 5.2 miles

**CONFIGURATION:** Loop

**DIFFICULTY:** Moderate

**SCENERY:** Waterfalls, canyons, river views, flowers, a spring, big trees

**EXPOSURE:** In the forest all the way

**TRAFFIC:** Heavy use, especially on weekends; on weekdays and on the trail away from Multnomah Falls, use is moderate.

**TRAIL SURFACE:** Pavement, gravel, packed dirt with some rocky sections

**HIKING TIME:** 3 hours

**SEASON:** Year-round, though it gets muddy in spots during winter and spring

**ACCESS:** No fees or permits required.

**MAPS:** Trails of the Columbia Gorge

**FACILITIES:** Full service at Multnomah Falls

**SPECIAL COMMENTS:** Trails in the gorge often suffer from slides and flooding in winter and spring, so call ahead to make sure this trail is available: Columbia River Gorge National Scenic Area, (541) 386-2333.

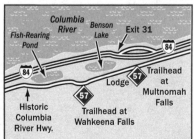

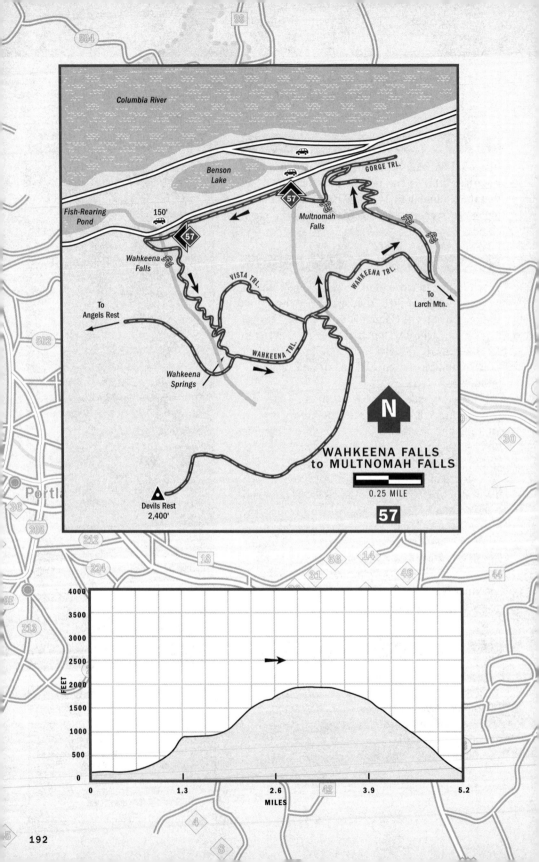

Columbia River

Benson
Lake

Fish-Rearing
Pond

150'

57

57

Multnomah
Falls

GORGE TRL.

Wahkeena
Falls

VISTA TRL.

WAHKEENA TRL.

To Larch Mtn.

To
Angels Rest

Wahkeena
Springs

WAHKEENA TRL.

N

WAHKEENA FALLS
to MULTNOMAH FALLS

0.25 MILE

57

Devils Rest
2,400'

4000
3500
3000
2500
2000
1500
1000
500
0

FEET

0          1.3          2.6          3.9          5.2

MILES

the way, comes primarily from a spring up on the ridge that you'll see later. To start the loop, follow the paved trail across the creek and then 0.2 miles up to a footbridge at the base of the upper falls. Take a nice, deep breath of that cool, moist air; your workout is about to begin.

In the next 0.4 miles of graveled switchbacks, you'll gain about 400 feet in elevation; such quick climbs are the trademark of gorge hikes. When you get to a lookout point on the right with a great view of the Columbia, the worst is over. You can rest a few minutes later on a bench at lovely Fairy Falls, sort of a miniature version of Ramona Falls (Hike 38 in this book).

There's still come climbing to do; it's just that now it's more gradual and you have the creek and some lovely old forest of ferns, cedars, hemlocks, and firs to take your mind off it. Fairly recent fires took out smaller growth, blackened the trunks of bigger trees, and opened the forest floor for berries and wildflowers to move in. Just above lovely Fairy Falls, you'll encounter the Vista Point

Top of Wahkeena Falls

Trail; turn right here, staying on the Wahkeena Trail (#420). In 0.4 miles you'll come to an intersection with the Angels Rest Trail (#415). The sign here has an interesting quirk: it lacks the word "trail" after Vista Point, Devils Rest and Larch Mountain. So the distances listed are to those trails, not to the destinations. At any rate, you should at least take a detour here on the Angels Rest Trail for about 100 yards to see Wahkeena Spring.

The spring is a sort of magical place, where cool, clear (and in my opinion drinkable) water comes right out of the ground. There are several big, moss-draped cedars there, two of them on nurse logs and one in the creek, and in April there are trilliums blooming all over the place. There's also a little trail that goes off down the stream, but it goes nowhere in particular.

You can turn back, of course, and continue towards Multnomah Falls, but if you want to add some fun (and a small dose of effort), you're only 2.6 miles from Angels Rest at this point. Or you can just see some sights along the way. In 100 yards, there's a little creek which, for some reason, is filled with red rocks. The next half mile on that trail gains 400 feet, but then it's basically flat the rest of the way to Angels Rest. A mile up, you'll come to a clearcut area where the Foxglove Trail cuts off (and up) to Devils Rest, and a half mile past that you'll come to a nice campground with little-bitty picnic tables and more nice cedars (and also a birdhouse—see if you can find it). After another half mile, you'll get to another intersection with the Foxglove Trail, and just below that Angels Rest.

Devils Rest is worthwhile, and there are three ways to get there. The Foxglove Trail (from the clearcut on the Angels Rest Trail) goes up through the clearcut for half a mile, then it turns left onto a trail and climbs for another half mile. It gains 800 feet in that mile. Technically, Devils Rest is the summit of the ridge, but it's a nondescript pile of rocks with no view. The real view is just below the summit on the east-bound Devils Rest Trail (#420C); look for the trail going off to your left as you head downhill.

Meanwhile, back at the intersection of the Wahkeena and Angels Rest Trails, back near the spring, take the Wahkeena Trail up the hill 0.4 miles to a four-way intersection. Coming up the hill from your left is the Vista Point Trail; ignore it. Going up the hill to your right is the Devils Rest Trail. And straight ahead is the Wahkeena Trail.

Continuing east on the Wahkeena Trail, you'll soon start downhill and, in 0.9 miles, intersect the Larch Mountain Trail (#441). This trail (see page 76) connects Multnomah Falls with Larch Mountain. For our purposes here, turn left and head down rock-filled Multnomah Creek. In the next mile, you'll pass several waterfalls in a gorge filled with ferns and large, old-growth Douglas firs.

A well-marked (and well-traveled) paved trail to the left leads 0.1 mile to the top of Multnomah Falls, where a wooden platform offers an ego-building view of the camera-toting throngs below. "Yeah," you can say later at the bottom, "I've been up there." This brings me to why I like to do this hike this way. From this point on, especially on a weekend, you'll be among hundreds of people. From my perspective, it's better to move downhill (hence, more quickly) through this scene, arriving at Multnomah Falls and the Benson Bridge a mile later.

The highest falls in Oregon at 542 feet, upper Multnomah Falls is indeed quite a sight. Be sure to stop in the information office at the lodge to see the pictures of various floods and a massive rockfall that occurred there in years gone by. Now for the final reason I like to start this hike at Wahkeena Falls but park at Multnomah Falls: When you're all done, you can get yourself an ice cream cone or an espresso, cruise the gift shop if you're into that, and your car is right there waiting for you.

► **NEARBY ACTIVITIES**

The 1925 Multnomah Falls Lodge is well worth checking out, with its skylights and fireplace in the restaurant and old-style stone and wood construction. The food is excellent as well, especially the Sunday brunch. The smoked salmon omelet is out of this world.

# WASHINGTON PARK/ HOYT ARBORETUM

A family could spend a weekend in Washington Park and never run out of things to do. The park has a zoo, a children's museum, the World Forestry Center, the Oregon Vietnam Veterans Memorial, a world-class Japanese garden, the Hoyt Arboretum, and miles of hiking trails. TriMet runs a shuttle bus that connects it all. The loop described here is only a suggestion.

## ▶ DESCRIPTION

This loop hike can be your base for exploring and an introduction to all that Washington Park has to offer. From a hiker's perspective, the heart of the park is Hoyt Arboretum (literally meaning "tree museum"), founded in 1928 on land that was completely clear-cut in the early twentieth century. Be sure to stop in the Visitor Center (which is on this loop) for their helpful maps.

Beginning your walk at the Oregon Vietnam Veterans Memorial, follow the trail under and then across the bridge and through a circular series of memorials describing events at home and in Southeast Asia from 1959 to 1972.

## ▶ DIRECTIONS

The best way to get to this trailhead is actually to take the Max Light Rail. It takes you from downtown to the deepest transit station in North America (260 feet—second deepest in the world) with artwork and displays on the geological history of the region. An elevator puts you right next to the World Forestry Center. To drive from downtown Portland, head west on US 26 and take Exit 72/Zoo after 1.3 miles. At the end of the ramp, turn right on SW Canyon Road. Then stay to the left, circling the parking lot, and turn left at the MAX station. The trailhead is at the Vietnam Veterans Memorial on your left 0.1 mile later. Driving time is 5 minutes.

## ⓘ KEY AT-A-GLANCE INFORMATION

**LENGTH:** 4 miles

**CONFIGURATION:** Loop

**DIFFICULTY:** Easy

**SCENERY:** 950 species and varieties of plants, with labels on more than 5,000 trees and shrubs

**EXPOSURE:** Shady, with occasional open spots for city views or contemplation

**TRAFFIC:** Use is heavy on weekends but moderate during the workday or when the weather is inclement.

**TRAIL SURFACE:** Pavement, packed dirt, gravel

**HIKING TIME:** 2 hours for the recommended loop

**SEASON:** Year-round

**ACCESS:** No fees or permits needed.

**MAPS:** The Hoyt Arboretum Visitor Center offers a trail guide.

**FACILITIES:** Water and rest rooms are available throughout the park.

**SPECIAL COMMENTS:** For more information, contact the Portland Parks and Recreation office at (503) 823-7529.

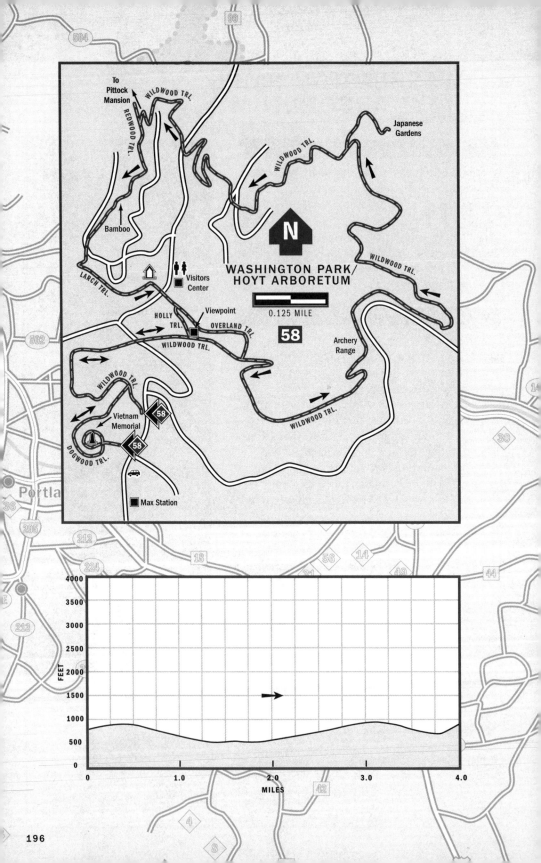

To
Pittock
Mansion

WILDWOOD TRL.

REDWOOD TRL.

Bamboo

LARCH TRL.

WILDWOOD TRL.

Japanese
Gardens

WILDWOOD TRL.

**N**

**WASHINGTON PARK/
HOYT ARBORETUM**

0.125 MILE

**58**

Visitors
Center

Viewpoint

HOLLY
TRL.

OVERLAND TRL.

WILDWOOD TRL.

Archery
Range

WILDWOOD TRL.

WILDWOOD TRL.

**58**

Vietnam
Memorial

DOGWOOD TRL.

**58**

■ Max Station

4000

3500

3000

2500

2000

**FEET**

1500

1000

500

0

0          1.0          2.0          3.0          4.0

**MILES**

At this point, you're in the arboretum—specifically, on the Dogwood Trail. (Each arboretum trail is named for the trees that dominate it.) Follow the Dogwood Trail out of the memorial, and then turn left onto the Wildwood Trail. (To your right is the beginning of this 28-mile "wondertrail" that wanders through Washington Prak and Forest Park for some 30 miles.

Stay on the Wildwood Trail for 0.4 miles as it circles to the right and climbs a small hill to a viewpoint between two water towers. Look for Mount St. Helens and Mount Rainier, and then turn left on the Holly Trail and walk 100 yards to the Visitor Center, where there's water, rest rooms, and a mountain of information. Return to the viewpoint and turn left on the Wildwood Trail. In about 200 feet you'll come to the Magnolia Trail on the left; take it 0.3 miles to the Winter Garden if you'd like to cut about 1.6 miles off your hike and stay in the arboretum. For a pleasant, woodsy stroll and access to other Washington Park attractions, stay on the Wildwood Trail.

The wide, flat Wildwood Trail loops out for 1.5 miles, with access along the way to the Cherry, Walnut, and Maple Trails. At the 1.2-mile mark, you will have a view down to the right at the waterfall area of the Japanese garden; just after that a trail leads to the garden, the largest in the world outside Japan and a must-see. Just down a hill beyond that is the International Rose Test Garden, with 8,000 rose bushes in more than 550 varieties. Did I mention you could spend quite a while in Washington Park?

Back on the Wildwood Trail, 0.3 miles past the Japanese Garden Trail you enter the Winter Garden, where the Magnolia Trail cutoff re-enters. Just 0.6 miles later on the Wildwood Trail, take a left on the Redwood Trail for an exploration of the sequoia collection. Just beyond that, you'll enter the redwood collection, which includes a specimen of the dawn redwood, thought to be extinct until a few decades ago. This tree was the first of its species in the Western Hemisphere to produce cones in 60 million years.

Note: If you were to stay on the Wildwood Trail here, you would add a 2.4-mile out-and-back trip to the Pittock Mansion, which is at the top of the Macleay Trail (see page 96).

Back on the Redwood Trail, when you come to a trail on the right marked To Creek Trail, take that, and you'll be in the middle of the bamboo collection. From redwoods to bamboo—culture shock is now a possibility. The Creek Trail dead ends at a road; pick up the Redwood Trail at the far side, and you'll pass through the larch collection on your way to the picnic shelter. Cross the road, and you're back at the Visitor Center. Turn right, take the Holly Trail back to the Wildwood Trail, turn right on it, and follow it a half mile back to your car.

▶ **NEARBY ACTIVITIES**

Of all the attractions in Washington Park, the Children's Museum is the newest and hottest. It opened at this location in 2001 and features hands-on exhibits in a "center for creativity, designed for kids age 6 months through 12 years old." Kids can climb, swim, toss balls, and even produce a movie there.

# WILDWOOD RECREATION AREA

## KEY AT-A-GLANCE INFORMATION

**LENGTH:** The two loop trails total 1.75 miles.

**CONFIGURATION:** Loop

**DIFFICULTY:** Easy

**SCENERY:** Wetlands, meadows, streams

**EXPOSURE:** Alternating between shady and open

**TRAFFIC:** Moderate to heavy use on summer weekends, light otherwise

**TRAIL SURFACE:** Gravel, pavement, boardwalk

**HIKING TIME:** 2 hours to do both loops

**SEASON:** Open year-round, but the road is gated from November to April. During those times, you'll have to walk in.

**ACCESS:** $3 parking fee per vehicle

**MAPS:** Free hiking maps are available in a kiosk at the parking area.

**FACILITIES:** Water and rest rooms at the parking area; area is wheelchair-traversible.

**SPECIAL COMMENTS:** For more information, call the Mount Hood Visitor Information Center at (503) 622-7674.

## ▶ IN BRIEF

As much an educational experience as a hiking one, this is a glimpse into the natural world of birds, fish, plants, and water that is in fact all around the Pacific Northwest. The crown jewel of Wildwood is the Underwater Viewing Structure, especially when various species of salmon and trout are returning to the area to spawn.

## ▶ DESCRIPTION

The 33-mile-long Salmon River is the only river in the lower 48 states that is designated as a National Wild and Scenic River from its headwaters to its mouth, in this case, from Mount Hood to the Sandy River, three miles below Wildwood. As far from the sea as it is, it gets several runs each year of anadromous fish—fish that are born in fresh water, go to the ocean, and return to the fresh water of their birth to spawn and die. Although salmon are the most famous of these—and this bend of the Salmon River does get runs of salmon—steelhead do the same thing and beyond even that, there are native trout in this stretch of the river.

To get a sample of this natural wonderland, hike two different loop trails, the 1-mile Wildwood Wetland Trail and the 0.75-mile Cascade Streamwatch Trail. To start the Wetland Trail, start to the left of the parking lot kiosk, where there are rest rooms and free maps available. You'll cross a 190-foot-long wooden bridge over the lovely Salmon River, where in fall and winter you just

## ▶ DIRECTIONS

From Portland on US 26, drive 33 miles east of I-205 and turn right at a large sign: CASCADE STREAMWATCH. It's half a mile past the Mount Hood Visitor Information Center. Following the Trailhead sign, drive a mile ahead to the parking area for both trails. Driving time is 50 minutes.

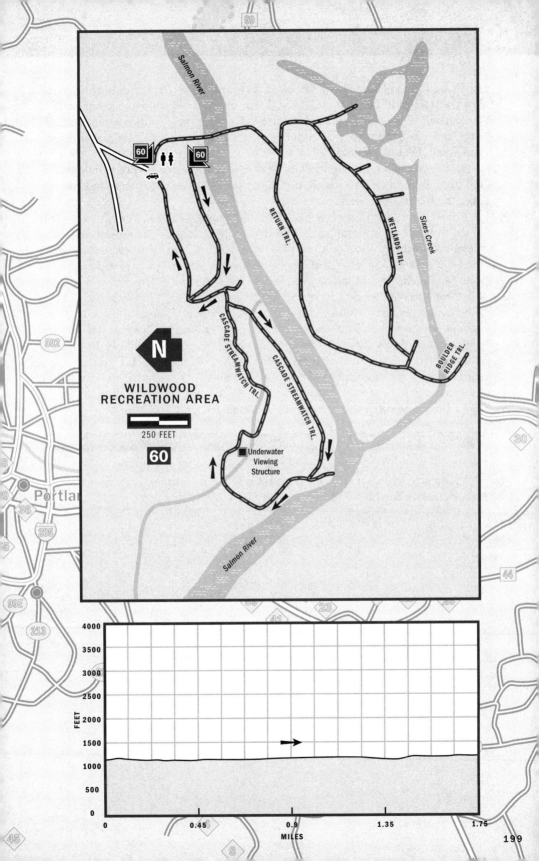

Salmon River

60 ♟♟ 60 🚗

RETURN TRL.

WETLANDS TRL.

Sixes Creek

BOULDER RIDGE TRL.

**N**

WILDWOOD RECREATION AREA

250 FEET

60

CASCADE STREAMWATCH TRL.

CASCADE STREAMWATCH TRL.

■ Underwater Viewing Structure

Salmon River

Portland

4000
3500
3000
2500
2000
1500
1000
500
0

FEET

0    0.45    0.9    1.35    1.75
MILES

might see Chinook salmon and steelhead spawning below. Once over the bridge, follow the signs onto the boardwalk. You'll visit several lookouts onto various parts of the wetland: a cattail marsh, an overgrown beaver dam, an area filled with skunk cabbage, and a wetland stream. At each one there's a notebook-style informative display describing the area's wildlife. Also, if you're quiet and go in the morning, there's a good chance you'll see some wildlife. Be sure to take the gravel Return Trail back to the parking lot, if only to admire the size of some 80-year-old stumps and contemplate the fact that they were cut by hand.

The Cascade Streamwatch Trail starts at the same kiosk and takes you on a tour of the world of an anadromous fish. In fact, to navigate the trail you just follow the metal fish in the pavement. Along this trail, you'll visit an overlook of the river, a three-dimensional model of the Mount Hood area, several great picnic areas with grills, and then the fantastic Underwater Viewing Structure. Here, you can see tiny fish most times of the year and try to identify them using the chart on the wall. From late October to mid-December you might even catch a glimpse of an adult Coho salmon. You have a better chance of seeing bigger spawning fish a little later on the trail, when it drops down to the riverside. Look for winter steelhead in January; spring Chinook salmon in March and April; summer steelhead in May; and Coho and fall Chinook from late September to mid-November. In case you're wondering, the Salmon River is closed to salmon fishing; you can fish for native trout at limited times, but it's all catch-and-release with artificial lures only.

## ▶ NEARBY ACTIVITIES

Wildwood is actually a full-service 600-acre recreation area, with picnic areas available for rental, ballfields, and a play area. For rental information, call the Salem District of the Bureau of Land Management at (503) 375-5646.

# WILLAMETTE RIVER

### ▶ IN BRIEF

Take a tour of central Portland and the Willamette River on a series of interconnected paved walkways. You can piece this one together on different days, mixing in tourist activities, or do it all in a pleasant day of wandering.

### ▶ DESCRIPTION

Portland is so cool. Whether it's tearing out a major road and replacing with it a park, or building a floating walkway in the middle of downtown, the city just takes care of its walkers.

Here's a loop through downtown and the area to the south that takes in river views, hustle and bustle, entertainment, education and even some solitude. There are numerous places to start, but I've decided to start at the west end (downtown side) of the Hawthorne Bridge—for the simple reasons that it's my favorite bridge in town and the park just to the south of it is a great place to be. How many downtowns have Canada geese hanging out in them?

The big platform on the south side of the bridge has a great view of the boats at RiverPlace, as well as a sign talking about Tom McCall Waterfront Park, which stretches from here north to the Steel Bridge. In the early 20th Century a plan was

### ▶ DIRECTIONS

There are numerous ways to access this hike. A parking lot between SE Madison and Salmon Streets, with entrances at Main and Salmon, was scheduled for completion in 2003. The easiest way to access it is via public transit. From Downtown Portland, take bus #4, 10, or 14 on SW Fifth Avenue and get off at SW Madison and First Avenue, then walk one block towards the river. You could also park at Sellwood Park and walk down the hill towards Oaks Amusement Park. Driving time is 5 minutes.

### ⓘ KEY AT-A-GLANCE INFORMATION

**LENGTH:** 11 miles to do the whole thing

**CONFIGURATION:** Loop

**DIFFICULTY:** Easy

**SCENERY:** Condos and cormorants, highrises and herons, bridges and beavers, boats and butterflies . . .

**EXPOSURE:** Open most of the way, occasionally in the shade, with one mildly nerve-wracking bridge crossing.

**SOLITUDE:** Use is heavy on summer weekends and after work on a nice day, moderate otherwise.

**FACILITIES:** Water and toilets at numerous locations

**TRAIL SURFACE:** Paved

**HIKING TIME:** 5 hours

**SEASON:** Year-round

**ELEVATION:** About 300 feet all around.

**ACCESS:** No fees or passes required.

**MAPS:** There's no good map of the whole thing (other than in this book). Portland Parks and Recreation has a map of Waterfront Park and the Eastbank Esplanade at www.parks.ci.portland.oregon.us.

**SPECIAL COMMENTS:** Portland Parks and Recreation, (503) 823-7529

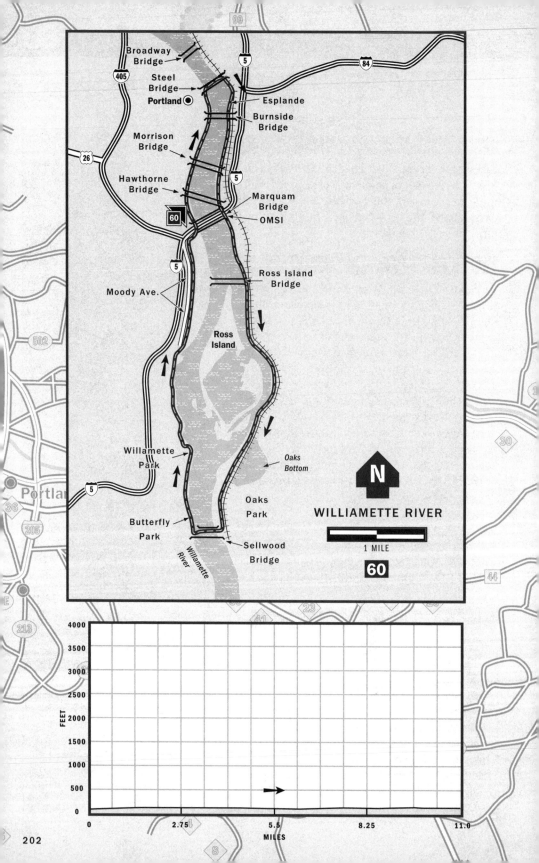

Broadway
Bridge

405

Steel
Bridge

**Portland** ◉

Esplande

Burnside
Bridge

Morrison
Bridge

26

Hawthorne
Bridge

60

Marquam
Bridge

OMSI

5

Moody Ave.

Ross Island
Bridge

Ross
Island

Willamette
Park

Oaks
Bottom

5

Oaks
Park

Butterfly
Park

Willamette
River

Sellwood
Bridge

**N**

**WILLIAMETTE RIVER**

1 MILE

**60**

4000
3500
3000
2500
2000
FEET 1500
1000
500
0

0          2.75          5.5          8.25          11.0
MILES

proposed to make this a waterfront park, but in the 1920s a seawall was built to control floods, and then Harbor Drive was built in the 1940s. But when the Marquam (I-5) Bridge opened in 1966, Harbor Drive was made obsolete. So Governor Tom McCall proposed a public open space to go there, and that park opened in 1978. The city named it for McCall in 1984.

There are restrooms under the Hawthorne Bridge, if you need them; otherwise, walk north, dodging joggers and bikers and enjoying the many summertime festivals, if one is going on. You'll also pass by Salmon Street Springs, which usually has kids romping in it.

Look, on the left, for the Battleship Oregon Memorial, built in 1956 to honor an 1893 ship nicknamed "the Bulldog of the United States Navy." On July 4, 1976, a time capsule was sealed in the base of the memorial; it's set to be opened July 5, 2076. Look, also, for The Founders' Stone, which honors Portland's founders (William Pettygrove and Asa Lovejoy), who tossed a coin to decide

The Esplanade crosses the Steel Bridge; Convention Center in the background

whether the new town would be named New Boston or Portland (for the city in Maine). You'll also see the Oregon Maritime Center and Museum, housed in the sternwheeler Portland.

Under the Burnside Bridge, and one block to the left, you can hit Saturday Market, open weekends from March through Christmas, for food and hand-made crafts. You can also cross the river by taking a flight of steps located in the market onto the bridge. Just before the Steel Bridge, you'll come to the Japanese American Historical Plaza and its wonderful cherry trees. Come here in March and be amazed by the pink blossoms.

The walkway crosses the Steel Bridge, but it's worth it to take a little detour to the north. Just follow the walkway as it goes under the bridge near the steps, then cross the railroad tracks and continue in front of the condominiums along the river. There's a little beach here, and rocks and pilings which often host herons, geese, and ducks. I've even seen salmon jump in this stretch of river. The path passes in front of the condos (does it make you feel like a voyeur?), visits a lookout platform, goes under the Broadway Bridge, and eventually reaches a big deck with a nice view north towards the Fremont Bridge.

Now go back to the Steel Bridge (built in 1912) and cross over it, either down on the lower level or up on top. You might choose based on the view, or because the lower section is raised to let a boat through. The Steel Bridge is one of the few in the world (and the only one in the U.S.) with two lift spans; the lower part lifts into the upper part. The total weight lifted between the two spans is nine million pounds.

At the east end of the 890-foot walkway, turn right, and you'll be on the 1.5-mile-long Eastbank Esplanade. Enjoy some of the 280 trees and 43,695 shrubs (most native) planted along the trail; local beavers sure did when they first went in, so now many of them are covered by fence—the plants, not the beavers. Also, enjoy the 13 "urban markers" along the way; they mark where streets are, and each one has a unique light fixture on it, as well.

In just a few minutes you'll come to the fanciest feature of the Esplanade, the floating walkway. At 1,200 feet, it's the longest in the world. It's held in place by 65 pylons, each one sunk 30 feet into the bottom of the river. Each section of the walkway weighs 800,000 pounds, and you can still feel it bobbing up down when the wind is tossing up the river.

If you want to head back to the west side, you can do so on the Burnside Bridge via a staircase on the south side.

Just north of the Morrison Bridge, you'll see what looks like a strange rock formation; in fact, this is leftover concrete, dumped when the Morrison Bridge was being built. What kind of fines do you think that would generate these days?

If you're wondering about some other oddities—the little bumps on the seats of benches—those are to keep skateboarders from practicing tricks on them.

Just past the Hawthorne Bridge, which has a nice lookout point on the north side and access to cross back over the river, you'll come to the Oregon Museum of Science and Industry (OMSI). The path goes right across the front of OMSI (past the submarine), and if you like, you can step inside for a snack, a drink, or some education. (The Omnimax Theater is especially recommended).

You've now officially left the Esplanade, but don't worry. Just follow the path as it loops around to the left and turns into Southeast Carruthers Street Take a right on Southeast Fourth Avenue, and in two blocks you'll be on the Springwater Corridor Trail. This trail will eventually run all the way to the town of Boring, and possibly even to Estacada, and maybe even into the National Forest along the Clackamas River—all depending on which enthusiastic civic leader you ask.

Just past a lovely concrete plant on the right, you'll come to an area that was replanted with native shrubs and flowers from the fall of 2003 to the spring of 2004, so you can see how it worked out—and enjoy the first real taste of quiet on the trip. For most of the next three miles, you will feel free of the city.

Just under two miles along, you'll come to a trail that goes under the railroad tracks to the left; this is a connector to the Oaks Bottom Trail (see page 122). Soon thereafter, you'll come to Oaks Bottom on the left; I've seen as many as two dozen herons in there at once. On the right, you'll pass Oaks Amusement Park, then just before the Sellwood Bridge turn left onto Spokane. Look for a cute little church in the trees on the left; that's Oaks Pioneer Museum, which was originally the 1851 St. John's Episcopal Church and was moved to this location in 1961.

Go two blocks and turn right on Southeast Sixth, then you'll arrive at Southeast Tacoma. If you need a break, there's a coffee shop four blocks to your left; otherwise, turn right and head over the 1925 Sellwood Bridge. Look for a statue of an owl on a roof to your right, and then look out for traffic. This is a pretty nervous bridge crossing, especially when a big truck goes by and the whole bridge bounces.

At the west end of the bridge, take some steps down to the right, cross under the road, then follow signs for the Willamette Greenway Trail. You'll walk along the side of Macadam Avenue, then turn right at a sign for the Macadam Bay Club. Just before the gate for this club, turn left to get back onto the trail.

In less than half a mile, you'll come to Butterfly Park, which is really just an undeveloped piece of riverside, filled with cottonwood trees, where a lot of butterflies live. Volunteers maintain it to keep it attractive to the winged critters. An interpretive sign explores more, but it's nice to know you live in a city that has a Butterfly Park.

About a quarter-mile north, you'll come into 30-acre Willamette Park, where the trail hugs the riverside next to fields full of dogs, discs and barbecuers. At the north end of that park, you'll come into an area of condos and office buildings—and enough "Stay on the Trails" signs to make you crazy. Pay attention to the trail, because at times you have to hug buildings and duck through parking lots, but it's all well-marked with the Willamette Greenway Trail signs.

Eventually, you pop out onto Southwest Moody Avenue in a light industrial area. Follow it north under I-405, then turn right onto Southwest Sheridan. Before you know it, you'll be walking through the shops and marinas of RiverPlace, and just north of that is where all this adventure started, the Hawthorne Bridge.

# 60 Hikes within 60 MILES

## PORTLAND

## APPENDICES
## & INDEX

# APPENDIX A:
# HIKING STORES

What good is hiking without the chance to break in boots, try out a new kind of sock, or see how the latest piece of outdoor wicky-wacky works? If you're looking for gear, here's where to go in Portland:

## ▶ CONTACT INFORMATION

**Columbia Sportswear**
911 Southwest Broadway
(503) 226-6800

**G.I. Joe's**
3900 Southeast 82nd Avenue
(503) 777-4526

**Next Adventure**
*(includes used items)*
426 Southeast Grand Avenue
(503) 233-0706

**Oregon Mountain Community**
60 Northwest Davis Street
(503) 227-1038

**Patagonia**
907 Northwest Irving Street
(503) 525-2552

**REI–Portland**
1405 Northwest Johnson
(503) 221-1938

**The Mountain Shop**
628 Northeast Broadway
(503) 288-6768

**US Outdoor Store**
219 Southwest Broadway
(503) 223-5937

# APPENDIX B:
# PLACES TO BUY MAPS

## ▶ CONTACT INFORMATION

**Nature of the Northwest**
800 Northeast Oregon Street
    Suite 177
(503) 731-4444

**Oregon Mountain Community**
60 Northwest Davis Street
(503) 227-1038

**REI–Tigard**
7410 Southwest Bridgeport Road
(503) 624-8600

# APPENDIX C:
# HIKING CLUBS

## ▶ CONTACT INFORMATION

**BergFreunde Ski and Activities Club**
(503) 245-8543
www.bergfreunde.org

**Columbia River Volkssport Club**
www.ava.org/clubs/crvc

**Friends of Forest Park**
(503) 223-5449
www.friendsofforestpark.org

**Mazamas**
909 Northwest 19th Avenue
(503) 227-2345
www.mazamas.org

**Trails Club of Oregon**
(503) 233-2740
www.tco.citysearch.com

**Oregon Chapter Sierra Club**
2950 Southeast Stark Street
  Suite 110
(503) 238-0442
www.oregon.sierraclub.org

**Portland Parks and Recreation**
(503) 823-7529
www.parks.ci.portland.or.us

**Ptarmigans**
1220 Northeast 68th Street
Vancouver, Washington
Meet at 7 p.m. on the second Tuesday
of each month at the First Congrega-
tional Church in Vancouver.
www.ptarmigans.org

# INDEX

# INDEX

# INDEX

# INDEX

# INDEX

# INDEX

# INDEX

# INDEX

# American Hiking Society

## THE VOICE OF THE AMERICAN HIKER... THE HEART OF THE HIKING COMMUNITY.

Join the national voice for America's Hikers.

Visit **www.AmericanHiking.org**

or send a $25 check to:

American Hiking Society

Attn: Membership

1422 Fenwick Lane

Silver Spring, MD 20910

# Looking For More Info?

Menasha Ridge Press has partnered with Trails.com to provide additional information for all the trails in this book, including:

- Topo map downloads
- Real-time weather
- Trail reports, and more

To access this information, visit:

**http://menasharidge.trails.com**

In Partnership With

 Trails.com

219

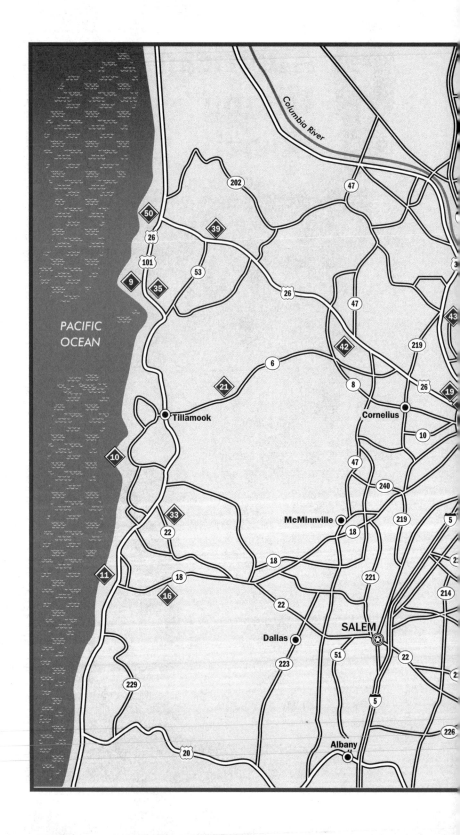